JOURNAL OF LEGAL PLURALISM
and Unofficial Law

NUMBER 63 / 2011. SPECIAL ISSUE

INTERNATIONAL DEVELOPMENT INTERVENTIONS

Bibliographic information published by the Deutsche Nationalbibliothek
The Deutsche Nationalbibliothek lists this publication in the Deutsche Nationalbibliografie; detailed bibliographic data are available in the Internet at http://dnb.d-nb.de.

ISSN 0732-9113
ISBN 978-3-643-99873-6

A catalogue record for this book is available from the British Library

Zweigniederlassung Zürich 2012
Klosbachstr. 107
CH-8032 Zürich
Tel. +41 (0) 44-251 75 05
Fax +41 (0) 44-251 75 06
e-Mail: zuerich@lit-verlag.ch
http://www.lit-verlag.ch

LIT VERLAG Dr. W. Hopf
Berlin 2012
Fresnostr. 2
D-48159 Münster
Tel. +49 (0) 2 51-620 320
Fax +49 (0) 2 51-23 19 72
e-Mail: lit@lit-verlag.de
http://www.lit-verlag.de

Distribution:

In Germany: LIT Verlag Fresnostr. 2, D-48159 Münster
Tel. +49 (0) 2 51-620 32 22, Fax +49 (0) 2 51-922 60 99, e-mail: vertrieb@lit-verlag.de

In Austria: Medienlogistik Pichler-ÖBZ, e-mail: mlo@medien-logistik.at

In Switzerland: B + M Buch- und Medienvertrieb, e-mail: order@buch-medien.ch

In the UK: Global Book Marketing, e-mail: mo@centralbooks.com

JOURNAL OF LEGAL PLURALISM
and Unofficial Law

POLICY

The Journal of Legal Pluralism and Unofficial Law (JLP) is a refereed, independent, inter-disciplinary, international journal devoted to scholarly writing, documentation, information on current developments, and communications about all aspects of legal pluralism and unofficial law anywhere in the world and at any time. Issues 1-18 bear the name *African Law Studies*.

MANUSCRIPTS

Manuscripts for the Journal of Legal Pluralism should be submitted to the editor-in-chief:

Melanie G. Wiber
Department of Anthropology, University of New Brunswick
P.O. Box 4400, Fredericton, N.B.
Canada E3B 5A3
Fax: (+ 01) (506) 453-5071
Email: wiber@unb.ca

or to one of the associate editors. Unless the editors are otherwise informed, submission of a manuscript implies the undertaking that it is not currently being considered by another journal and that if accepted it will be available for publication.

Manuscripts must conform to the style and other instructions contained in the JLP 'style sheet' (to be found on the JLP web site under the title 'Author guidelines'), and should generally be submitted in electronic form.

SUBSCRIPTIONS

From nr. 49 (2004) the Journal of Legal Pluralism has been published by LIT Verlag, Münster-Hamburg-Berlin-Vienna-London, whose address for inquiries about subscriptions and for orders is Grevener St./Fresnostr.2, D-48159 Münster, Germany, Fax (+49) (0)251 23 19 72, vertrieb@lit-verlag.de.
Back numbers of African Law Studies and the Journal of Legal Pluralism to nr. 48 are available from William S. Hein & Co., Inc., 1285 Main Street, Buffalo, New York 14209-1987, USA..

INDEXES AND DATABASES

Articles appearing in the Journal of Legal Pluralism are indexed in the principal legal and social science indexes and online data-bases. It is planned to make available the full text of all articles published more than two years previously on the website of the Journal of Legal Pluralism at www.jlp.bham.ac.uk . Currently the site contains the full text of all articles in nrs. 15 to 57, and abstracts of articles in nrs. 43 to the current number.

CITATION

The Journal of Legal Pluralism and Unofficial Law should be cited as: *Journal of Legal Pluralism*.

CONTENTS

FROM THE EDITORS

As was announced in Number 62 of the *Journal of Legal Pluralism*, Melanie G. Wiber has assumed the position of editor-in-chief as of Number 63 (this volume). The transition period has been one of an enormous learning curve, and Melanie Wiber is deeply indebted to Gordon R. Woodman for his continuing support and hard work on behalf of the journal.

As many readers know, this is a challenging time for journal publications, with many new publishing venues and arrangements being developed, including ejournals and blended hard copy and electronic journal options. Gordon Woodman and Melanie Wiber have been actively researching ways to better serve our readership, and hope to have some options in the near future that will provide for a wide variety of readers' needs.

Melanie Wiber would like to thank the new and continuing members of our Board of Associate Editors, who have been invaluable in providing feedback and advice on both manuscripts and publishing options. It is also worth thanking our many peer review scholars who have given freely of their time and effort to review and in many cases substantially improve the manuscripts the journal has been receiving.

About this Number

This issue represents the additional contribution of Helene Kyed, as guest editor. Dr. Kyed is a researcher at the Danish Institute for International Studies. She has selected papers for this volume from those presented at the 1-3 November, 2010 Conference in Copenhagen with the title: *Access to Justice and Security. Non-State Actors and Local Dynamics of Ordering*. Her introduction to the volume gives an excellent summary of the many contributions of this set of readings to the concepts and manifestations of legal pluralism in the security and order field.

This number also introduces a new innovation in the *Journal of Legal Pluralism*, as it is the first issue which provides contact information for the corresponding author of each paper. We hope that readers will find this and other innovations to come useful in creating and/or enhancing a lively and interactive space for research and scholarly communication.

ABSTRACTS OF ARTICLES

JLP 63: 25-47

JUSTICE AND SECURITY ARCHITECTURE IN AFRICA: THE PLANS, THE BRICKS, THE PURSE AND THE BUILDER

Bruce Baker

This article examines international interventions in policing and justice in Sub-Saharan Africa. It calls for increased local ownership and realistic plans that are based on what is available, affordable, effective and legitimate whether this is state provision or not. Yet international development agencies, even when they recognise the importance of so-called 'non-state' actors, are still primarily concerned with building state provision. When, however, the categories of 'state' and 'non-state' are examined more critically, it is seen that the boundary between these categories of actors is blurred, dynamic and subject to local negotiation. The indications are that the distinction between 'state' and 'non-state' is maintained because it serves the interest of powerful actors, including international donors. Conversely, the distinction makes little sense to ordinary citizens, who are more concerned with who actually provides quality policing and justice, not with who authorises it. Based on these observations, the article supports an alternative, 'multi-layered' approach to policing and justice, which is based on the inclusion of a plurality of providers and which has an emphasis on networks.

JLP 63: 49-72

RECONFIGURING STATE AND NON-STATE ACTORS IN THE PROVISION OF SAFETY IN (SOUTH) AFRICA: IMPLICATIONS FOR BOTTOM-UP POLICING ARRANGEMENTS AND FOR DONOR FUNDING

Monique Marks, Jennifer Wood, Julian Azzopardi and Thokozani Xaba

In this article we seek to move beyond conventional understanding of the state as the central provider of security and justice to think in a broader way about what donors might do to improve policing. We take a critical look at the nature of the state in South Africa today with an emphasis on policing being delivered through pluralized arrangements of state and non-state actors. Given that non-state actors carry out most forms of 'everyday policing' (Buur and Jensen 2004), we address the question of how the South African state might best position itself in this plural world. We argue for a circumscribed role for the public police that can both complement and strengthen everyday policing arrangements. We further argue that this policing system, broadly defined, be 'anchored' (Loader and Walker, 2007) at the local level through a municipal structure of strategic planning and regulation. We suggest some implications of this framework for international donor funding.

JLP 63: 73-109

NEITHER STATE NOR CUSTOM – JUST NAKED POWER: THE CONSEQUENCES OF IDEALS-ORIENTED RULE OF LAW POLICY-MAKING IN LIBERIA

Stephen Lubkemann, Deborah Isser and Peter Chapman

In this article we provide an empirically grounded critique of the internationally-driven 'Rule of Law' policy approach in post-conflict Liberia by highlighting the consequences of policy-makers difficulties in coming to terms with the realities of legal pluralism. Informed by a 'progressive' intent to establish a single formal justice system for all Liberians, this approach has promoted policies that ignore or seek to constrain customary justice institutions because they are seen as violating human rights and falling short of international justice standards - even though they are preferred by most of the population. These efforts also involve a top-down approach to reconstituting and reforming the formal legal system that, to date, has largely neglected capacity-building at the local level while emphasizing narrow technical remedies (such as legislation revision) that fail to account for social, economic, and political realities. This approach has undermined the customary justice systems without improving the capacity or performance of the formal justice system - resulting in a growing 'justice vacuum'. For most Liberians the quest to obtain justice in this 'vacuum' has increasingly become little more than an effort to secure advantage over opponents through the mobilization of social networks, by exercising political and/or economic power, or through other extra-judicial means. In this context 'customary and 'state/formal' justice institutions are not approached by most Liberians as distinct avenues for seeking justice but rather as poles in a single power topography. This topography includes a wide array of other actors and institutions that are not a part of either the formal or the customary justice systems but who are often appealed to and frequently affect justice outcomes. In conclusion we consider several political effects of the constraint of customary justice and the broader implications of dismissing pluralism for Liberia's delicate post-conflict peace building and political development processes.

JLP 63: 111-142

THE POLITICS OF CUSTOMARY LAW ASCERTAINMENT IN SOUTH SUDAN

Cherry Leonardi, Deborah Isser, Leben Moro and Martina Santschi

This article focuses on a strategy produced by the Government of Southern Sudan and the UNDP in 2009 for a written ascertainment of customary law. It argues that this strategy reflected a legalistic desire to regulate and order the hybrid, composite practices and laws of the local courts and to ensure certainty, predictability and substantive requirements such as equality and due process. Based on empirical research into local justice in 2009-10, the article argues that the goal of ascertainment was driven more by multiple - often contradictory - political agendas than by the actual needs of litigants. The universalising discourse of international rule of law programming can mask the politics of interventions. But in South Sudan, the politics of justice intersected with broader debate over decentralisation of government and over ethnic and cultural rights, at both national and local levels. The contradictions within the ascertainment strategy were in turn a product of long-standing tensions between local culture and universal norms, tensions that litigants and justice providers were exploiting creatively by employing multiple logics and laws to argue cases. The article explores the question of whether more certain or fixed laws would strengthen or hinder access to justice for the weak or poor, arguing that in the current context in South Sudan the interests of the latter were served more by the accessibility and flexibility of the law and justice provided by chiefs and by some county-level magistrates. The article explores the nature of this living law as it was manifest in actual court cases, and argues that it differed from the normative assertions of customary law that recording has tended to produce. Finally the article uses an example of recent tensions over customary law and justice in Rumbek to illustrate some of the potential pitfalls of trying to introduce greater certainty of judicial outcomes, and to reinforce our arguments for the politicised nature of law.

JLP 63: 143-177

HYBRID AND 'EVERYDAY' POLITICAL ORDERING: CONSTRUCTING AND CONTESTING LEGITIMACY IN SOMALILAND

Louise Wiuff Moe

A number of recent post-colonial liberal peace critiques have moved beyond the counter-positioning of 'liberal/Western' versus 'communal/non-Western' peace and political order. Instead, they draw attention to the *interstices* - the processes of contestation, repulsion and accommodation - between these approaches. Some argue that the most promising, if contentious, forms of political ordering and peace building take place exactly in a hybrid of state-based and liberal practices, and local customs and 'everyday' life in post-conflict settings.

Through a case-study of Somaliland, this article examines the potentials and limits of such a hybrid approach to advancing peace and political order. The analysis in particular engages with the largely uncharted issue of how political legitimacy is constructed or undermined, in the context of post-conflict hybrid political orders.
Somaliland's reconstruction process was characterised by very low international intervention when compared to other so-called 'fragile states' and post-conflict settings. The article looks at how political institutions and structures of governance were constituted from *within* Somaliland through local agencies and formation of alliances, which cut across the dichotomies of 'state/non-state' and 'liberal/traditional' forms of governance and legitimacy. It illustrates the advantages, as well as some of the challenges, of this process of political ordering and hybridization, where the domestic sphere was allowed to be constitutive for the creation of legitimacy.

Examining a small-scale international-local initiative of peace dialogues and community policing in Somaliland, the article also discusses how international support may engage with 'everyday' strategies of self-securing, and deliberately 'facilitate' hybridity in the context of conflict management and justice.

The analysis offers an empirical anchoring of the concepts of 'hybridity' and the 'everyday', but also demonstrates how the case of Somaliland speaks more broadly to post-colonial liberal peace critiques and the call for new approaches to peace and political order.

JLP 63: 179-205

SPINNING A CONFLICT MANAGEMENT WEB IN VANUATU: CREATING AND STRENGTHENING LINKS BETWEEN STATE AND NON-STATE LEGAL INSTITUTIONS

Miranda Forsyth

This article argues that increasing the quality of conflict management in legally plural countries requires creating and strengthening linkages between state and non-state legal systems. Given that the resources relevant to conflict management are currently held by both state and non-state actors and institutions, this will facilitate a more efficient and effective sharing of these resources. It will also help to eliminate the problems involved with forum shopping, and promote the development of more autochthonous and legitimate conflict management institutions as each legal system learns from and adapts to the other. The article discusses a number of initiatives that have taken place in Vanuatu, a country in the South Pacific, that have forged such linkages, and draws out lessons from them about how to better create and strengthen such linkages. The final section of the article proposes a new conceptual framework to help to centralise the analysis of links in conflict management reform. The conflict management web framework presented here approaches reform in a holistic way, taking account of *all* the actors and institutions involved in this field in a given jurisdiction. It emphasises the need to develop and strengthen the links between institutions and actors whose actions directly or indirectly affect one another in order to help them to work together better. This means both between state, non-state and hybrid actors and institutions, and also between international donors, academics and NGOs.

JLP 63: 207-230

DECENTRALISED POWER AND TRADITIONAL AUTHORITIES: HOW POWER DETERMINES ACCESS TO JUSTICE IN SIERRA LEONE

Paul Jackson

This article explores how international donor-supported decentralisation efforts and justice and security sector reform in Sierra Leone's post-conflict reconstruction process have intersected with local power dynamics and ordinary citizens' access to justice and security. Decentralisation efforts have introduced democratically elected local governments, but also retain a significant role for traditional chiefs, which have created the grounds for conflicts between chiefs and councillors over power and resources. In terms of justice provision, this leaves the citizen with a nominally wide choice, but with rivalries and unpredictable actors to choose from. This has been further complicated by new internationally supported paralegal programmes run by NGOs, which also provide a threat to the chiefs and their virtual monopoly of power in local justice. The article argues that the micro-political processes of actors existing in a space between 'state' and 'non-state' effectively mean that there has been a tendency of elite capture of the decentralisation efforts at the local level as well as a continuation of chiefdom power. This result acts to the detriment to those who have always lost out on access to justice and security. Based on these insights, the article provides a solid critique of international development agencies' tendency to assume that the traditional and formal systems are somehow unaffected by local power structures. It also challenges the perceived dichotomy between 'modern' and 'traditional' systems, instead arguing that within Sierra Leone there is a hybrid network of institutions that constantly change and are subject to a variety of controlling bodies. The problem with this network is that to a greater or lesser degree all of the institutions are occupied by the same groups of people and so the excluded may remain excluded whilst the local elite may retain and extend their power over a mix of different institutions.

JLP 63: 231-262

DELIVERING JUSTICE: THE CHANGING GENDERED DYNAMICS OF LAND TENURE IN BOTSWANA

Anne Griffiths

This article argues for the important role of social networks in legal pluralism contexts, and in doing so for the importance of moving beyond abstract assertions about law and legal processes. It is based on an in-depth study (2009-2010) of women's access to and control over land in Botswana, within a legal pluralist context where the state is highly heterogeneous and where customary and statutory law administer land through varying institutions that derive their power from a constellation of sources. The article shows that a much higher proportion of women now gain formal customary land titles and certificates than was the case 25 years ago. This overall reflects that access to land is no longer influenced as much by gender as by "class". The latter represents a constellation of factors that contribute to the accumulation of human, social as well as economic capital. While improvements in women's access to land are partly owed to changes in land law, the role of Land Boards, and the influence of human rights NGOs, access to land is strongly influenced by social networks and informal transactions. What is crucial are the factors that contribute to the social networks that individuals can draw on, which have an impact on their capacity to negotiate poverty and access to justice in both formal and informal domains. Legal pluralism within this context reflects mutually constitutive processes that draw on and intersect with the social dimensions of everyday life. These insights ought to have an important bearing on the strategies of international development agencies' focus on the linkages between poverty reduction, access to justice and property rights.

ABOUT THE CONTRIBUTORS

Julian AZZOPARDI is Head of Education and Training at Inspire - The Foundation for Inclusion, an NGO providing services to persons with disability in Malta and Gozo. Previously, he has worked in the socio-economic development sphere both in a professional and voluntary capacity in India, South Africa and various countries in South America. Between 2000 and 2006, Mr. Azzopardi worked with various European Institutions in Brussels addressing competition, employment and development issues. He holds a BA (Hons) in International Relations from the University of Malta and an MA (Cum Laude) in Development Studies from the University of KwazuluNatal in Durban, South Africa. This is Mr. Azzopardi's second collaboration on a book chapter whilst having previously published a book review in Transformation in 2010. Contact Julian.azzopardi@inspire.org.mt.

Bruce BAKER is Professor of African Security and the Director of African Studies Centre at Coventry University. He has published widely on non-state policing. His latest book is: *Security in Post-conflict Africa: The role of non-state policing* (CRC Press, 2009). Contact bruce@bakerbrum.co.uk.

Peter CHAPMAN is a consultant with the Justice for the Poor Program in the Justice Reform Group of the World Bank. From 2009 to 2011 he worked on a legal empowerment and local justice program with the Carter Center in Liberia. Prior to that, he worked on issues of accountability, human rights and civil society in Cambodia and East Africa along with environmental law in the United States. Contact pfchap@gmail.com.

Miranda FORSYTH, BA/LLB (Hons) (University of Melbourne), LLM (University of Connecticut), PhD (Australian National University) is a Postdoctoral Fellow at the Regulatory Network in the College of Asia and the Pacific at the Australian National University. Previously she spent eight years working in Vanuatu, first as a Public Prosecutor and then as a lecturer in criminal law at the University of the South Pacific. Her doctoral research investigated the relationship between the state criminal justice system and the customary justice system in Vanuatu and proposed a new method to allow the two systems to work in a more mutually supportive way. The results of this research have been published in the book *A Bird that Flies with Two Wings: State and Kastom Justice Systems in Vanuatu* (2009) ANU ePress. In 2010 Miranda was awarded an ARC Discovery grant to investigate ways in which intellectual property laws can be used to promote development in the Pacific Island Countries. Contact Miranda.Forsyth@anu.edu.au.

Anne GRIFFITHS is professor and holds a personal chair in the Anthropology of Law at the School of Law at Edinburgh University. Her research focuses on anthropology of law, comparative and family law, African law, gender, culture and rights and juvenile justice. Her most recent publications include *The Power of Law in a Transnational World: Anthropological Enquires* (2009); *Spatializing Law: An Anthropological Geography of Law in Society* (2009) and *Mobile People, Mobile Law: Expanding Legal Relations in a Contracting World* (2005) co-edited with F. and K. von Benda-Beckmann. Over the years she has held visiting appointments at various institutions including Senior Research Fellow, International Research Centre on Work and the Human Lifecycle in Global History (IKG), Humboldt University, Berlin (2010-2011), Distinguished Visiting Professor, Faculty of Law, University of Toronto, the Max Planck Institute for Social Anthropology, Halle/Saale, Germany, The International Institute for the Sociology of Law Oñati - Gipuzkoa, Spain. The University of Texas at Austin, School of Law and the Southern and Eastern African Regional Centre for Women's Law at the University of Zimbabwe. She is currently a member of the Executive Body of the Commission on Pluralism, a branch of the International Union of Anthropological and Ethnological Sciences, of which she was President from 2003-2009. Her current research, funded by the Leverhulme (2009-2010) is on the *Gendered Dynamics of Land Tenure in Southern Africa*. Contact Anne.Griffiths@ed.ac.uk.

Deborah ISSER (JD) is Head of the Justice for the Poor Programme in the World Bank. Previously she was a Senior Rule of Law Advisor at the United States Institute of Peace, where she directed the project on Customary Justice and Legal Pluralism. Her work has involved field research, policy analysis and facilitated dialogue in Liberia, Southern Sudan, Afghanistan and Melanesia. She is the editor of *Customary Justice and the Rule of Law in War-Torn Societies* (USIP Press, 2011), and the author of numerous articles and book chapters on justice reform in conflict affected states. Contact disser@worldbank.org.

Professor Paul JACKSON is currently Head of the International Development Department at the University of Birmingham in the UK. He has expertise in post-conflict reconstruction, state building, governance, decentralisation and security governance. He has a body of research, policy work and training on the relationships between state and non-state actors, decentralisation, institutional development and governance, particularly in situations where the state has collapsed or is fragile. Recent experience includes Nepal, Northern Uganda, Sierra Leone, Rwanda, and the Caucasus. As Director of the Global Facilitation Network for Security Sector Reform, Paul Jackson has been involved in providing research support and training to FCO, MOD and DFID officials. He sits on the Geneva DCAF Advisory Board, is a member of the Folke Bernadotte Institute working group on Security Sector Reform and directs the International Development Department's postgraduate programme in Conflict, Security and Development. His evaluation, with Peter Albrecht, of the UK Government's involvement in post-conflict Sierra Leone, *Rebuilding Sierra Leone: Security Sector Reform,* was published at the end of 2010 by Palgrave Macmillan. Contact p.b.jackson@bham.ac.uk.

Helene Maria KYED is a researcher at the Danish Institute for International Studies. She has a Master Honours degree in Social Anthropology and a PhD degree in International Development Studies. Kyed has extensive research experience within the field of legal pluralism, including long-term fieldwork in Mozambique on the state recognition of traditional authorities and the interaction between state and non-state justice and security providers. Particularly, Kyed has addressed the political implications of state-non-state engagements, and addressed theoretical questions concerning competing forms of sovereignty, social ordering and claims to authority. Current research also engages with the topic of community policing in Mozambique and Swaziland. She has co-edited four book anthologies, *State Recognition and Democratization in Sub-Saharan Africa. A New Dawn for Traditional Authorities?* (New York: Palgrave-Macmillan 2007); *State Recognition of Local Authorities and Public Participation: Experiences, Obstacles and Possibilities in Mozambique* (Maputo: Kapicua 2007); *Perspectives on Involving Non-State and Customary Actors in Justice and Security Reform* (Rome: IDLO 2011); and *The Dynamics of Legal Pluralism in Mozambique* (Maputo: Kapicua 2012). She has also published articles in peer-reviewed international journals and book chapters on the topics of traditional authority, citizenship, sovereignty and local forms of justice enforcement and policing. Contact hmk@diis.dk.

Cherry LEONARDI (PhD, History) is a Lecturer in African History at Durham University, UK. Her research and publications since 2001 have focused on the historical and contemporary role of chiefs in Southern Sudan, and what this reveals about governance, state-society relations and political and judicial cultures. She is currently writing a book on this subject based on a combination of fieldwork, oral histories and archival sources. Contact d.c.leonardi@durham.ac.uk.

Stephen LUBKEMANN is Associate Professor of Anthropology, International

Affairs, and African Studies at The George Washington University. He has conducted fieldwork in Mozambique, South Africa, Liberia, and Angola and among African refugees and migrants in Europe and in the U.S. From 2007-10 he partnered with USIP on the project Customary and Informal Legal Systems in Liberia: Rule of Law Options for the First Post-Conflict Decade and is currently directing a research project on urban justice in collaboration with the Carter Center. He has authored numerous articles and book chapters, co-edited three volumes and authored the book *Culture in Chaos: An Anthropology of the Social Condition in War* (Chicago, 2008). His research focuses primarily on social and political change in protracted conflict settings and on the interaction amongst international, local, and transnational actors in war-torn contexts. Contact sl02@gwu.edu or Stephen.Lubkemann@gmail.com.

Monique MARKS is based in the Community Development Programme at the University of KwaZulu-Natal in South Africa. She is also a Research Associate of the Centre of Criminology at the University of Cape Town. She has published widely in the areas of youth social movements, ethnographic research methods, police labour relations, police organizational change, and security governance. She has published three books: *Young Warriors: Youth Identity, Politics and Violence in South Africa*; *Transforming the Robocops: Changing Police in South Africa;* and *Police Occupational Culture: New Debates and Directions* (co-edited with Anne-Marie Singh and Megan O'Neill). Her fourth book (co-edited with David Sklansky) *Police Reform from the Bottom Up: Police Officers and their Unions as Agents of Change* is to be published by Routledge. Contact marks@nu.ac.za.

Leben Nelson MORO received his M.Sc. in forced migration and D.Phil. in development studies from the University of Oxford. Currently, he is an assistant professor at the Center of Peace and Development Studies, University of Juba, Sudan, where he teaches graduate courses in forced migration and development and primarily conducts research on development-induced displacement and resettlement, focusing on oil-induced displacement in Sudan. He has conducted fieldwork in the oil areas of South Sudan and among Sudanese refugees in Egypt, Uganda and Kenya. Some of the findings of his studies appeared in the *Journal of Refugee Studies* (Oxford University), *St. Anthony's International Review* (Oxford University), *Forced Migration Review* (Oxford University), *New Internationalist* and *Pambazuka News*. Contact lebenmoro@hotmail.coml.

Martina SANTSCHI is a PhD researcher at Swisspeace. She holds an MA in social anthropology, ecology and biology from the University of Bern. Her PhD research focuses on the ways in which actors, including traditional authorities, negotiate statehood and authority in the local arenas of postconflict South Sudan. She has been working as a consultant for the Swiss government on councils of traditional authorities in South Sudan. During her studies her main research interests were ethnicity and conflicts in Eastern and Central Africa. She conducted field research in northern Uganda and eastern Democratic Republic of Congo. Contact martina.santschi@swisspeace.ch.

Louise WIUFF MOE is a Ph.D. candidate at the School of Political Science and International Studies, University of Queensland. She holds a Master's degree in International Studies from the University of Stellenbosch under an exchange agreement with the International Peace Research Institute, Oslo (PRIO). In 2008, Ms. Wiuff Moe was a visiting researcher at the Academy for Peace and Development in Somaliland (northwest Somalia). Subsequently, she worked as a junior researcher for the Finnish Institute of International Affairs and the Crisis Management Initiative in Helsinki. Research areas include: peace processes; political legitimacy and governance capacities in fragile settings; interfaces between state and non-state forms of governance. Contact louise.wiuffmoe@uqconnect.edu.au.

Jennifer WOOD is an Associate Professor of Criminal Justice at Temple University (Philadelphia, USA) and is a Methods Core member of Robert Wood Johnson's program for Public Health Law Research. Her work focuses on the delivery of policing and security in the context of wider shifts in regulation and governance. Her current research examines the nexus between security and public health. She teaches courses on qualitative research, criminal behaviour, crime and social policy, and policing. She is the author of *Imagining Security* (2007; with Clifford Shearing), co-editor of *Democracy, Society and the Governance of Security* (2006; with Benoît Dupont), and co-editor of *Fighting Crime Together: The Challenges of Policing and Security Networks* (2006; with Jenny Fleming). Prior to joining Temple University in 2007, Dr. Wood was a Fellow at the Regulatory Institutions Network, Australian National University. Contact woodj@temple.edu.

Thokozani XABA is the Dean and Head of School of Built Environment and Development Studies at the University of KwaZulu-Natal. He has a PhD from the University of California, Berkeley. His areas of specialization are the sociology of knowledge, ancient African history, community development and power and authority in urban and rural development. Contact Xabat@ukzn.ac.za.

INTRODUCTION TO THE SPECIAL ISSUE

LEGAL PLURALISM AND INTERNATIONAL DEVELOPMENT INTERVENTIONS

Helene Maria Kyed (Guest Editor)

Introduction

The concept of legal pluralism is no longer solely an analytical concept, used by socio-legal scholars to describe the plurality of normative orders and institutions that enforce order within a political organization. It is today an explicit 'policy concept' applied in the policies of international development agencies and of some governments. Such has been the case especially during the past five to ten years. This special issue is about the influence of international development intervention on situations of legal pluralism as part of Western donors' support to justice and security reform in so-called 'fragile states' and in developing countries undergoing democratic transition.[1] It therefore explores one aspect of legal pluralism as a

[1] The articles in this special issue are revised versions of a selected number of the papers presented at the 1-3 November, 2010 Conference in Copenhagen with the title: *Access to Justice and Security. Non-State Actors and Local Dynamics of Ordering*. The conference was organised by the Danish Institute for International Studies (DIIS) with support from the Danish Ministry of Foreign Affairs and with additional funding from the International Development Law Organisation (IDLO)

newly emerging 'policy field' - that is, as a field for problem definition, intervention, reform and regulation (Shore and Wright 1997). [2] In international development intervention, this is exemplified by donor agencies increasingly recognising the importance of 'non-state', 'informal' and 'customary' institutions, practices and norms in the 'delivery of justice and security' (see DFID 2004; Chirayath et al. 2005 (World Bank); OECD 2007; UNDP 2009; OHCHR 2006; Danida 2010; USAID 2005, 2009). In some contexts this has led donors to advocate for "the need to incorporate customary systems in justice reform strategies" (Isser 2011: 325). This new tendency marks a fundamental departure from past international donor policies, which focused on formal state institutions, in effect supporting a kind of legal centralism (see Griffiths 1986; von Benda Beckmann 1997).[3]

Yet the question still remains: how is legal pluralism actually applied in the policies and programmes of international development agencies? And when we look closer at international interventions: what are their underlying objectives and what repercussions does their recognition of legal pluralism have in practice for the different actors involved?

The contributions to this special issue engage with these questions by providing empirically grounded and critical analyses of the interface between international development intervention and local mechanisms of justice and policing in a number of predominantly African countries (Northern Somalia/Somaliland, South Sudan, Liberia, Vanuatu, Botswana, Sierra Leone, and South Africa). They do so in

(for other outputs from the conference see Albrecht and Kyed (2010); Albrecht, Kyed, Harper and Isser (2011)). I am strongly indebted to Peter Albrecht (DIIS) for discussions of the issues presented here and for collaboration in organising the conference and in developing its ideas.

[2] The shift in international development policies towards more inclusion of legal pluralism was also discussed in an earlier issue of this Journal, which differs from this issue because it focused specifically on human rights (see vol. 60, 2010, guest edited by Yüksel Sezgin).

[3] The concept of legal centralism refers to the ideologically informed claim that "[...] law is and should be the law of the state, uniform for all persons, exclusive of all other law, and administered by a single set of state institutions" (Griffiths 1986: 3).

different ways. Some analyse how internationally-supported reforms have been implemented locally. Others explore local initiatives that can inspire future international intervention in alternative ways. The article on Somaliland also provides an example of a very low level of international intervention. Moreover, while some articles focus predominantly on dispute resolution and justice issues - the classical focus of legal pluralist studies - others also deal with policing and local security groups.

In common for the articles is a critical stance towards state-centric and legalistic models of intervention and reform. A number of the articles illustrate the negative consequences of such models for ordinary citizens' access to justice and security in post-conflict contexts (Liberia, Sierra Leone and South Sudan). Others give examples of alternative approaches that are small-scale and locally grounded (in Vanuatu, Somaliland, and South Africa) and which may be strengthened by legislative changes and the support of NGOs (in Botswana on land access). In common is the argument that the ideal-typical understanding of 'the State', which informs the state-centric model of intervention, is so far removed from empirical realities - and may actually stumble upon change 'from within' - that there is a need to fundamentally change the way that statehood is (still) conceptualised by international agencies.

Against this background the contributions to this issue bring into play a number of alternative concepts such as 'hybridity', 'plurality', 'networks', 'nodes' and 'webs'. These can be seen as a critique of how international development agencies currently apply the concept of legal pluralism. The issue also highlights the need to focus on 'the politics of legal pluralism' (Kyed 2009), both empirically and as a policy field. This is informed by an understanding of justice and security provision, and by extension social ordering, as deeply political phenomena, being both the product of broader power relations as well as part of (re)producing such relations. However, before discussing the alternative thinking proposed in this issue, it is worth looking briefly at past state-centric models of intervention, how the shift was brought about and how legal pluralism is currently applied in international development programmes.

International Development Policies on Justice and Security: From Past to Present

Until very recently, international support to justice and security reform was directed almost exclusively at formal state institutions (e.g. courts, legislature, the police and correctional services). Some funding was also given to those civil society organisations that fit the image of their Western counterparts, such as human rights leagues. The objective was to build states along Euro-American lines, based on Western definitions of the rule of law and an ideal Weberian model of state sovereignty (Weber 1978).[4] In this optic 'state building' is equal to strengthening state monopoly on security and justice functions. Simultaneously, justice and security reforms were presented as technical legal tasks rather than deeply social and political processes (see Isser 2011: 3-5; Harper 2011: 34).[5] This state-centric, legalistic approach became the subject of internal critique from the mid-2000s. In a World Bank background paper it was for instance stated that:

> Justice sector reforms have frequently been based on institutional transplants, wherein the putatively 'successful' legal codes (constitutions, contract law, etc.) and institutions (courts, legal services organizations, etc.) of developed countries have been imported almost verbatim into developing countries [...] Local level context and the systems of justice actually operating in many contexts were largely ignored. As such, justice sector reformers have failed to acknowledge, and thus comprehend, how the systems—which, at least in rural areas, are predominantly customary, idiosyncratic to specific sub-regional and cultural contexts, and residing only in oral form—by which many people (if not most poor people) in developing countries order their lives function. (Chirayath et al. 2005: 1)

Moreover, customary, or other institutions that divert from ideal 'rule of law' templates were seen as representing "[...] archaic, 'backward', or rigid practices

---

[4] This focus on state institutions does not mean that international agencies have been unaware of the predominance of non-state and customary justice institutions in many of the countries where they intervene. For instance, of the 78 assessments of legal systems undertaken by the World Bank since 1994, many mention the prevalence of traditional justice, yet none of the World Bank projects deal explicitly with traditional legal systems (Chirayath et al. 2005: 3).

[5] Stephen Golup (2003) has referred to this as 'rule of law orthodoxy' driven by legal professionals, who prefer working within familiar-formalist settings and who view institutions outside of the state as too 'messy' and complex.

that are not amenable to modernization, efficient market relations, or broader development goals" (Chirayath et al. 2005: 4), and as frequently violating the international human rights that most donor agencies commit themselves to promoting (Harper 2011: 34).

Today by contrast the majority of multilateral and bilateral donor agencies including the United Nations and the World Bank, officially embrace the legal pluralist position.[6] There are different reasons for this apparently drastic shift. One is the poor success rate of interventions aimed at transforming formal state institutions into well-functioning systems. Another is the realisation that international agencies need to accommodate the empirical fact that 'non-state actors' or 'informal systems' are the primary locus of dispute resolution and often the most accessible and effective justice providers in the eyes of most citizens. This not least concerns poor and marginalized citizens, who are commonly the intended beneficiaries of donor supported reforms. Moreover, there seems to be increased agreement that donors need to engage constructively with 'customary systems' because it "can improve the legitimacy of the state and its formal institutions, whereas repressing them can exacerbate tensions" (Isser 2011: 326). This argument also supports efforts to *de jure* broaden the entire system of justice and security provision, by expanding the number of providers, rather than 'investing' in the state alone. Finally, many donor agencies now see involvement with for instance customary leaders as a way to stem human rights violations, i.e. by 'targeting' the places where they occur (Harper 2011: 36).[7] In short, the shift in donor policies reflects in part a genuine wish to be more inclusive of plurality, and in part a pragmatic reaction towards 'targeting' more beneficiaries, expanding the number of 'service providers', and working with 'what is there' in contexts with

[6] During the past three years there have also been a growing number of comprehensive studies for guiding international donor policies and programmes, some commissioned directly by the donors themselves, others with some financial support from donors. The most significant ones have been produced respectively by the United States Institute for Peace (USIP), International Development Law Organization (IDLO); International Council for Human Rights Policy (ICHRP); Danish Institute for Human Rights (DIHR); International IDEA; and the Netherlands Institute for International Relations, 'Clingendael'.

[7] For more details on the reasons behind the donor shift towards recognising legal pluralism, see Albrecht and Kyed 2011; Chopra and Isser 2011; Harper 2011; Isser 2011.

'weak' state capacity. As addressed next this can lead to a rather contradictory application of legal pluralism as a 'policy concept'.

How is 'legal pluralism' used by international agencies today?

Overall the contributors to this issue agree that international development agencies have come a long way in accepting the importance of including non-state legal orders in any policy-discussion of justice and security reform.[8] However, the approach to legal pluralism is surrounded by ambiguity and ideological baggage. Some even suggest that the recognition of legal pluralism remains by and large rhetorical. The actual support to non-state legal orders are marginal and often is simply a 'transitional strategy' towards - or as a pragmatic means to pursue - conventional (i.e. Euro-American style) state-building (Isser 2011: 325; Albrecht 2010). In other situations international agencies recognise the role played by customary or informal 'systems', but support government efforts to constrain their areas of jurisdiction. Or they try to 'fix' customary 'systems' according to rule of law principles so as to make them more like formal state justice (Harper 2011: 38). As such, international donors may actually contribute to suppressing the very plurality that they have otherwise now (officially) come to recognise.

As Bruce Baker argues (this issue), an idealized version of the Weberian state seems to remain the end-goal. [9] Ultimately this makes it difficult for donors to envision a genuinely plural system. Often when informal institutions are in fact

[8] I realise the danger of lumping together 'international development agencies', as if they all share identical agendas and programme approaches. There is indeed variety among agencies in how they approach legal pluralism, not least if we also include the projects and programmes of International and National Non-Governmental Organisations (NGOs). Here I am therefore providing a generalised picture. In the individual contributions to the issue, variety will come to the fore.

[9] This is also reflected in, for instance, the World Bank's overall approach to development and security, as represented in the very recent World Development report. Despite a new turn towards recognizing non-state institutions the World Bank still holds onto a specific model of statehood where the state has a clear monopoly on security provision (World Bank 2011); see also Nordic Africa Institute comments by Finn Stepputat and Louise Riis Andersen, at http://www.nai.uu.se/forum/entries/2011/08/22/a-small-step/index.xml).

included into justice programmes they are 'targeted' to provide civic education about the formal system and human rights or are themselves seen as targets of such education. Even when more 'pluralistic approaches' are *de facto* used, there is still a tendency for a continuity of the legalistic approaches of the past. Predominantly, resources have been used to: 'sensitize' traditional leaders to state law and international human rights; 'harmonize' customary practices with Western law; develop the capacity of customary systems through training or infrastructure; establish oversight mechanisms for customary justice processes to ensure compliance with human rights; support national or local processes of codifying or ascertaining 'customary law' so as to make it more broadly known and compatible with a system of appeal with the formal court system; efforts to expand the participation in customary decision-making, e.g. by introducing elections or quotas into the membership of dispute resolution forums, and develop institutional linkages to state systems, which is believed to improve the effectiveness of customary justice (Isser 2011: 342-3; Harper 2011: 41-51; Ubink and van Rooij 2011: 12-14).[10] In short, these all include activities that would - if successful – 'adjust' or 'reform' the non-state legal orders to the main principles and standards of international agencies, however in the very 'name' of recognising pluralism.

Commonly, arguments by international agencies for reforming non-state legal orders are that the latter, among positive attributes, also represent 'negative' aspects, such as gender discrimination and other kinds of human rights violations. In fact, justice reform practitioners, who today recognise legal pluralism, typically work with an approach that seeks to (1) minimize the 'negative' aspects of non-state legal orders, while (2) 'preserving' their 'positive' aspects such as accessibility and effectiveness and (3) 'improving' their ability to meet Western rule of law notions of certainty, predictability and substantive requirements such as equality and due process. Importantly, what is seen here as 'negative' and 'positive' is based on international criteria of what is 'good' justice; not on those notions of justice grounded in local realities and experiences.

Such, essentially ideologically-driven programming, has also informed why many donor agencies, including international NGOs, have actually ended up doing what a World Bank paper recommended in 2005: to focus *not* on supporting already

[10] For detailed accounts of the different international donor approaches to engage with customary and informal justice systems, including empirical examples, see Harper 2011; Ubink and McInerney 2011.

existing non-state legal orders - because "doing so would be hugely time consuming" (Chirayath et al. 2005: 26) - but to aim at "creating new mediating institutions wherein actors from both realms [state and customary] can meet—following simple, transparent, mutually agreed-upon, and accountable rules—to craft new arrangements that both sides can own and enforce" (ibid.). This has supported the establishment of new 'hybrid institutions' or new 'alternative dispute resolution' (ADR) forums, such as community mediation schemes, paralegals and community policing forums. What characterises these, according to donors, is that they draw on a 'mixture' of the 'positive' aspects of informal or customary justice – i.e. mediation, participation, conciliation, cost-effectiveness, flexibility and so forth - and international human rights (Harper 2011: 59-78; see also Albrecht and Kyed 2011).[11] To international agencies such new institutions should usually involve 'community' volunteers from outside of established local power structures, who can be trained in human rights from the outset, while also draw on those local norms and customs that do not violate human rights. They represent a 'fresh' beginning, so to speak (Albrecht and Kyed 2011). At the same time they are seen to fill a 'gap' where the formal state courts are inaccessible and/or non-responsive to local justice needs, and where customary courts violate human rights, and are seen as 'too problematic to reform'. Moreover, it is often envisioned that such new institutions can help to improve linkages between 'formal' and 'informal' justice systems, including assisting citizens in better accessing the formal courts (Harper 2011: 59-60). Such efforts certainly support legal pluralism. In fact, they enhance plurality in terms, at least, of expanding the number of dispute resolution fora available to citizens (ibid.: 71).

The critical issue is that such efforts tend to be, ultimately, driven by concerns for uniformity and standardisation, or as Louise Wiuff Moe (this issue) puts it, by a desire to 'manage diversity'. This is not least critical, because the choice to establish new hybrid institutions typically means that locally legitimate justice practices and already existing providers are excluded from programming, although they are significant in the plural legal reality, whether donors like them or not.

---

[11] Such new 'hybrid institutions' established by international donors or NGOs, often in alignment with national governments, can be contrasted with new 'community-driven' or organically developed local initiatives, which have come about as the result of groups of citizens themselves responding to changing demands for alternative justice and security solutions. Examples of the latter are for instance provided in the article by Marks et al. in this issue.

Technical and timeline constraints are certainly among the factors that help explain why international agencies may find it easier to establish new institutions (on this issue see Albrecht and Kyed 2011; Isser 2011). However, the desire to 'manage diversity' also runs through the programmes that do include existing non-state providers. The crux of the matter is that even when donors recognise legal pluralism the objective is still, it seems, to eventually see a unified justice system under the regulation of a familiar sovereign authority – i.e. the state. Thus the ideological and bureaucratic-logics of state-building continue to inhibit international agencies from thinking in terms of genuine pluralistic alternatives. While reform efforts now open a space for a plurality of actors in delivering justice and security, they simultaneously close the spaces for *de facto* forms of diversity. Importantly, the latter spaces include those ongoing negotiations, contestations and interactions that are so central to locally anchored processes of change in pluralistic settings. This includes changes of those mechanisms of justice that discriminate certain groups, like women. Consequently, in their efforts to 'manage diversity' - according to pre-defined templates from the 'outside' - internationally-supported reforms, can easily end up marginalising processes of change from 'within' as well as contribute to a denial of the politics involved in such processes (Isser 2011: 5).

Against this background, it seems that international development intervention currently contributes to replicating a kind of 'weak' legal pluralism (Griffiths 1986; Merry 1988; von Benda-Beckmann 1997) whereby the central state (with support from international agencies) withholds the ultimate power - i.e. undivided sovereignty - to acknowledge or refuse the existence of different bodies of law (Merry 1988: 871). Applied in this way legal pluralism policies can be used to assert state monopoly on the production of legal norms and to tame non-state legal orders (ICHRP 2009: 93). This was very much the case with colonial indirect forms of rule, giving way to a state-enforced dualistic system (Mamdani 1996). Currently, it is also not difficult to see the politics behind policies that lead to 'weak' legal pluralism, when analysed empirically – i.e. how national governments have a political interest in 'managing diversity' under a centralised authority. However, today such politics tend to be masked by the universalising discourse of international rule of law programming. Although it may be argued that current international recognition of legal pluralism does not follow the same repressive political agendas of colonial rule, there is a clear continuity of the same state bureaucratic-logic. This logic is concerned with hierarchical ordering, centralisation and boundary-marking. It supports a de-politicisation of the justice and security fields, even as it serves ideological-driven agendas.

Central to the state bureaucratic-logic is a dichotomous conceptualisation of legal pluralism, which reinforces thinking into distinct, separate 'systems'. As Harper (2011: 37-8) points out about international development programmes that include customary 'systems': "at the strategic level, the topic [of legal pluralism] continues to be approached from a dichotomous perspective - juxtaposing the formal [state] and the informal [non-state] systems by highlighting their differences and evaluating customary systems in terms of how closely they align to state justice precepts." In this sense, international donor agencies seem to replicate what Merry (1988) refers to as 'classic' legal pluralism theory, which viewed state law as separate from other forms of social ordering, instead of viewing each as part of "a continuum of differentiation and organization of the generation and application of norms" (Merry 1988: 877; see also Allott and Woodman 1985).[12] As discussed next, empirical reality calls for much more flexible conceptualisations of legal pluralism, dominated by "mutually constitutive relations" (Merry 1988: 889) rather than distinctive separations. The critical point is that policies, which rely on such separations, run the risk, not only of strengthening those specific power-holders who represent the distinct 'systems, but also of undermining the justice views and needs of those very users of the 'systems' that donors claim to have as their beneficiaries. This calls for alternatives.

Alternative Concepts and Approaches

The contributions to this issue suggest different alternative ways of approaching legal pluralism by international agencies, reflecting variety in disciplinary backgrounds and in the contexts they are dealing with. Yet, even if not explicitly using the concept, they share an emphasis on 'strong' legal pluralism (Griffiths 1986): i.e. they argue for the need to take in at the outset empirical manifestations of diversity and the experiences of ordinary citizens, rather than begin with a pre-defined state model. Moreover, they share a critique of the legalistic approach to reform - i.e. of the idea that laws and prohibitions can change behaviour and beliefs - instead arguing for the need to engage with those social and political

[12] Sally Falk Moore (1973) has strongly contributed to this debate, such as by critically scrutinizing the strict separation between 'systems' with her concept of the 'semi-autonomous social field'.

processes of negotiation and contestation that are taking place in specific contexts. This is, as Lubkemann et al. (this issue) suggest, based on an understanding of justice and law as always deeply implicated in social and political relations, as well as informed by culturally differentiated concepts and hierarchies of value. Another aspect that unites the contributions is an emphasis on relations rather than on separate systems or orders, thereby challenging the dichotomous perspective on 'state' versus 'non-state' systems. This focus forms part of efforts to rethink 'the state' and to use more empirically-grounded conceptualisations of the wider political order within which 'the state' is situated.

The socio-legal literature on legal pluralism since the 1980s, in particular, has much to offer in terms of alternative thinking. This issue draws on such scholarly work, and also expands it by drawing on peace and conflict studies as well as on the security governance literature on plural policing (see Boege et al. 2009; Wood and Shearing 2007; Jones and Newborn 2006). In this sense, the issue hopefully adds further insights to the scholarly debate on legal pluralism, which has tended to focus very little on policing actors, and much more on justice forums, despite the many overlaps that occur in practice.

Relational concepts and approaches – hybridity, networks and webs

A key concept running through many of the contributions to this issue is 'hybridity'. While certainly not a new concept in the socio-legal literature (see, e.g. Merry 1988), hybridity is here used not only in the sense of 'legal hybridisations' or as 'interlegality' to describe the complex combinations of different types or sources of *law* within legal orders and individual justice institutions (Santos 2003, 2006). It is also used to describe the wider sphere of political ordering, of which the legal domain, and justice and security provision are seen as integrated elements.[13] This is for instance captured under the concept of

[13] There is also an extensive literature on the hybrid nature of chieftaincy or traditional authority in Africa, which extends beyond the legal domain, however this literature tends not to include formal state institutions as equally hybrid, instead approaching 'the state' as more or less monolithic (see for instance van Rouveroy van Nieuwaal and van Dijk 1999; and a 1996 special issue of this *Journal of Legal Pluralism*, guest edited by Ray and van Rouveroy van Nieuwaal 1996).

'hybrid political order' (Boege et al. 2009; Brown et el. 2010; Clements et al. 2007; Lambach and Kraushaar 2008), which is applied to describe pluralistic contexts "in which diverse and competing claims to power and logics of order co-exist, overlap and intertwine" (Boege et al. 2008: 10).

Hybridity is here understood as more than the sum or pooling together of distinct and remnant sources. It rather implies the coming into being of a different political order, with new institutional arrangements as well as new types of contestations, as for instance shown by Wiuff Moe (this issue) with regards to the merger of different sources of authority and legitimacy in the new political order of Somaliland. Thus, processes of hybridisation create new forms of meaning and action, not a simple co-existence of 'pure' elements, from distinct 'systems'. An 'order' or 'system' does not have a 'pure', 'autonomous' identity, but can only be defined in relation to the wider constellation of which it is a part. The term 'system' is itself seen as problematic: it denotes structured and relatively comprehensive bodies of law, which do not correspond with the often much more loosely structured mechanisms of justice and security, overlapping and negotiated jurisdictions, as well as clusters of rules that bridge local, national and global frontiers (see Woodman 1998; Griffiths 1986: 12). In line with this thinking, a number of the articles in this issue argue that empirical reality is better understood in terms of networks and webs between different sets of actors and sources, rather than in terms of co-existing entities. Often such networks are continuously negotiated and revised, and therefore both dynamic and productive of new constellations.

The concept of 'hybrid political order' also challenges a static view of pluralistic contexts, incorporating the idea that justice and security institutions are not only plural, but continuously overlap, influence and transform each other. Like the concept of 'strong' legal pluralism, it does not grant the 'state' a "privileged position as the political framework that provides security, welfare and representation; [rather] it has to share authority, legitimacy and capacity with other structures" (Boege et al. 2008: 10). This opens up for new ways of viewing the state, as itself more plural, or multilayered, and therefore as more capable of sharing responsibilities with other institutions, than is the case with the monolithic state model used by international agencies today. It also supports approaches that build on and work with - rather than seek to overcome or manage - already existing forms of diversity. The latter are seen as significant assets in reform processes, not as problems of 'disorder' and 'state weakness'. Thus, the challenge becomes not one of 'taming' or 'managing' diversity, but of supporting "appropriate forms of complementarity and interaction" (Boege et al. 2008: 16) between a variety of actors and institutions. The result may or may not be new forms of hybrid governance arrangements, but in common will be "networks of governance, which are not introduced from the outside, but embedded in the societal structures on the ground" (Boege et al. 2008: 17).

In line with this 'relational' thinking, a number of the articles in this issue provide different suggestions to how international agencies can aid mutually supporting linkages between different actors actively involved in policing and conflict resolution (see the articles by Bruce Baker, Miranda Forsyth, Louise Wiuff Moe and Marks et. al). Such linkages can facilitate a more efficient sharing of resources, and should be done in a non-hierarchical way, which leaves more room for creative compromises than if a top-down approach is adopted. The approaches proposed do not *per se* undermine state building, but support a kind of state building where state authorities work with local orders of governance rather than try to impose their supremacy over them (see also Boege et al. 2008: 15). Marks et al. (this issue) in fact argue that with 'pluralised arrangements' state 'weakness' – here in the sense of a lack of state monopoly on providing justice and security – can actually be a 'strength', because state legitimacy is enhanced when state institutions accommodate local orders of governance. The challenge, nevertheless, is to 'convince' state authorities, and not least central government departments, that pluralism can also be to their advantage. It is thus imperative to take into account the political interests at play when supporting linkages, networks and webs.

The political dynamics of legal pluralism

There is a real risk of depoliticising the fields of justice and security when applying the concepts of networks, webs and hybridity, and when approaches rely on partnerships and 'divisions of labour' within pluralistic arrangements. Supporting linkages does not erase power interests and political contestations, as people enter them with their own agendas. The incentives for collaboration can be countered by, or at the very least co-exist with, overlapping claims to authority. This may not least be the case if the 'division of labour' is perceived by the involved actors as instituting a hierarchy of responsibilities, associated with greater authority, such as for instance between dealing with petty versus serious crimes. Formal arrangements based on 'division of labour' can particularly run into problems in those contexts where sovereignty is *de facto* shared - i.e. where the state does not have a monopoly on violence and on claims to final authority over significant areas of social life - such as in many Sub-Saharan African countries (Hansen and Stepputat 2005).

When considering policies on legal pluralism it is therefore pertinent to ask: Are the different implicated authorities, and notably centrally placed state representatives, willing to *de jure* share sovereignty? And are international development agencies able and willing to support that? It is here important to keep in mind that international agencies are strongly influenced by a view of sovereign power as equal to the assertion of territorial sovereignty by states, i.e. through the monopolisation of violence and permanent and visible military and police forces (Hansen and Stepputat 2001). As suggested by Hansen and Stepputat (2005) sovereign power can however be approached as particular claims and practices that may be a dimension of different forms of authority, including non-state ones. Such power encompasses the claim to superior authority within a given political organisation and it covers the capacity to define and enforce the normal situation of a particular order. Sovereign power can therefore exist independently of a 'state'. However, whether a state or a non-state order the question is still the extent to which more decentralised, shared and indeed pluralistic arrangements are conceivable. Such could for instance be organised on a set of shared principles, which are not defined or determined by specific centres, but based on broad-based and continuous negotiations.

What is significant to keep in mind is that even the most pluralistic arrangements contain asymmetries, hierarchies, and double standards (Zips and Weilenmann 2011). While it is important to critically question dichotomies, such as 'state' versus 'non-state', we should not erase differences but "shift them from the zone of timeless oppositions" into that of empirical political issues, including negotiations, contestations and interactions across differences (Brown 2009: 80, quoted in Wiuff Moe's contribution to this issue). Thus when using the concepts of hybridity and networks, 'the political' should not be downplayed, but in contrast be brought more out in the open where differences can be discussed and negotiated. In doing so, as Pieterse (2001) notes, it is important to take note of the historical specificity of hybridity and its continuous interaction with efforts to establish boundaries between different entities, such as 'state' and 'customary'. He stresses: "We can think of hybridity as layered in history, including pre-colonial, colonial and postcolonial layers, each with distinct sets of hybridity, as a function of boundaries that were prominent, and accordingly different pathos of difference" (Pieterse 2001: 231). In short, hybridity is only noteworthy when fixed categories and boundaries are being produced, and boundaries are only produced and notable because there are always patterns of hybridity and border-crossing (Pieterse 2001: 234).

The concept of hybridity can therefore encompass a variety of sources and their combinations, without pretending that distinctions no longer matter for the actors concerned. This is evident in the article on South Sudan by Leonardi et al. (this issue), where the emphasis on distinct 'systems' in the debates about ascertaining customary law was informed by the competition for power at both national and local levels. However, this co-existed with *de facto* amalgamation of norms and procedures in local justice forums. Thus, while ordinary citizens made no clear line between state and non-state judicial institutions, but perceived them as part of a hierarchy within a single system, politically powerful actors had an interest in establishing clear boundaries. Jackson (this issue) also shows for Sierra Leone how different justice institutions at the local level are entangled within the same networks of power, despite past and present reform efforts to 'single' out the state and new democratic institutions from 'customary' ones.

Lund (2006: 673) captures this apparent paradox in his general discussion of the 'twilight' character of public authority in Africa: "On the one hand, actors and institutions in this [political] field are intensely preoccupied with the state and with the distinction between state and society, but on the other hand, their practices constantly befuddle these distinctions". Consequently, "we should pay careful attention to *how* concepts and distinctions are produced, instrumentalized and contested" (Lund 2006: 678, emphasis in original), and thereby "problematize the distinctions we tend to accept as given" (Lund 2006: 679).

While it is empirically often difficult to exactly specify what "is 'state' and what is not [because] many institutions have a twilight character" (Lund 2006: 673), it is important to take seriously the continuous and inherently political efforts by the actors involved in networks/linkages to mark out boundaries between distinct 'systems' – such as 'state' versus 'traditional' (Kyed 2007). One type of actor here is the international donor community itself, but also state authorities, customary authorities and other powerful players often have an interest in such boundary-marking. Noteworthy, as Baker suggests (this issue), is that the state versus non-state distinction is mostly important to the powerholders and the legislators, because it is part of consolidating their specific kind of authority. It is much less, if at all, significant in the eyes of ordinary citizens. To them it is less important *who* provides justice or public safety, and much more important *how* such justice is provided (see also Leonardi et al. this issue).

Central here is to recognise that justice and security provision are fields where power is contested, authority is reconfigured and constituted, and where different actor interests are at stake over power, resources and 'clients' (Kyed 2009; Tamanaha 2008). Part of this is the intensely political nature of 'law' itself - whether state or customary or other forms of law - exemplified by continuous negotiations and contestations over the meanings of justice and law (see Forsyth and Leonardi et al. in this issue). The contexts we encounter embed contradictory conceptions of justice, not alone because of differences in cultural values and beliefs, but also due to the distinctive socio-economic situations within which people live (see Lubkemann et al. in this issue).

Another factor is that justice institutions and policing actors are often tightly linked into political power structures, locally and nationally. In Sierra Leone, for instance members of the local elite use their power to manipulate cases in the formal courts, and court cases sometimes become subject to political party disputes (see Jackson this issue). Importantly, certain groups in society do not have the ability to negotiate the power networks within which courts and dispute resolution forums are embedded, and therefore do not have equal access to justice. This is irrespective of whether there are well-functioning linkages or not between (state and non-state) providers. Similarly in Liberia, the vast majority of citizens view the justice system as little more than arenas where the more powerful can assert their interests, not for a fair outcome, but rather to leverage personal resources. Economic and political resources are constantly at stake. Class differentiation and (in)justice coincide, and makes everyday forms of case resolution highly political and often overtly unjust (see Lubkemann et al. in this issue).

The relationship between legal pluralism and unequal power relations is not, however, given. Von Benda-Beckmann et al. (2009) suggest that legal pluralism can reinforce inequality by decreasing the binding power of the law over the more powerful. Greater flexibility can also work against the weaker parties because the strong tend to determine the choice of forum or rules. In other situations, however, weaker parties can manipulate and exploit the contradictions in the rules to pursue 'creative strategies', which may push for changes in established power hierarchies and of discriminatory practices.

They key issue here is that any reform efforts should realise and make explicit the political dynamics of pluralistic arrangements, rather than try to 'remove' or ignore politics. There are at least three dimensions of such politics to consider: first, the competition for authority between providers, often marked by efforts to articulate distinctions, even as (or at times exactly because) they collaborate and have overlapping jurisdictions; second, contestations over the meanings of justice and law, which reflect power relations and the socio-economic situation, but that can also lead to changes 'from within' to the benefit of weaker groups; and third, unequal access to justice due to differences in the resources and skills people have available for negotiating the power networks within which justice and security institutions are embedded.

Such political dynamics are commonly ignored or poorly understood by international development agencies, as are the political implications of their interventions (Isser 2011). In fact, in some situations internationally supported reforms contribute to reinforcing unequal power relations, as the Sierra Leone and Liberia cases in this issue suggest. Rather than trying to 'depoliticise' the field of justice and security, it is better to constructively engage with the ongoing contestations over legal norms and practices between individuals and groups of individuals within and across localities. This can for instance be done by facilitating forums and arenas for debate (see for instance Forsyth and Leonardi et al.). International agencies can also support the empowerment of less resourceful groups to navigate and negotiate within both formal and informal power networks. These suggestions are informed by an understanding of legal orders as the result of internal processes of contestation, competing interests and changing socio-economic circumstances.

The Contributions

The first article by Bruce Baker represents a general critique of the state-building approach to security and justice sector reform in Sub-Saharan Africa. He calls for increased local ownership of reform efforts and approaches that are adjusted to what is available, affordable, effective and legitimate in the eyes of ordinary citizens in each specific context, whether this is state provision or not. In general, however, this would imply a 'multi-layered' approach, which is based on the inclusion of a plurality of providers and which has an emphasis on networks. This suggestion is given empirical depth in the article on South Africa by Monique Marks, Jennifer Wood, Julian Azzopardi and Thokozani Xaba. They address the significant role of community safety groups in the 'everyday policing' of neighbourhoods in Durban. Here the state police *de facto* play a minimal role, either relying on non-state actors or allowing them to perform policing activities independently. This empirical reality, the authors argue, ought to be formalised. They therefore support a minimalist state, but within a framework where locally elected governments ensure democratic control of policing actors. It is also at the decentralised level that international development agencies ought to concentrate their support, rather than at central state level.

The article by Stephen Lubkemann, Deborah Isser and Peter Chapman on the internationally-supported post-conflict efforts to reform the justice system in Liberia also provides an empirically grounded critique of the state-centric perspective, and of the 'rule of law' policy approach. By promoting a 'single justice system' this approach clearly undermined legal pluralism, and with this, ignored ordinary Liberian's justice preferences and experiences. It also had the consequence of perpetuating the power of elites over justice institutions rather than promoting, as intended, more equal access to justice. A similar critique of the 'Rule of Law' approach is provided in the article by Cherry Leonardi, Deborah Isser, Leben Moro and Martina Santschi on the joint UNDP-Government plan to ascertain customary law in South Sudan. A key difference here is that legal pluralism is recognised by the reformers. However, this is compromised by a legalistic desire to regulate and order the hybrid, composite practices and laws of the local courts. The risk is that a 'fixing' of customary laws not only fuels ethnic divisions, but also undermines those local contestations over legal norms, which challenge discriminatory practices and elite power.

The Somaliland case, presented by Louise Wiuff Moe, supports the case for international engagement with internal processes of change, including the facilitation of linkages and spaces for negotiations between a diverse set of actors. She focuses on how a 'hybrid political order' has *de jure* been institutionalised as a result of an internally driven peace-building process, rather than one driven by international agencies. The process has not been without tensions and conflicts, as different claims to political legitimacy have been allowed to come into play. However, the plural, hybrid governance arrangements that have resulted from the process has helped sustain peace, strengthened government, and improved local security and justice provision. The article also provides a number of concrete examples of how international NGOs have supported the internal processes of political ordering, including within the areas of conflict resolution and policing. In the next article, Miranda Forsyth similarly argues for more incremental, locally-grounded, international engagement with justice reform processes, which focuses on enabling dialogue and linkages between actors and initiatives, resulting in what she terms a 'conflict management web'. She bases this on an analysis of a range of different initiatives by international donors, academics, the government and community leaders over the past few years in Vanuatu, which have all sought to align the *Kastom* (customary) and state systems of conflict management.

Paul Jackson's article on Sierra Leone criticises internationally supported post-conflict reforms for failing to address the political dynamics of justice and security provision. He shows how decentralisation reforms have contributed to a further consolidation of local elite power, which ultimately acts to the detriment of those who have always lost out on access to justice. Jackson argues that international agencies should support mechanisms to enhance the ability of ordinary citizens to negotiate the power networks and justice structures at a local level. Anne Griffiths' article on women's improved access to land in Botswana, also supports the case for 'empowering' vulnerable groups' ability to better access social networks and engage in informal transactions. Legal reforms and reformed institutions have certainly contributed to the substantial increase in land titles to women over the past 25 years. Yet just as important have been factors that contribute to women's capacity to negotiate poverty and access justice in both formal and informal domains, namely: education, employment and changing social dynamics of families and households. In Botswana such socio-economic developments owe much to the strong lobby work of NGOs, some of which are supported by international development agencies. The article by Griffiths also points to the fact that processes of legal and institutional change take a very long time, and therefore require not only longitudinal research to be comprehended thoroughly, but also long-term engagement with reforms, rather than quick, pre-defined 'fixes', based on abstract models. This is not least because justice and security issues, being far from neutral, apolitical fields, are deeply embedded in political power structures and diverse socio-economic situations.

COPENHAGEN,
November 2011.

References

ALBRECHT, Peter

2010 'Betwixt and between – chiefs and reform of Sierra Leone's Justice Sector.' *DIIS Working Paper* 2010: 33

ALBRECHT, Peter and Helene Maria KYED

2010 'Justice and Security. When the State isn't the main Provider', *DIIS Policy Brief*, December 2010, Copenhagen: Danish Institute for International Studies (DIIS).

2011 'Introduction: Non-State and Customary Actors in Development programs'. Pp. 3-2 in Peter Albrecht, Helene Maria Kyed, Erica Harper and Deborah Isser (eds.), *Perspectives on Involving Non-State and Customary Actors in Justice and Security Reform*. Rome: International

Development Law Organisation (IDLO).

ALBRECHT, Peter, Helene Maria KYED, Erica HARPER and Deborah ISSER (eds.)

2011 *Perspectives on Involving Non-State and Customary Actors in Justice and Security Reform*. Rome: International Development Law Organisation (IDLO).

ALLOTT, Antony and Gordon WOODMAN (eds.)

1985 *People's Law and State Law*. Dordrecht, Holland: Foris Publications.

BENDA-BECKMAN, Franz von

1997 'Citizens, Strangers and Indigenous peoples: Conceptual Politics and Legal Pluralism.' *Law and Anthropology*, 9: 1-42.

BENDA-BECKMANN, Franz von, Keebet von BENDA-BECKMANN and Julia ECKERT (eds.)

2009 *Rules of Law and Laws of Ruling: on the governance of law*. Farnham: Ashgate.

CLEMENTS, Kevin .P.; Volker BOEGE; M. Anne BROWN; Anna NOLAN and; Wendy FOLEY

2007 'State Building Reconsidered: The Role of Hybridity in the Formation of Political Order.' *Political Science* 59(01): 45-56.

BOEGE, Volker, M. Anne BROWN and Kevin P. CLEMENTS

2009 'Hybrid Political orders, Not Fragile States.' *Peace Review* 21/1: 13-21.

BROWN, M. Anne

2009 'The pursuit of grounds'. Pp.55-90 in M. Anne Brown (ed.), *Human Rights and the Borders of Suffering*. Manchester: Manchester University Press.

BROWN, M. Anne; Volker BOEGE, Kevin P. CLEMENTS and Anna NOLAN

2010 'Challenging statebuilding as peacebuilding - working with hybrid political orders to build peace.' Pp. 99-116 in Oliver P. Richmond (ed.), *Palgrave Advances in Peacebuilding. Critical Developments and Approaches*, Basingtoke: Palgrave Macmillan.

CHIRAYATH Leila, Caroline SAGE and Michael WOOLCOCK

2005 'Customary Law and Policy Reform: Engaging with the Plurality of Justice Systems' (World Bank Background Paper, July 2005).

CHOPRA, Tanja and Deborah ISSER

2011 'Women's Access to Justice, Legal Pluralism and Fragile States'. Pp. 23-38 in Peter Albrecht, Helene Maria Kyed, Erica Harper and Deborah Isser (eds.), *Perspectives on Involving Non-State and Customary Actors in Justice and Security Reform*. Rome: International Development Law Organisation (IDLO).

DANIDA
2010 *How to Note on Informal Justice Systems.* Copenhagen: Danish Ministry of Foreign Affairs.
DFID (DEPARTMENT FOR INTERNATIONAL DEVELOPMENT)
2004 *Non-State Justice and Security Systems.* London: DFID.
GOLUP, Stephen
2003 'Beyond Rule of Law Orthodoxy. The Legal Empowerment Alternative'. *working papers*, Rule of Law Series 41, October, Washington DC: Carnegie Endowment for International Peace.
GRIFFITHS, John
1986 'What is Legal Pluralism?' *Journal of Legal Pluralism*, 24: 1-50.
HANSEN, Thomas Blom and Finn STEPPUTAT (eds.)
2001 *States of Imagination. Ethnographic Explorations of the Postcolonial State.* Durham & London: Duke University Press.
2005 *Sovereign Bodies. Citizens, Migrants and States in the Postcolonial World.* Princeton and Oxford: Princeton University Press.
HARPER, Erica
2011 *Customary Justice: From program Design to Impact Evaluation.* Rome: International Development Law Organisation (IDLO).
ISSER, Deborah (ed.)
2011 *Customary Justice and the Rule of Law in War-Torn Societies*, Washington: United States Institute for Peace.
JONES, Trevor and Tim NEWBORN
2006 *Plural Policing. A Comparative Perspective.* London and New York: Routledge.
ICHRP (International Council for Human Rights Policy)
2009 *When Legal Worlds Overlap: Human Rights, State and Non-State Law.* Geneva: ICHRP.
KYED, Helene Maria
2007 *State Recognition of Traditional Authority. Authority, Citizenship and State Formation in Rural Post War Mozambique*, PhD dissertation. Roskilde: Roskilde University.
2009 'The Politics of Legal Pluralism: state policies on legal pluralism and their local dynamics in Mozambique.' *Journal of Legal Pluralism and Unofficial Law* 59: 87-120.
LAMBACH, Daniel and Maren KRAUSHAAR
2008 'Hybrid Political Orders. the Added Value of a New Concept', Occasional Paper, Australian Center for Peace and Conflict Studies. http://www.issr.uq.edu.au/acpacs-publications (visited Oct 2010).

LUND, Christian
2006 'Twilight Institutions: An Introduction.' *Development and Change* 37(4): 673-684.
MAMDANI, Mahmood
1996 *Citizen and Subject. Contemporary Africa and the legacy of late colonialism.* Princeton: Princeton University Press.
MERRY, Sally Engel
1988 'Legal Pluralism.' *Law & Society Review* 22/5: 869-895.
MOORE, Sally Falk
1973 'Law and Social Change: The Semi-Autonomous Social Field as an Appropriate Subject of Study.' *Law & Society Review* 7: 719-746.
OECD (ORGANISATION FOR ECONOMIC CO-OPERATION AND DEVELOPMENT)
2007 *Handbook on Security System Reform – Supporting Security and Justice.* Paris: OECD.
OHCHR (OFFICE OF THE HIGH COMMISSIONER FOR HUMAN RIGHTS)
2006 *Rule-of-Law Tools for Post-conflict states: mapping the justice sector.* New York & Geneva: OHCHR
PIETERSE, J.N.
2001 Hybridity, So What? The Anti-hybridity Backlash and the Riddles of Recognition, *Theory, Culture and Society*, 18 (2-3): 219-245.
RAY, Donald I. and E. Adriaan B. van ROUVEROY VAN NIEUWAAL
1996 'Introduction. The New Relevance of Traditional Authorities in Africa.' *Journal of Legal Pluralism and Unofficial Law* 37-38: 1-38.
ROUVEROY VAN NIEUWAAL, E. Adriaan B. van, and Rijk van DIJK (eds.)
1999 *African Chieftaincy in a New Socio-Political Landscape.* Leiden: African Studies Centre.
SANTOS, Boaventura de Sousa
2003 'O Estado heterogéneo e o pluralismo jurídico'. Pp. 47-128 in Boaventura de Sousa Santos and João Carlos Trindade (eds.) *Conflito e Transformação Social: Uma Paisagem das Justiças em Moçambique.* Porto: Afrontamento.
2006 'The Heterogeneous State and Legal Pluralism in Mozambique'. *Law and Society Review* 40(1): 39-76.
SHORE, Chris and Susan WRIGHT
1997 *Anthropology of Policy. Critical Perspectives on Governance and Power.* London and New York: Routledge.
TAMANAHA, Brian Z.
2008 'Understanding legal pluralism: past to present, local to global.' *Sydney Law Review* 30/3: 375-411.

UBINK, Janine and Thomas MCINERNEY (eds.)
2011 *Customary Justice: perspectives on Legal Empowerment.* Leiden: University of Leiden, Faculty of Law. Rome: International Development Law Organisation (IDLO).
UBINK, Janine and Benjamin von ROOIJ
2011 'Towards Customary Legal Empowerment: An Introduction.' Pp. 7-28 in Janine Ubink and Thomas Mclnerney (eds.), *Customary Justice: perspectives on Legal Empowerment.* Leiden: University of Leiden, Faculty of Law. Rome: International Development Law Organisation (IDLO).
UNDP (UNITED NATIONS DEVELOPMENT PROGRAMME)
2009 *Community Security and Social Cohesion. Towards a UNDP Approach* (2009) 9.
USAID (UNITED STATES AGENCY FOR INTERNATIONAL DEVELOPMENT)
2005 *Field Study of Informal and Customary Justice in Afghanistan and Recommendations on Improving Access to Justice and Relations between Formal Courts and Informal Bodies*, Washington DC: USAID.
2009 *Security Sector Reform* (February 2009). Washington DC: US Agency for International Development, US Department of Defence, and US Department of State.
WEBER, Max
1978 *Economy and Society: An Outline of Interpretive Sociology*. (2 volumes). Guenther Roth and Claus Wittich (eds.). Berkeley: University of California Press.
WOODMAN, Gordon R.
1998 'Ideological combat and social observation: recent debate about legal pluralism.' *Journal of Legal Pluralism* 42: 21-59.
WORLD BANK
2011 *World Development Report 2011: Conflict, Security, and Development.* Washington DC: The World Bank.
WOOD Jennifer and Clifford SHEARING
2007 *Imagining Security*. Portland: Willan Publishing
ZIPS Werner and Markus WEILENMANN (eds.)
2011 *The Governance of Legal Pluralism. Empirical Studies from Africa and Beyond*. Wein and Berlin: Lit Verlag.

JUSTICE AND SECURITY ARCHITECTURE IN AFRICA: THE PLANS, THE BRICKS, THE PURSE AND THE BUILDER

Bruce Baker

Introduction

A bricklayer likes to know before beginning a new project, what bricks are to be used and what the building looks like that is to be constructed. These are essential questions for justice and security development in Africa as well. What is being built, with what, by whom and for whom? These are the issues being addressed by this article. The 'bricks' on offer are very varied and are often divided into 'state' and 'nonstate-informal' actors, though this is not a fully accurate distinction from an empirical perspective. Concerning the 'architectural plans' for the 'bricklayer' to follow, there are several plans on the drawing table. For some, security and justice architecture is about creating a state strong enough to hold a monopoly of effective justice and security provision. Others offer plans based on local security and justice inputs. It helps, also, to be reassured that however good the plans are, someone can pay for the construction. It might also be worthwhile consulting the people who are going to use the security and justice 'building' as to whether they are happy with it. In the final analysis, however, which 'bricks', which 'plan' and whose money are choices made by the one who is commissioning the building. Yet even that is not clear in the case of justice and security architecture in Africa. Is it an African project seeking donor support, or a donor project hoping for African ownership?

To set aide the analogy for a moment, this article is about the dilemma presented by legal pluralism in Africa. Is its prevalence to be welcomed and its opportunities exploited or is it a handicap to justice that should be eliminated? In seeking to present an overview of what is happening in security and justice programmes in Africa and the issues that they are raising, this article begins by examining the security and justice providers in Africa, with particular emphasis on policing; the providers being the bricks of security architecture. It notes that given the few resources available to most African countries, the state police and judiciary are inevitably limited. However there are many other providers, commonly termed 'nonstate' or 'informal', though, as the article explains, the terminology does not do justice to their diversity, local nature and their complex relationships with the state. These providers, it is argued, can in some cases be effective, and often have widespread local support. Next the article considers the benefits and drawbacks of two approaches by donors and African states to security and justice provision; the architectural plans. The more widely used is statebuilding and a less widely used is the multi-layered approach. The next section explores the cost implications of the two plans; the purse. It argues that statebuilding is not only very expensive but may well be unsustainable in a way that using nonstate-informal actors is not. Finally and briefly, the article asks whose security architecture is it that is being built in Africa? Who is the builder? Amid disputes about what is meant by local ownership, the article calls for the security and justice users to design an affordable architecture.

The Bricks

Looking at what the state police and judiciary have to offer in Africa one realises that it is very limited. It is not just the quality of the 'bricks', which perhaps can be improved. It is also the actual numbers. There are very few 'bricks' and they are expensive. The numbers of police, judges and magistrates per head of population are often quite small, and they are usually urban based and may be beyond sustaining at current levels given the resource implications.[1] But the state police and judiciary are not the only 'bricks' on offer. It is not always appreciated just how many groups are present in Africa providing security and justice. Though most have come to recognise the rapid growth of private security since the 1990s (Abrahamsen and Williams 2008) the long standing provision of everyday policing

[1] My own research estimates that the ratio of police officers to population is: Guinea Bissau 1: 2,403; Uganda 1: 1,839; Rwanda 1: 1,454; Liberia 1: 857; Nigeria 1: 722; Sierra Leone 1: 625 (cf. England and Wales 1: 402).

and dispute resolution by community collectives has been relatively overlooked by governments, international donors and academics working in policing and security studies.

I have argued many times before that it is these nonstate-informal actors that are the dominant and preferred policing and dispute resolution providers of most Africans most of the time (Baker 2009). These are the most common and popular 'bricks' available, as the World Development Report (Chirayath et al. 2005), UNDP (Wojkowska 2006), OECD (2007) and DFID (2004) have acknowledged. It is estimated that these nonstate-informal actors provide at least 80 per cent of justice services in sub-Saharan Africa (OECD 2007: 17). Customary courts probably cover 90 per cent of Africa's population (Chirayath et al. 2005: 3). In a UNDP report it is argued that these networks "are the cornerstone of dispute resolution and access to justice for the majority of populations, especially the poor and disadvantaged" (Wojkowska 2006). Indeed, Nigeria's national crime victimization survey shows that 50 per cent of Nigerians use nonstate-informal policing to protect them from crime (CLEEN 2005). In two states surveyed in Nigeria, nonstate-informal actors were the preferred choice of delivery 88.9 and 62.5 per cent of the time (Alemika and Chukwuma 2004: 6).

Such widely available 'bricks', however, vary in their quality and shape. To name some, there are: private citizens organized on a voluntary, as needed, basis (locally called 'vigilance' or 'vigilante' groups, though they do not necessarily have the negative aspects that these words convey in the West); security groups organized by and for the benefit of trading communities; informal local government security structures providing everyday policing; customary chiefs who prevent or resolve customary, civil and often criminal cases; religious police (especially Islamic) overseeing moral conduct; anti-crime groups that are semi-commercial in their operations; restorative justice community-based organizations; and ethnic or clan militias acting to protect a distinct way of life.

Despite their great variety, it is common for donors and security scholars to classify all such groups under the terms 'nonstate' or 'informal'; in other words to make their defining characteristics either that they are not state providers or that they are not methodical and recognised. These are categorisations that subtly question whether they are or ever can be professional, effective, reliable or authorised. It is worth asking not only whether the terms are accurate, but why security and justice should be viewed from a state and formal perspective any way. What makes the terms additionally problematic is that security and justice providers are not always clearly separated and distinct in their authorisation, formality or even in their activities. It is true that there are plenty of examples of, for instance, nonstate-informal security and justice groups acting autonomously with no reference to other providers. However it is equally true that Africa has many examples of security and justice activities that are shared by groups from either side of the state boundary, whether as a result of sanctioned or unsanctioned arrangements. Johnston talks of these cross-boundary relationships as 'hybrid' (Johnston 1992). In the case of policing groups, some realize there is much to gain from tapping into the knowledge, capacity and resources of others so as to achieve their own agenda. The strength of the policing actors varies, that is, in terms of the capital available to them, whether symbolic, cultural, economic and social, to use the terminology of Bourdieu (Bourdieu and Wacquant, 1992). Hence the transactions and interactions will vary according to the perceived capital of the actors by others.

The state police will, by its size and resources and legal standing, tend to dominate internal security networks and assume an asymmetrical relationship with other security actors. Its dominance is based on its economic capital, that is, its state and donor finances; its cultural capital, that is its corporate knowledge and skills acquired by training and experience; and its social capital, that is all that it has gained through possessing a longstanding officially recognised role. Only private security companies may be able to compete with the police in economic and cultural capital. Where the nonstate-informal actors may score, however, is in symbolic capital, that is, in prestige, honour and attention. Thus, for instance, the source of power of chiefs or ethnic militia leaders or imams is their standing in the local or ethnic or religious community as revered 'big men' and their unchallenged local legitimate authority. In many parts of Africa the state police have, in comparison to these local leaders, little power.

The recognition of capital in others draws providers together into security and justice networks. It is no surprise that many instances can be found of state and nonstate-informal actors carrying out joint patrols and operations or exchanging information about crime and criminals. Take, for instance, the case of a South Sudan market association in Yei. It has arranged with the police that when the police arrest any traders, they are to be handed over to the association on request for the association itself to resolve the issues. The details of their resolution are then reported to the police. Both parties express their satisfaction with the arrangement. Then there are cases of community-based groups working with state police in dividing the work according to whose modus operandi is best suited for the required task. The state may also provide nonstate-informal policing groups with equipment or training and it is not unknown for commercial security to supply the police with resources. The boundary, then, between state and nonstate-informal is blurred and dynamic. The ties are repeatedly negotiated and revised. What may be official policy may be countered by unsanctioned local practice between policing group leaders. This is how the Uganda police on the Uganda/DRC border find themselves, contrary to official policy, working with local youth groups. The value of the youths' intelligence about trans-border crime is worth the price of offering them immunity regarding their 'other affairs' as long as these affairs are conducted away from the border town and out of sight (Titeca 2009).

Neither the term 'nonstate' nor 'informal', therefore, fully characterise those that are so labelled. In fact many do have some degree of authorisation by certain levels of the state and do undertake what in official state law and in Western notions of the state is seen as the state's security business. The terms also fail to acknowledge those in tactical alliances or government sponsored partnerships. To my understanding the thread running through nonstate-informal groups is not so much that they have nothing to do with the state, but that they are *local* security and justice providers. That is, they operate in a geographically and politically defined sub-national and sub-regional space; enforce the prevailing order of that locality; and use as 'foot soldiers' volunteers recruited from that locality. Though there is obviously some indeterminacy or contestation about the spatial extent of what constitutes local, the locality's heartland is likely to be agreed by the majority of inhabitants living in an area. There is also likely to be a shared awareness by locals of where 'others' are found, and logistically most voluntary groups are constrained in the area of their influence by lack of resources. Even when recruits, support or perhaps legitimacy, come from beyond these bounds, the needs and available volunteers of the immediate locality define the group. Whilst the state may well have police and justice officers working at the local level, their authority, orders and procedures are all determined by those outside the locality: this is not the case for nonstate-informal providers.

In these circumstances the persistence of the terminology of 'state'-'nonstate-informal' is perhaps surprising. Yet as Bourdieu (1989: 7) has observed, classifications are the product of social structures and domination, however much they might have the appearance of objective necessity. In this case the classification suits many policing actors. Cooperation may have its advantages, but sometimes both sides have reservations about being associated with their 'partner' and do not want to be 'contaminated' by their unacceptable actions. The state police like to reassert that they are the professionals and 'real' police. They are keen to perpetuate the myth that they hold the monopoly of service provision or at least should be at the centre of donor aid. Likewise not all local policing groups like to be seen to be working too closely with a state police that might be deemed corrupt and predatory and closely associated with an unpopular regime.

The dichotomy of state/nonstate-informal also serves the interests of donors. As state agencies whose attention is on building state security and justice, this terminology marks the border of acceptable area of work from the unacceptable or at least the doubtful and controversial. A review of 78 assessments of legal and justice systems undertaken by the World Bank since 1994 noted that: "many mention the prevalence of traditional justice in the countries looked at, but *none* explore the systems in detail or examine links between local level systems and state regimes" (Chirayath et al. 2005: 3). The donors by definition come from a political culture that is pre-occupied with the state and its strengthening, and so inevitably it is the state providers that are the principal object of their security reform programme. Anything that falls under 'nonstate-informal' is therefore problematic; it is outside their remit or if it is not, it is outside the sphere of *professional* security and justice. The UK's Department for International Development (DFID), for instance, may be sympathetic in principle to working with nonstate-informal justice and policing, however it is quick to note that 'common problems' associated with nonstate systems include, "corruption and abuse of power; non-compliance with international human rights standards, such as discrimination or inhuman and degrading punishments; lack of accountability" (DFID 2004: 3). It warns programme managers that: "particular attention should be given to whether nonstate justice and security (NSJS) systems respect individual rights. For example, where NSJS systems discriminate against women and marginalised groups" (ibid). It is surprising how often donors quickly list perceived problems with nonstate-informal actors, such as gender discrimination and human rights abuses - all of which are major issues in Africa's state police forces and courts as well (e.g. on Nigeria Police, see Human Rights Watch 2010).

Interestingly, the actual users of policing and justice services are less concerned about the blurred boundaries. Indeed, the state/nonstate-informal boundary is not one recognized by most African citizens as fundamental. Issues of effectiveness and accessibility trump concerns over the nature of the authoriser. An individual may according to circumstances move from the arena of one security and justice provider to another and from state to nonstate-informal. In the village the headman or maybe the imam is there to bring a settlement regarding 'men-women problems'. To settle the land dispute there is the paramount chief or there may be a restorative justice organization. On the visit to the town a neighbourhood committee will be on the watch for armed robbers; a commercial security guard will protect the entrance to the bank; and a taxi-drivers' association will deal with any pickpocket at the bus station. Finally, if there is a serious crime and a 'shedding of blood', there is the state police. The boundary, so important to the state and international donors, is far less significant to users and is crossed without concern. The issue crucial to them is not focused on authorisation, but on effectiveness. It matters less who has authorised the security, than how good the provider is at protecting them and their property and resolving disputes. In terms of the building analogy, they are looking for what good 'bricks' are available at the site; they don't care too much who made the 'bricks'.

For Africa's security architecture, therefore, there are only a few state police 'bricks' and a lot more of the nonstate-informal kind available. Some of those nonstate-informal 'bricks' are of too poor a quality to use. But many are very popular locally and widely respected. Research by the United States Institute for Peace (USIP) in Liberia found that:

> even if the formal justice system were able to deliver affordable, timely and impartial results [which most Liberians doubt] it would still not be the forum of choice for many rural Liberians (Isser et al. 2009: 8).

The Plans

Beyond the bricks, what of the architect's drawings for the building project; beyond the providers of security and justice in Africa, what plans for security and justice in the future are on the table? It may well be that nonstate-informal providers are currently the principal ones, but *should* that continue? Is it what the people want; is it what the governments want; is it what the police and judges want; is it what the donors want? What is the big plan; and are all the stakeholders agreed on it? Is it a plan that seeks to replicate Western security architecture or at least offers a less sophisticated version of it; or does it have very distinct features, necessary because we are dealing with developing countries or because this is Africa? In this plan, what is the role of the state police and judiciary; and where, if at all, does nonstate-informal fit in?

There are different security and justice plans for Africa. The UK, which alone carried out Security and Justice Sector Reform (SJSR) in 20 countries in sub-Saharan Africa in 2000 to 2007, has set out its architectural drawing. Its Security Sector Reform policy paper (DFID n.d.) has as its goal: "increasing partner countries' ability to meet the range of security needs within their societies in a manner consistent with democratic norms and sound principles of governance, transparency and the rule of law". What might be questioned is their assumption that there is only one way to achieve that: reform of the state security services. In fact there are at least two plans currently circulating: statebuilding and multi-layered support.

The State Building Approach

The first and currently preferred plan by governments and donors is the statebuilding option (Call and Wyeth 2008; UNDP/USAID 2007; Whaites 2008). This option takes as its starting point the assumption that most states in Africa are weak or even fragile. They currently lack the capacity for control, regulation and implementation, particularly in the core fields of statehood such as basic public goods. Given that the statebuilding option sees justice, security, and policing as foundational state activities, it cannot conceive a legitimate state other than one that is performing these functions. The overall aim is, therefore, to support the building of, "effective and legitimate states able to fulfil key international responsibilities and to provide core public goods and services, including security" (OECD 2008: 3). Ideally the state security institutions, as far as possible, should achieve a state monopoly of justice and security provision.

The state-building option means essentially building a state in the image of rich OECD countries. The 'weaknesses' detected in the African states' provision of policing and justice are measured by the standards of Western state police services and courts. This means ignoring the main policing and justice providers in Africa, the nonstate-informal actors. Hence the plan is to provide assistance so that in the future African countries can reach something like Western levels of police and court provision. The vision means nothing less than building a form of statehood, one where the state is the main provider of justice and security, that has never and still does not exist beyond the OECD world. This is a very ambitious plan. For a continent where more than 26 states since 1980 have endured the suffering and destruction of conflict over all or part of their territory, this is particularly challenging (Baker 2009: 3-4).

If the 'building sites' are examined to see how this plan has fared, it is found that for post-conflict and weak states the almost universal conclusion of studies and reports on statebuilding in the security and justice sector is that little has been achieved. Call and Cousens (2007: 8) admit that efforts to build security institutions have not been "especially encouraging". Englebert and Tull (2008: 106) argue that the results of UN peace operations in Africa "have been paltry, particularly as regards the establishment of self-sustaining state institutions". Despite large investment of resources, it is admitted in a World Bank report that "the numerous rule of law assistance programs in post-conflict or fragile countries have so far resulted in few lasting consequences" (Samuels 2006: 15). An internal review of UK Security Sector Reform programmes found that, "interventions have been partially effective within different programmes... 'Partial effectiveness' means that programmes generate some useful outcomes but cannot produce a multiplier effect given political blockages" (Ball et al. 2007: xi).[2] The statebuilding plan might be thought easier in countries *not* coming out of conflict, but in fact the absence of transition can tend to reduce the sense of urgency for reform. Ball, Biesheuvel and Olanisakin's review of security reform in Nigeria noted that:

> At the best of times, the Nigerian government is difficult to engage at any level, not least at the Federal level. Obtaining the political commitment of the Inspector General of Police and the Federal Minister of Justice, for example, would require consistent high-level engagement [...] It does not appear that such intensive involvement was factored into the design of the Security, Justice and Growth Programme. It certainly has not been manifest in programme implementation over the last two years [...] [T]he programmes have suffered from insufficient buy in from senior Nigerian officials (Ball et al. 2007: 24-25).

Not only has the statebuilding plan often failed to reform state security services or expand them to a level where they can provide nationwide service, but they have of course largely ignored the main players in the security and justice sector, namely nonstate-informal. This not only "alienates citizens from the rebuilding of their states and undermines democratic accountability" (François and Sud 2006: 128), but means that the primary task of enhancing security for the majority has not been achieved. The tragedy is that in fact, "traditional and local authorities

[2] They were more positive about Sierra Leone, but see Baker (2010).

may be key channels for public service delivery as well as critical actors in re-establishing post-war stability and social reconciliation" (Call and Cousens 2007: 9).

The Multi-Layered Approach

A second and alternative plan for security architecture is the multi-layered option that some donors are expressing an interest in, although as yet not many donors are undertaking programmes that incorporate the concept, following through in terms of many programmes.[3] This plan recognises that across much of Africa, it is nonstate-informal authorities that are primarily responsible for the distribution of public goods such as security and justice. This recognition is based on the assumption that in the developing world there is rarely a case of a unified state monopolising public core services and controlling all its territory. Instead, a very different political order exists where there are overlapping layers of state and nonstate-informal spheres of power. These at times provide parallel forms of order and governance and at times, as a result of a mutual influence, distinct hybrid forms (Boege et al. 2008: 2; see also Louise Wiuff Moe's contribution to this special issue). In Africa the reality is often one of a political order where people, in the absence of the state, define themselves first and foremost as members of a kin group, tribe, village or neighbourhood and offer their primary loyalty to its rules and rulers. This loyalty owes much to the fact that these same local arenas have long provided order, security and basic services and the state has appeared a distant even alien external force (Boege et al. 2008: 10). In other words, "the processes and institutions freely associated with Western experiences of democracy may easily co-exist with social and political relations and practices which may continue much as before" (Roberts 2008: 71). In such a polity there are no strict boundaries between 'public' and 'private', 'state' and 'society', or 'public good' and 'private benefit'. Many post-colonial states have retained "indigenous mechanisms of socio-legal and political organization from their own historical experiences" since these "are considered more appropriate" than those offered by international donors (Roberts 2008: 79).

[3] Examples of donors who have given verbal support are : OECD (OECD 2007: 17); DFID (DFID 2004); DCAF/ Geneva Centre for the Democratic Control of Armed Forces (Law 2006: 2); World Bank Conflict Prevention and Reconstruction Unit (Samuels 2006: 18).

Starting from an analysis of the African state along these lines, a very different plan for the future emerges. It is one that does not insist on a normative position about the necessity for a state monopoly of violence. It recognises the existing multiple policing and justice providers, some of which are linked. Support is conditional, not on the nature of the authoriser, but on the nature of the provision. Whether a service provider is customary, community-based or commercial, is not the key issue. Central is whether the provider is offering a locally supported and acceptable standard of policing and justice. I use 'acceptable' as opposed to 'currently fully compliant with international standards' in the same way that election monitors say 'relatively free and fair' and not 'perfect'. Such is to recognise that in a poorly resourced situation development has to be progressive. Acceptable is a measure that has reference to what the provision was in an earlier period, rather than having reference to some absolute standard. Put simplistically, it means 'good enough for now' in the eyes of donors, states and local populations. It is, of course, the standard used to justify supporting the state police in Africa.

The multi-layered support option assumes that many African states will in the foreseeable future continue to struggle to find the human and financial resources to deliver security and justice to the majority of their populations. The demand for security and justice outstrips the provision capacity of governments. So this plan shifts the attention from who *should* be providing policing, to who *is* providing it. It does not ask, how state policing can be extended to areas where it is currently absent, but, how existing nonstate-informal policing active on the ground can be supported and enhanced. It is not a plan that is trying to build security and justice from scratch. Nor is it trying to exclude state policing and courts. As noted before, there already exist linkages between state and nonstate-informal providers and these links are a key intervention point to begin support that will deliver improved security and justice to the populations that they serve. A multi-layered support to policing and justice providers offers assistance to all those offering a service that is welcomed by the majority of the local population and judged acceptable by states and donors. It is not a strategy of abandoning support for the state providers. Instead, it is one that helps all effective policing and justice provision so that what is within reach of Africans is steadily improved, irrespective of who provides it (Baker and Scheye 2007, 2009). As the OECD notes, programmes that support "either state or non-state institutions, one to the exclusion of the other, are unlikely to be effective" (OECD 2007: 17).

The multi-layered approach to security and justice governance has been promoted by Wood and Shearing (2007) as 'nodal governance'. They argue that there should be recognition of the multiplicity of authorisers and providers of policing, "that co-exist in multiple ways to produce diverse security outcomes" (Wood and Shearing 2007: 13). Social network analysis by governments or donors may reveal that for any given security network the state may or may not be the dominant provider; the nodes may or may not be linked in that network; the links may or may not be sanctioned by the state; the nodes may or may not currently co-operate. From that understanding of the network, the next logical step is to ensure that across its entirety resources are distributed and managed fairly and efficiently so as to promote the effectiveness and accountability of not just individual groups, but of the network as an entire system. Such a total programme would suit the plurality of security and justice in Africa, although it would be very hard to achieve, for recognizing multiple providers is not the same as integrating them into a single network. Questions of skills, roles, availability, authority, legality, legitimacy and co-ordinating processes abound.

One way forward has been suggested by Herbert Wulf (2007). He identifies two issues facing multi-layered policing. The first is the problem of legitimization, given the competitive nature of legitimation. Second, is the problem of apportioning authority so as to avoid disputed sovereignties and yet to achieve a clarity of functions. His solution is to hold fast to two principles, namely subsidiarity for practice and supremacy for norms. "The monopoly of violence should be exercised according to the *subsidiarity principle*, that is, the lowest level should be the starting point" (Wulf 2007: 20; italics in the original). Only when that level is not capable or cannot be tasked with exercising the monopoly of force should a higher state or regional or even global level undertake the task. Concerning supremacy in norm setting, he argues for it to be top-down, so that norms of a higher level prevail over those of a lower level. Wulf, therefore, sees "a legitimate multi-level public monopoly of force, with a division of labor between the different levels and acceptable and agreed norms for the application of force" (Wulf 2007: 29).

Specialization is another, although related, approach to integrated security and justice across the state and nonstate-informal spectrum. Some have noted that state police have taken on more and more roles within the community (e.g. problem solving and mediation) to the point where their limited numbers are stretched even further and the skills required of them multiply (Altbeker 2007). The response offered to this overload is 'minimalist policing' (see also Marks et al. in this special issue). This calls for the police to intervene only when there is criminal (or perhaps serious criminal) activity and then to do so using their legal powers and the criminal justice system. In other words, "instead of widening the reach of the police, we need to confine them to what they are trained and resourced to do and what interventions they are inclined towards" (Marks et al. 2009: 150). For the remainder, nonstate-informal providers can be authorized by the state to provide, drawing upon their expertise of local knowledge and conciliatory processes and upon their local availability and legitimacy. The focus, then, of this approach is clarifying roles according to skills so that all in the network are clear about what they can individually contribute and what they can realistically expect from others. Menkhaus (2007: 106) calls it a "negotiated division of labour". When each provider concentrates on what they do best, it only furthers their legitimacy unless, of course, their authority is contested.

For Western states and the Western educated African leaders to envisage offering support for a different political order from the one they have been familiar with is obviously challenging, but some have made a move in that direction. For example the UK through the British Council is currently not only supporting police reform in Sierra Leone, but is also engaged in strengthening chiefs' courts and assisting paralegals in a concerted effort to broaden access to justice. Yet this is still a long way from an integrated security and justice system. Even if an integrated system could be built, it is acknowledged that practical difficulties would arise. For instance, it might be questioned whether the African state has the capacity to undertake a steering function of ensuring the quality, efficacy and accountability of all policing agencies and dispute resolution mechanisms.

Underlying this debate concerning which overall approach to follow in security and justice seems to be lack of clarity regarding how the categories of 'public' and 'private' are used. In common usage public goods are services for the common good and are provided free by the state to all citizens according to certain standards. Private goods are services offered to those who can pay since they are for the profit and in the interest of the providers. The one is assumed to be universal and free, the other localised and costly thus excluding the poor. This is a travesty of reality in security and justice in most of the world. No one who knows anything of African police forces would describe them as offered to all citizens and offered freely without discrimination or favour. Moreover, an objective account of nonstate-informal security and justice providers would not find them all self-regarding and serving only private and largely elite interests. Rather, many would be found to be universal to their local 'public' irrespective of status and power and offered at minimal cost to the user. As Samuels observes, non-state providers "may be more effective and less costly" (2006: 18) as there are networks that are already in every village and township and (in case of commercial security) around every economically valuable location. A public good is not to be mistaken for a good provided by the state; nor does its availability have to be nationwide. A public good can apply to a non-exclusionary service provided to all within a more localised context. Public goods and services can and are provided by nonstate-informal actors to their communities.

There are then at least two plans of security architecture, but they have very different objectives and different outcomes. Part of the process of deciding the merits of the two plans concerns what can be afforded by the client, assuming we know who exactly the client is.

The Purse

Architects' plans can look stunning, but before we get carried away let us ask if the proposed structures for Africa's policing and justice are affordable and therefore achievable and sustainable?

The security and justice reform carried out by the UK in 20 countries in sub-Saharan Africa 2001-2005 cost more than £240 million (Ball et.al. 2007: 10). In just one country, Sierra Leone, the reform process cost £145 million 2001-2005 (Ibid). For DFID and the UK government the Sierra Leone police reform programme came to be a test bed of their latest thinking on police reform policy and practice. As it evolved it went far beyond seeking simply to assist the police force to stand on its feet again. It sought explicitly to transform the police structure, function, values, legitimacy, service delivery outcomes, accountability, discipline and relationship with the public. The three police reform programmes spanning 1999-2010 represent the single most important effort by the agency worldwide to fundamentally reconstruct a police service in a post-conflict state.

The police in Sierra Leone reached their designated ceiling of 9,500 officers and an evaluation of the Sierra Leone police suggested many positive gains from the programme.[4] With hindsight, however, I and other observers would conclude that

[4] In particular, operational capability has been built in terms of numbers of trained personnel, and available buildings and vehicles and communications. Further, the management structure has been overhauled to reflect merit, streamlined to maximize efficiency and trained to impart key management skills. However it is still a very urban force and is still short of uniforms, equipment and especially

one overarching mistake stands out. The reform programme was simply too ambitious. The statebuilding option attempted too much too quickly. It is a common accusation across donor programmes. Scheye (2004: un-numbered), commenting on international post-conflict police programmes says: "To try to do too much leads to failure. To be over-ambitious is not financially, politically or culturally viable and there will be no real national control or ownership". Moreover, statebuilding that is financed from outside has eventually to come to an end. The UK financial commitment to Sierra Leone was remarkable for its endurance, but now it is winding down.[5] Its investment has been substantial and prolonged by international standards, yet as it withdraws, the Sierra Leonean government is unlikely to be able to sustain the investment.

In addition to doubts about the degree to which international policing programmes have permanently changed police culture and practices,[6] police forces in Africa frequently have low ratios of officers per head of population. For some, the answer to low numbers is simply that security reform "may have to be accompanied by increases in the costs of at least some types of uniformed forces" (Brzoska and Heinemann-Gruber 2004: 10). Yet even if, as a result of donor-funded reforms, police officers are increased in numbers, it is doubtful that such numbers will be sustainable, well managed, or able to provide crime protection and crime investigation for all citizens. One study suggested that sector-wide approaches to justice and security programmes were not yet achievable in any fragile states, partly due to serious shortfalls of human capital (Stone 2005). Further, shortfalls in public revenues raise questions as to whether countries can sustain security reform after donor money ceases (Sedra 2007). Security reform

accommodation. As regards the perception of the Sierra Leone police by the public, the message is mixed. There is evidence that the police are more trusted now than they were before by the public but concerns remain that the police and courts connive to allow corrupt officials to escape justice (ICG 2008).

[5] The next programme will continue with the broader perspective under the name of Improved Access to Security and Justice in Sierra Leone 2010-13. Beyond that it is uncertain, but support for policing by itself is seen as a decreasing priority by the UK.

[6] Professor Etannibi Alemika, says the evidence demonstrates that the police forces in most African countries are 'significantly brutal, corrupt, inefficient, unresponsive and unaccountable to the generality of the population', IDASA 2007.

that is promoted by donors too often miscalculates the resources available to weak states. By definition weak states, particularly post-conflict states, lack the capacity to deliver core functions, such as safety and security provision, in an effective and accountable manner. Their finances are over-committed and dependent on uncertain revenue streams.[7] In addition, they face severe shortages of human skills and training facilities and the basic infrastructure (physical, constitutional, legal, and administrative) required for effective service provision is often lacking. Further, the African state is in "transition towards both down-sizing and redefinition, given two decades of neo-liberal conditionalities" (MacLean and Shaw 2001, quoted in Shaw 2003: un-numbered). The diminished African state is not in a strong position to maintain large expensive services.

Against this financial background, it is surely in the interests of all to look again at the nonstate-informal sector, which requires minimal financial support. In other words, there is a need to evaluate the contribution that these policing providers might make, since they may well remain sustainable after the donors have reached donor fatigue and gone. Security and justice provision literally cannot afford to remain confined to the state services alone. Having said that, the volunteerism of nonstate-informal actors, though attractive in terms of running costs, does have issues regarding the sustainability of personnel. Young men, for instance, that run the vigilance groups in Monrovia's suburbs are all too likely to remain only as long as no other employment opportunities arise.

The Builder

Finally, there has to be agreement as to whose building this is; who is commissioning the bricklayer, architect and finance. Whose construction is this? Donor documents seem to suggest that security and justice programmes are being built by the country governments themselves. The documents highlight that the

[7] An informant revealed that the 2007 estimated budget of the southern Sudan Police Service was approximately $50 million. Salaries for the 20,000 strong (some say 10,000) service consume nearly 88 per cent. Operating and capital costs are both projected to be 6 per cent, with only 1 per cent allocated for fuel and vehicle maintenance, restricting the police to urban centres. In such circumstances, the police service will remain under-trained, under-equipped, and essentially paralyzed because of the lack of operating funds.

project is and must be, 'people-centred and locally owned'. Laurie Nathan (2007) is blunt as to why so often donors use "local ownership" as a mere "rhetorical device". He says donor governments in fact impose their own programmes since:

> The donors are imbued with a sense of superiority [...]; they lack respect for local actors and regard them as incompetent; they underestimate the difficulties of state building and transformation, and become overly frustrated with the slow pace or lack of reform; their financial and bureaucratic systems require programmes with a high level of pre-determined detail [...]; their short-term funding cycles require deliverables within unrealistic time frames; they are sometimes intent on pursuing their own political agendas at the expense of local interests (Nathan 2007: 2).

Unfortunately it has been proved too often that security architecture that is not commissioned by local 'builders' but by foreign ones is unsuitable for local needs. Hence the 600 or so vehicles bought for the Sierra Leone police after the civil war were for the most part quickly out of service because of poor usage, poor maintenance and lack of fuel. The state finances and the police training were not ready for that technical leap (Baker 2005). Lack of local ownership is likely to become even pronounced as Western donor governments demand that their aid programmes first and foremost contribute to their own national security through 'upstream' prevention that helps to stop potential terrorist threats arising in developing countries.[8] Unsurprisingly such external projects meet a lack of enthusiasm if not hostility. It is not that local actors will necessarily develop the very best security architecture imaginable. Nevertheless, "a process-oriented approach that respects and empowers local actors is more likely to yield good results in the long-term than a product-oriented approach that undermines local actors and is not sustainable" (Nathan 2007: 3).

It has often been pointed out that there are several versions of what 'local ownership' means. It might be ownership by the government; the security and

[8] In the UK a new National Security Council, which oversees all aspects of foreign policy, is requiring that the Overseas Development Administration budget should make the maximum possible contribution to national security. http://www.guardian.co.uk/politics/2010/aug/29/protests-uk-security-aid-policy.

justice agencies; or the political and educated elites. It rarely means ownership by the majority of the people who will be using the security and justice architecture constructed. So called 'buy-in' may well be possible from the local political elite when what is being constructed is an effective centralized, coordinated, state-provided security that can defend their interests. It may not, however, be what many of the members of the population had in mind. An improved police force in a distant city is of limited value to many. The pursuit of centralization secures no local ownership from the voiceless and powerless, who are likely to see themselves better served by local security systems. Their choices, in as much as they have them, are based on 'what is available', 'what works best', 'what supports local values' and 'what can be afforded' and that invariably leads them to preferring nonstate-informal providers (Baker 2009; Isser et al. 2009; Alemika and Chukwuma 2004). Many donors, assuming they themselves are the builders (since they have the cash), are looking for local support among the government for the plans they have drawn up. What would be more helpful would be for them to offer support for the builders chosen by local people to execute the plan that they have got to live with.

Conclusion

The argument of this article has been that there are other ways for donors and African states to build security architecture than by supporting state security and justice agencies with training, finance and equipment. The statebuilding route is necessarily an expensive route, one that raises serious questions about its sustainability. It is also one that has so far failed to bring greatly improved security and justice to the majority of Africa's citizens, who live their lives for the most part out of reach of these state services. An alternative, although not without difficulties, is the multi-layered approach. This would make use of some of the many local providers of security and justice that exist below the layer of the state - nonstate-informal groups. Though they may have significant local support, for the most part few of these nonstate-informal providers reach all the international standards, any more than the police and judges of the state criminal justice system do. Yet many are open to transformation and already have links with the state, so that it is not impossible to envisage their improvement being speeded by donor support.

There will no doubt be debates over the details of which nonstate-informal group to support and how, but the principle that local people should be the focus of donor desire for local ownership seems beyond challenge. A donor support for security and justice that was designed and approved by local people for their local needs might result in variations in levels of provision and standards nationwide, but the locally designed provision would have the advantage of legitimacy and support without which security and justice is unlikely to succeed.[9] In the terms of the analogy used in this article: the 'bricks' are there – some expensive ones (the police) and a lot of very inexpensive ones of varying quality (nonstate-informal actors). Alternative 'architectural plans' are on the table. The African client can afford very little in the way of building or running costs. Let the client design an affordable architecture - one that meets the expressed wishes of the population; one that will actually make security and justice better for the majority. And let friends of the client support them in any way they can.

References

ABRAHAMSEN, Rita and Michael WILLIAMS

2008 'Public/private, global/local: the changing contours of Africa's security Governance.' *Review of African Political Economy*, 35: 539-553.

ALEMIKA, Etannibi E.O., and Innocent C. CHUKWUMA

2004 *The Poor and Informal Policing in Nigeria. A Report on Poor Peoples' Perceptions and Priorities on Safety, Security and Informal Policing in A2J Focal States in Nigeria.* Lagos: Centre for Law Enforcement Education (CLEEN).

ALTBEKER, Antony

2007 *A Country at War with itself: South Africa's Crisis of Crime.* Johannesburg: Jonathan Ball.

BAKER, Bruce

2005 'Who do people turn to for policing in Sierra Leone?' *Journal of Contemporary African Studies* 23: 371-390.

[9] A study in South Sudan found that the strength and popularity of local policing and justice is precisely that it is 'tailored to the perceptions and needs' of local people. The variation not just between localities but also within localities is exactly what makes it successful in the eyes of users. "Each case is negotiated, argued and bargained out to come to a conclusion that is by no means predictable on the basis of the bare bones of the case" (Leonardi et al., 2010: 74).

2009 *Security in Post-conflict Africa: The Role of Non-State Policing*. Boca Raton: CRC Press.

2010 'Sierra Leone Police Reform: the role of the UK government.' Paper presented to the GRIPS State-Building Workshop 2010: *Organizing Police Forces in Post-Conflict Peace-Support Operations*, January 27-28th. Available: http://www3.grips.ac.jp/~pinc/data/10-06.pdf

BAKER, Bruce, and Eric SCHEYE

2007 'Multi-layered justice and security delivery in post-conflict and fragile states.' *Conflict, Security & Development* 7: 503-528.

2009 'Access to justice in a post-conflict state: donor-supported multidimensional peacekeeping in Southern Sudan.' *International Peacekeeping* 16: 171-185.

BALL, Nicole, Piet BIESHEUVEL and Funmi OLANISAKIN

2007 *Security and Justice Sector Reform Programming in Africa.* , Evaluation Working Paper 23. London and Glasgow: DFID.

BOEGE, Volker, Anne BROWN, Kevin CLEMENTS and Anna NOLAN

2008 *On Hybrid Political Orders and Emerging States: State Formation in the Context of 'Fragility'*. Berlin: Berghof Research Center for Constructive Conflict Management. Available at: http://www.berghof-handbook.net/uploads/download/boege_etal_handbook.pdf.

BOURDIEU, Pierre

1989 *La noblesse d'état. Grandes écoles et esprit de corps.*

BOURDIEU, Pierre, and Loïc J.D. WACQUANT

1992 *An Invitation to Reflexive Sociology.* Chicago: University of Chicago Press.

BRZOSKA, Michael and Andreas HEINEMANN-GRÜDER

2004 'Security Sector Reform and Post-Conflict Reconstruction under International Auspices.' In Philipp Furi and Miroslav Hadžić (eds.), *Sourcebook on Security Sector Reform.* Geneva and Belgrade: Centre for the Democratic Control of Armed Forces (DCAF) and Centre for Civil-Military Relations.

CALL, Charles T., and Elizabeth M. COUSENS

2007 *Ending Wars and Building Peace.* Coping with Crisis Working Paper Series. New York: International Peace Academy.

CALL, Charles T., and Vanessa H. WYETH (eds.)

2008 *Building States to Build Peace.* Boulder, CO: Lynn Rienner.

CHIRAYATH, Leila, Caroline SAGE and Michael WOOLCOCK

2005 'Customary law and policy reform: engaging with the plurality of justice Systems.' Prepared as a background paper for the *World Development*

Report 2006: Equity and Development.
CLEEN (Centre for Law Enforcement Education)
2005 *Criminal Victimization, Safety and Policing in Nigeria.* Lagos: Cleen Foundation.
DFID (DEPARTMENT FOR INTERNATIONAL DEVELOPMENT)
2004 *Non-State Justice and Security Systems.* Briefing. London: DFID.
n.d. *Understanding and Supporting Security Sector Reform* London: DFID, http://www.dfid.gov.uk/pubs/files/supportingsecurity.pdf.
ENGLEBERT, Pierre and Denis M. TULL
2008 'Postconflict reconstruction in Africa: flawed ideas about failed states.' *International Security* 32: 106-139.
FRANÇOIS, Monika and Inder SUD
2006 'Promoting stability and development in fragile and failed states.' *Development Policy Review* 24: 141-160.
HUMAN RIGHTS WATCH
2010 *'Everyone's in on the Game' Corruption and Human Rights Abuses by the Nigeria Police Force.* New York: Human Rights Watch.
ICG (INTERNATIONAL CRISIS GROUP)
2008 *Sierra Leone: A New Era of Reform?* Africa Report 143. Available at: http://www.crisisgroup.org/library/documents/africa/west africa/143 sierra leone a new era of reform.pdf.
IDASA
2007 *Conference Summary Report, Police Reform & Democratisation* http://www.idasa.org.za/index.asp?page=topics details.asp%3FRID%3D11.
ISSER, Deborah H., Stephen C. LUBKEMANN and Saah N'TOW
2009 *Looking for Justice: Liberian Experiences with and Perceptions of Local Justice Options.* Washington: United States Institute of Peace and George Washington University.
JOHNSTON, Les
1992 *The Rebirth of Private Policing.* London: Routledge.
LAW, David M.
2006 *The Post-Conflict Security Sector.* Policy Paper 41. Geneva: Centre for the Democratic Control of Armed Forces (DCAF).
LEONARDI, Cherry, Leben N. MORO, Martina SANTSCHI and Deborah H. ISSER
2010 *Local Justice in Southern Sudan.* Washington: United States Institute of Peace.

MACLEAN, Sandra J. and Timothy M. SHAW
2001 'Canada & New "Global" Strategic Alliances: Prospects for Human Security at Start of the Twenty-First Century. *Canadian Foreign Policy* 8(3): 17-36.
MARKS, Monique, Clifford SHEARING and Jennifer WOOD
2009 'Who should the police be? Finding a new narrative for community policing in South Africa.' *Police Practice and Research* 10: 145-155.
MENKHAUS, Ken
2007 'Governance without government in Somalia: spoilers, state building and the politics of coping.' *International Security* 31: 74-106.
NATHAN, Laurie
2007 *No Ownership, No Commitment: A Guide to Local Ownership of Security Sector Reform.* Paper commissioned by the Security Sector Reform Strategy of the UK Government's Global Conflict Prevention Pool, University of Birmingham, UK. Available at: http://www.ssrnetwork.net/documents/Publications/No Ownership No Commitment v2.pdf.
OECD
2007 *OECD DAC Handbook on Social Security Reform (SSR): Supporting Security and Justice.* Paris: OECD.
2008 *Concepts and Dilemmas of State Building in Fragile Situations: From Fragility to Resilience.* OECD/ DAC discussion paper. Paris: OECD. Available at: http://www.oecd.org/dataoecd/59/51/41100930.pdf.
ROBERTS, David
2008 'Hybrid polities and indigenous pluralities: advanced lessons in statebuilding from Cambodia.' *Journal of Intervention and Statebuilding* 2: 63- 86.
SAMUELS, Kirsti
2006 *Rule of Law Reform in Post-conflict Countries: Operational Initiatives and Lessons Learnt.* Social Development Papers no. 37. Washington: Conflict Prevention and Reconstruction, Social Development Department, World Bank.
SCHEYE, Eric
2004 *Report on the Wilton Park Conference S03/4, 'International Post-Conflict Policing Operations'*, held at Wilton Park, Steyning, West Sussex on 26-30 January.
SEDRA, Mark
2007 'Security Sector Reform in Afghanistan: An Instrument of the State-Building Project.' Pp. 151-176 in Louise Anderson, Bjørn Møller and

Finn Stepputat (eds.), *Fragile States and Insecure People: Violence, Security, and Statehood in the Twenty-first Century*. Houndsmill: Palgrave Macmillan.

STONE, Christopher

2005 *Supporting Security, Justice and Development: Lessons for a New Era*. New York: Vera Institute of Justice.

TITECA, Kristof

2009 'The "Masai" and "Miraa": public authority, vigilance and criminality in a Ugandan border town.' *Journal of Modern African Studies* 47: 219-317.

UNDP/USAID

2007 *First Steps in Post-Conflict Statebuilding: A UNDP-USAID Study*. Washington, DC: USAID.

WHAITES, Alan

2008 *States in Development: Understanding State-building*. A DFID Working Paper. London: Governance and Social Development Group Policy and Research Division, DFID.

WOOD, Jennifer, and Clifford SHEARING

2007 *Imagining Security* Cullompton, UK: Willan Publishing.

WOJKOWSKA, Ewa

2006 *Doing Justice: How Informal Justice Systems Can Contribute*. Oslo: UNDP Oslo Governance Centre.

WULF, Herbert

2007 *Challenging the Weberian Concept of the State: The Future of the Monopoly of Violence*. ACPACS Occasional Paper 9. Brisbane: ACPACS (Australian Centre for Peace and Conflict Studies).

RECONFIGURING STATE AND NON-STATE ACTORS IN THE PROVISION OF SAFETY IN (SOUTH) AFRICA: IMPLICATIONS FOR BOTTOM-UP POLICING ARRANGEMENTS AND FOR DONOR FUNDING

Monique Marks, Jennifer Wood,
Julian Azzopardi and Thokozani Xaba

Introduction

There is a curious paradox surrounding formal efforts to strengthen policing in South Africa. On the one hand, it has long been recognized that security is routinely delivered through pluralised, 'bottom-up' arrangements that co-exist with the more formalized system of state policing (Schärf and Nina 2001; Kyed and Buur 2006; Baker 2002; Steinberg 2008). On the other hand, numerous efforts on the part of the South African government, as well as external donor agencies, continue to rest on a state-centric approach to democratization and professionalization (World Bank 1998; Scheye 2009). Despite the empirical evidence of an historic and endemic pluralisation of policing, the state has positioned itself as the *key* provider and authoriser of security outcomes. It has done this through 'reinventing' itself as a 'developmental state', where primary emphasis is placed on government intervention and planning.

The international donor community has reinforced the state-centric view in that it has consistently framed police reform within western models of democratization, including the introduction of community policing principles and programmes

(Brogden 2004; Dixon 2007). International discourses about the future of policing in South Africa emphasize the improvement of formal police accountability and oversight (Bruce and Neild 2005), and the reintroduction of a designated and reinforced public order policing unit (Marks and Tait 2011). Very little, if anything, is mentioned by donor agencies about the real and potential contributions of less formal policing agents to the project of enhancing security.

Conventional, state-led views of the governance of policing in South Africa, and arguably in Africa more generally, overlook part of the landscape in which a range of actors play important roles in securing local communities. In this post-colonial plural policing landscape, the formal (state) police agencies are one of many policing actors. Much governance is carried out by groupings other than *the* police. We demonstrate this by showcasing 'everyday policing' in three urban spaces in Durban. These cases help us to think outside of the state-centric box about how policing can be regulated and about how plural policing resources can be mobilised.

We challenge the state-centric view that generally underpins African adaptations of the developmental state. Our goal in this paper is to emphasise the role that non-state actors perform in the advancement of African development, and this includes the provision of a safety. We argue that it is best to understand the state in Africa as 'hybrid', a term that we believe is gaining currency within the literature on African governance. In our view, 'hybrid' or 'plural' understandings of the state in Africa take us further in understanding the contemporary policing reality, and such an understanding helps us to frame a feasible normative solution to policing dilemmas in Africa.

Drawing on examples of three Durban-based groups actively involved in the delivery of community security, we seek to demonstrate that non-state actors routinely perform most policing functions across communities in South Africa. In the face of this reality, we suggest that the state's involvement in acknowledging the contributions of non-state providers, combined with efforts to coordinate and regulate their practices, can assist formal efforts to alleviate security deficits while strengthening the democratic character of security provision, and of state legitimacy more generally.

In this paper we articulate a vision of the state that emphasizes enhanced regulation of plural policing combined with a substantially scaled-down role for the state police. This circumscribed role involves a shift away from western imports of community policing models to a role that more squarely targets formal police resources on their core functions. We make the case, then, for a more minimalist view of the police. While potentially controversial, we suggest that this 'minimalist' view of the police role would allow for the more effective use of finite public police resources while engendering more positive perceptions of the police among the people they serve.

In proposing a more minimal approach to the state police we do not advocate a simple shifting of responsibility from the state to the 'private' realm. We are not advocating a neo-liberal agenda. Rather, we wish to advance a 'left-realism' approach which recognises that poor and working class people are the ones most badly affected by crime, and that security disparities are often amplified by state policing interventions that are overly punitive and out of alignment with local needs and conceptions of justice. In the left-realist view, practical solutions should be underpinned by democratised local control of the police, combined with active involvement of disempowered and marginalised citizens in resolving problems of insecurity (see Carlen 1992).

This vision requires the establishment of local safety organs to co-ordinate policing in the wider sense we describe here. Enhancement and formalisation of engagements between non-state actors and official bodies will require concurrent financial and material provision for local structures. We argue for a co-ordinated and mutually re-enforcing role on the part of international donor agencies to help promote such engagements. With this model in mind, there is scope for donor funding to have a significant impact both on policing specifically and on broader development goals of reducing governance disparities, provided that such funding is targeted to support local bodies tasked with co-ordinating plural policing and regulating non-state policing activities.

Plural Governance in Africa

The nature of the state on the African continent notoriously eludes definition (see van der Spuy 2000; Baker 2010); there are many state forms and state agendas in Africa. However, what is evident is that post-colonial centrist-state African countries are commonly measured, to their disadvantage, against 'stronger' western counterparts (Olayode 2005). All too often, they are deemed to be 'weak' in delivering basic services and goods, and as having 'failed' in sustaining citizen emancipation and equality, and being 'fragile' economically, socially and culturally. Western accounts of its structures and roles tend to close off from view significant elements of non-state governance and in particular the roles played by non-state actors in forging locally relevant solutions to the dilemmas of governance and development (Ellis 2009; Olowu and Wunsch 2004).

A range of common problems beset African states, including patrimonial, highly centralised, rent-seeking forms of politics (Chabal and Daloz 1999) and alienated 'subjects' (Hart and Padayachee 2010: 423). These troubles are the legacy of a combination of colonially imposed borders and bureaucratically invented identities (Appiah 1992); post-colonial leaders who were fixated on cementing allegiances with the former colonial regimes they had once sought liberation from (Olayode 2005); and externally-funded (and prescribed) initiatives (Wuyts 1996, cited in Mkandawire 2001b). Yet, it is quite wrong to regard the African state as having reached a catastrophic level of crisis. It is more useful to understand the state in Africa as actively reinventing itself to contend with the changing socio-political and economic changes of the global system (Olayode 2005).

A number of governments in Africa, including South Africa, have adopted notions of the 'developmental state' in their attempts at reinventing themselves and in shedding their colonial legacies. The key defining feature of the developmental state, as we understand it, is a state that commits substantial national resources to socio-economic development. Developmental states aim to balance economic growth and social development. While developmental state programmes value social partnerships in achieving their goals, at their core they are committed to state-led planning (see Mkandawire 2001b).

The ideal of a developmental state is laudable. However, for a developmental state to truly achieve its goals, government requires sufficient organization and the capacity to plan and regulate society and its institutions (Chang 1999; Wade 2003). Furthermore, a 'true' developmental state must have the capacity to mobilise and coordinate the resources and skills of its social partners (civic, labour, business) toward the realisation of common goals. At present, this does not seem to be the case in South Africa, arguably the country in Africa with the greatest economic and political capital. While social partners are recognised as important by advocates of the developmental state, the state (in Africa) remains the axis for all development and governance enterprises. This, we argue, has blinded developmental state projects to forms of social and cultural capital that could make governance (including of security) more effective, efficient and legitimate.

We are not critical of the notion of the developmental state as such. However, we are concerned about the way in which this has been interpreted and implemented.

We are equally concerned that developmental states in Africa will be unable to achieve their laudable goals because governments "lack the institutional attributes which enable it to act authoritatively in formulating and implementing programmes in order to achieve [them]" (Edigheji 2006: 4). This is as much the case for policing as it is for other areas of governance.

Attempts to mobilise non-state groupings, embedded in notional programmes such as the 'People's Contract' in South Africa, have failed because elites struggle to let go of bureaucratic and technocratic practices (Mangcu 2006; Cronin 2005, cited in Edigheji 2006). In South Africa, much like the rest of Africa, the mobilsation of community groupings is viewed concurrently as necessary and as burdensome. Government-led processes and institutions aimed at participation have become technocratic and are used to broaden the net of government, rather than to promote more pluralised forms of governance (Cronin 2005; Olowu 1994).

In order to release themselves from gridlock, any state self-reinvention in Africa needs to recognise that the state is "a facilitator, rather than a director, mobilizing and enabling social allegiances that are largely autonomous" (Appiah 1992: 169). African governments need to both take stock of established traditions of non-state, localised governance arrangements, and also find ways of actively mobilising and coordinating resources and capacities that lie outside of the state.

Mkandawire (2001b: 21) calls for a 'creative re-thinking' of socio-political progress in African development that considers governance arrangements that actually exist on the ground, taking care not to neglect existing capacities in the quest for 'new' ones. Based on these considerations, programmes for strengthening governance must be centred on utilizing, retooling and reinvigorating existing capacities, both state and non-state, that will deliver long-term developmental outcomes (Mkandawire 2001b).

To do this, it is useful to consider the state in Africa as 'hybrid' in nature (Boege et al. 2008; Baker 2009). Such a view recognises that while the state may provide some service and regulatory functions, African governments are often regarded by its citizens as an "alien external force, far away not only physically, but also psychologically" (Boege et al. 2008: 10). Thinking in terms of hybridity creates a space for governments to take serious account of non-state forms of governance that deploy varying logics and technologies. Hybrid thinking promotes the idea that different forms of governance "do not exist in isolation from one another, but [rather] permeate each other, and consequently give rise to a different and genuine political order" (ibid.). In this perspective, states do not automatically have ascribed to them a privileged position as *the* institution that provides public goods such as security, welfare, or health (see Olayode 2005).

Boege et al. (2008), who promote the idea of the hybrid state in Africa, point out that political entities in Africa consist of a range of customary and non-state institutions of governance that existed prior to the era of colonisation and still survive today, such as traditional court systems and co-operative community finance groupings like the 'stokvels' (community credit unions aimed at localised saving) and burial societies in South Africa (Lukhele 1990; Padayachee and Hart 2010). Accompanying these are new, localised, non-state groupings that take on certain governance responsibilities, such as home based care initiatives, particularly in regard to alleviating the localised affects of HIV and AIDS (Devereux and Lund 2010). In truth, many African societies have, and continue to be, governed "without reference to political entities that we would today recognize as states" (Ellis 2009:11).

Moving beyond a state-centric framework to one centred on hybrid political orders opens up new ways of conceiving how developmental goals might be achieved and how states might be strengthened (Boege et al. 2008: 3). A hybrid conception of the state suggests that alternative governance programmes are possible that deliver effective and legitimate outcomes while not downplaying the importance of the state and state-building exercises. A hybrid framework also suggests that local experience and responsibility that are built into such programmes open up more sustainable solutions to political and governance problems. State 'weakness' actually becomes a 'strength', because state legitimacy is enhanced when state authorities work with local orders of governance rather than wanting to dislodge them.

Hybrid accounts of governance promote a more minimalist conception of the state role, rather than viewing the state as *the* central authoriser and provider of public goods. A distinction is made between 'first-order functions' (e.g. enforcement of laws) that should be the responsibility of the state and 'second-order functions' (delivery of services) that may be undertaken by non-state actors, reflecting the hybrid reality frequently encountered in African societies (Menkhaus 2007). Menkhaus (2007), Boege et al. (2008), Stephens (2009) and others have suggested that assigning to the state a reduced and more narrowly specified role has a number of advantages. Such an approach acknowledges and empowers local communities and non-state actors who are already actively engaged in governance and service delivery projects. In addition, a more minimalist conception of the state allows us to think of the best possible way to make use of its real, finite resources and capacities.

In regards to security provision, African states are generally severely constrained in their resources, and are unable to distribute security in an equitable and efficient manner to all citizens. As a result, the citizenry seriously questions the legitimacy of state agencies such as the public police. This legitimacy deficit has been addressed through the (historic and current) activation of non-state providers of security that have complex and contradictory engagements with the state police (Baker 2002). This has occurred in Africa and also in 'more developed' countries.

The coming of different 'nodes' in the governance of policing is not unique to Africa, although it may be more pronounced in places where government deficits are very evident. The notion of the hybrid states fits well with ideas about plural or nodal governance, now well accepted in international criminological scholarship (Loader 2000; Jones and Newburn 2006; Shearing 2001; Johnston and Shearing 2003; Button 2008). We adopt the term 'plural' in this article, not only for the sake of conceptual consistency and its affinity with writings on legal pluralism, but also because it does not suggest that state and non-state entities necessarily 'permeate' each other, as suggested in the above conception of 'hybridity' (Boege et al. 2008). In considering pluralism in policing governance we look at how local forms of security delivery constitute a distinct apparatus, not necessarily present in the national public agenda, but rather in a form that 'bubbles up' (Braithwaite 2006) from citizens' perceptions of needs, rights, resource availability and effectiveness.

We now turn to three South African case studies, which demonstrate three of the important premises of this article. First, community groups are often the key providers of policing functions. Second, these groups interface in complex and contradictory ways with the state police; and finally, in promoting development goals, state and non-state policing providers need to acknowledge one another's contributions and limitations.

Plural Policing in Durban: Three Cases

The cases presented here illustrate ways in which people create security in their own communities when the state is either unable or unwilling to provide for such security. As elsewhere in South Africa (see, e.g., Singh 2008; Shearing 1994; Schärf 2000; Roche 2002), everyday policing groups emerging in neighbourhood or community contexts perform a wide-range of security functions. These cases illustrate the various ways in which state and non-state actors can co-exist in the delivery of security goods. While states may enlist local groups to help bolster state policing activities, community groups and organizations may 'steer' local arrangements, bringing together different actors in a horizontal system of resources and capacities. In some cases, forms of everyday policing may operate (mostly) independently of the state police, but nonetheless seek state recognition of their activities, in order to garner legitimacy and to help establish agreements for enlisting the support of state police when their unique capacities (e.g. use of legal authority and mandated use of force) may be required.

Our first example comes from Warwick Triangle, which is a transport node and trading district. The main occupants of Warwick Triangle are informal traders as well as working-class and underclass residents. Our second example is Newlands East, which is a lower-income residential area. While historically known for its 'coloured' (i.e. mixed-race) inhabitants, its inhabitants now come from a variety of racial backgrounds. We then turn to PalmRidge, which is a middle-class area straddling the suburbs of Berea and Overport.[1]

Warwick Triangle: traders taking charge

For many years, business people in Warwick Triangle have partnered to promote security and create a business-friendly environment. The initial group was called Traders Against Crime (TAC) and an offspring of TAC now refers to itself as the Warwick Triangle Community Policing Forum (CPF), although it has to formal connection to statutory community policing forums.[2] Traders formed these associations because frequent theft and armed robbery in the area were interfering with trade. As well, the local authority had not been responding to traders'

---

[1] PalmRidge is not the name of a suburb or area; it is abbreviated from the name of the organization formed in this section of the suburban Berea. Organized residents have called themselves the PalmRidge Neighbourhood Association. The name is drawn from two of the roads that form part of the boundary of the association.

[2] Ch. 7 of the South African Police Service Act (1995) requires that community police forums (CPFs) be established at every police station. Their functions are to promote accountability to the local community, monitor the effectiveness of the police locally, advise the service in regard to local priority policing, and evaluate the provision of visible policing services.

requests to repair traffic signals or install proper lighting. Due to feelings of insecurity, traders had resorted to closing their shops early and staying home at night.

TAC organizers claim that police were unresponsive when informed about criminal incidents. The police, it seemed, had a different agenda, which was to disrupt informal trade (which the municipality treated as nuisance behaviour). In responding to this security gap, informal traders and formal local business people collaborated in forming a street patrol system to keep watch of the area. Because TAC members know the area well and can respond quickly to incidents, they became de facto 'first responders' for victims.

Even violent incidents were the focus of TAC's efforts. Because they often served as first responders, TAC members felt the need to arm themselves. Even though members do call the police when a violent crime occurs, they feel they must respond (often with force) if the police are not responsive. Their usual course of action is to conduct a citizen's arrest and take the alleged perpetrator to the nearest police station. In this capacity, TAC members undertake a quasi-investigative role; they try to ensure that when they hand over an arrested person they provide enough evidence to help advance the case through the justice system.

TAC members acknowledge that they do not always respect human rights, and at times they do operate above the law. Some members revealed that they do use force to 'teach offenders a lesson'. The severity of the 'punishment' depends on what TAC members see as just in accordance with the gravity of the offence.

TAC is volunteer-driven, but they would like to be able to register formally as an organization. They would like this formal authority as a platform for raising funds. So far, however, they have not received this formal recognition, which means that their long term sustainability is constantly in doubt. Nonetheless, our research respondents claim that TAC has been successful in fostering pride in the Warwick area. Local officials agree, and TAC won a mayoral award for its contribution to crime reduction (Robbins and Skinner 2009). This formal recognition is symbolically important, especially given that TAC work can be dangerous, and sometimes life-threatening. Some have been shot and stabbed, and a leading TAC member was fatally shot while he was tackling a violent offender in 2009. While TAC had been working independently from the statutory community police forums, they are now seeking a formal relationship with the police, one that would help establish legitimacy in the eyes of local authorities and persuade police to be more responsive to calls for intervention.

Newlands East Street Committee: filling governance gaps

The 2008 African National Congress (ANC) Polokwane Conference resolved that street committees should be formed in all communities to support the state in the 'war against crime'. The first such committee was established in August 2008 and was launched in the presence of President Jacob Zuma (Mthembu 2008). The formation of street committees in South Africa can be traced back to the efforts of African National Congress supporters seeking to establish alternative governance structures during the Apartheid era. Although street committees aren't as active as they were in the mid to late 1980s, some original groups continue to function to this day (see Steinberg 2008).

Newlands East was a predictable location for a public launch because street committees were already active in the area. As well, some tragic events had occurred in the area including the fatal shooting of a pastor and numerous rapes and armed robberies. Even in these situations the police were unresponsive. The street committee now patrols the community between 6 and 9 pm, keeping an eye out for problematic behaviour.

In principle, street committees are meant to operate within the law and be non-punitive. In practice however, force is sometimes used. One Newlands East street committee respondent informed us in an interview, without reservation, that they will give a 'good hiding' to suspected criminals before they hand such persons over to the police. Similar to the TAC, the street committee does make efforts to produce evidence that can assist with a formal criminal investigation. It is not unheard of that a serious offender would be 'eliminated' (killed). As is the case with TAC members, street committee members see it as a necessity to arm themselves, especially when they are patrolling the informal settlements bordering Newlands East where most violent crime occurs. According to street committee leaders, the police are aware that street committee members carry guns. This was confirmed in an interview with the Newlands East Station Commissioner.

The street committee has broader concerns beyond violent crime in the area. They also address issues of community governance, such as problems of disorder and nuisance associated with the operation of illegal *shebeens* (informal drinking establishments). *Shebeens* operate until the early hours of the morning and drunken patrons can be 'troublesome'. The street committee chooses not to turn to the police as a first resort in such situations; rather, they look for what we might term 'softer' strategies because they recognize that *shebeens* are an important part of the social and economic life of the community. In one case, the street committee set up a meeting between the *shebeen* owners and community members to decide how to move forward with a solution. They reached an agreement where the *shebeen* owners would close at 9 pm and they would make sure that they did not sell alcohol to minors. This agreement was reached with the understanding that if *shebeen* personnel did not comply, the street committee would mobilize the police and liquor regulation agencies.

From the perspective of the police, this arrangement works well because the problem of disorderly behaviour associated with *shebeens* is not a high priority on the spectrum of criminal behaviour that requires police attention. The police also realize that even though they have authority to close down *shebeens,* this is not a long-term solution because other more covert *shebeens* will pop up in the community due to the demands for this enterprise.

Street committee members also respond to other problems that the state police have very little time for, including infrastructure issues such as broken streetlights and potholes. They even play a social service role in assisting vulnerable members of their community. For instance, they identify families that are unable to afford school fees and attempt to negotiate reduced fees with schools. They also check on the needs of elderly residents and other isolated members of the community. In short, the street committee seeks to fill governance gaps at the local level.

PalmRidge: partnering with the police

Although the PalmRidge Neighbourhood Association (PRNA) fulfils similar functions to the other two groups, it differs in the sense that it developed in 2006 at the suggestion of the local state police commissioner. It also differs because it does not have a street patrol component and members do not carry arms, at least officially.[3] Another unique aspect of this group is that they work closely with a private security company called ADT. This (multi-national) company is a major service provider in the area, providing security services privately to residents who can afford this extra protection. The Palm Ridge policing arrangement therefore differs from the police-community partnership model that is typical in state-led initiatives. It is a three-way horizontal partnership between the community, the commercial security sector and the police.

[3] It is possible that some members may choose to carry firearms at their own behest, but we don't have the evidence to confirm or deny this.

The PRNA meets monthly and ADT representatives report to members on what they have been doing in the community. These meetings serve as an opportunity for members to provide input into ADT services and priorities. PRNA members see ADT as more responsive and reliable than the police, and ADT recognizes the PRNA as a legitimate organization representing community interests.

The local police commissioner encouraged the formation of the PRNA at a time when there were serious concerns with violent crime in the area, including house robberies by an area gang, and a stabbing of a community member. Since its first meeting, approximately half of the houses in the area became members of the PRNA scheme, which works to manage and prevent crime, to improve local infrastructure/physical conditions, and to strengthen social cohesion in the area. Since its inception, the PRNA has strongly rejected the use of violence and extra-legal measures to fulfil its mandate. As is the case with the Newland East Street Committee, crime is not the only concern of the PRNA, even though it was the initial catalyst for its formation. 'Policing' functions derive from a broader mission to fill governance gaps.

The case studies discussed above represent, we suggest, at least a partial view of the plurality of policing in South Africa. These forms of everyday policing operate to promote localized conceptions of order, drawing on capacities available in their communities. Part of the variability in such arrangements stems from differences in the nature of the areas (residential, trade areas) as well as particularised concerns about security and governance issues. Related to differences in how such groups operate is the distribution of resources available to meet local needs. In areas with high concentrations of traders, concerns tend to be centred on problems of security that threaten the viability of business, as seen more broadly in Berg's work on Business Improvement Areas in Cape Town (Berg 2004).

If the above cases are indeed indicative of a wider field of plural policing, one might begin to develop a general typology depicting ways in which non-state actors co-exist with the state. In some cases, the state has formally promoted bottom-up solutions, while in other cases state policing co-exists independently from these organic arrangements, although state police may be enlisted when their coercive capacity is required. The pluralism we find therefore is both state-initiated and non-state initiated. There may be dynamics of mutual enrolment in fulfilling one another's agendas, but not always. The face of plural policing is therefore more complex than is suggested by a state-centred view of police-led partnerships, or a neo-liberal image of state delegation (Wood and Shearing 2007). In the next section we turn to the implications of this reality for re-imagining the transformation of policing.

Re-Positioning the State in Plural Policing

The above three cases raise the question of how the public police should formally position itself in this plural landscape of service delivery. This is a question for state government more generally, given that groups such as the ones highlighted here participate in larger governance processes. Responses to this question have implications for how internal police reform agendas are conceptualized as well as for how external donor agencies imagine their critical roles.

From a donor perspective, recognizing this reality of plural policing can lead to two general positions. Donors could continue to focus their efforts on improving state capacity, partly through emulating police-centred models of professionalization and democratization that have generally worked in western contexts. Alternatively, donors could expand their efforts to incorporate non-state policing institutions in their efforts, thereby de-centring the state in reform agendas. Both the state-centric and pluralist agendas come with costs and benefits, and with certainties and uncertainties. For Bayley (2011), a big uncertainty associated with a pluralist agenda is the failure to know which non-state arrangements to formally acknowledge and support, given that some reveal a history of extra-legal and even brutal policing practices. This normative concern alone may warrant an overall hesitation by donor agencies to fund and oversee entities, which may be difficult to regulate at a distance. At least with police-centred reform, donors can back up their efforts with evidence that state-centred approaches have suited other democratic contexts and carry fewer political risks.

In contrast to this thinking, Scheye (2009) argues for a 'pragmatic realist' approach to donor funding of justice and security in ways that suit the conditions of a 'multi-layered post-colonial state' (see also Bruce Baker's contribution to this issue). Scheye's approach centres on three pillars, which incorporate both state and non-state elements. First, donors should support efforts to strengthen the accountability of state policing. The second pillar involves a short- to medium-term emphasis on strengthening the capacity of non-state entities and networks to deliver security at the local level. The third pillar aims at bolstering links between the state and these localized entities. Scheye adds that the strength of the post-colonial state is not measured by pure state capacity alone but rather by the quality of "interlocking relationships between its different layers of authority - state and non-state" (Scheye 2009: ii).

As Scheye (2009) recognizes, and as our cases demonstrate, there are indeed important concerns about the capacity of non-state entities to violate human rights in their quests to promote security and justice. In the South African context, the same concerns have long held true for state police organizations. Given the decades-long track record of state police brutality that has been consistently documented, it's not necessarily the case, as Scheye points out, that non-state entities are more brutal. Rather, the most important factor to consider is the willingness on the part of non-state entities to become more effective and human rights-respecting. This is an empirical question, but so far, Scheye contends, there is no evidence to suggest that non-state entities prefer being brutal, especially at the expense of garnering wider political legitimacy for their efforts. That being said, Scheye (2009) proposes that donors think carefully about the policing arrangements they would acknowledge and support. Undoubtedly, some groupings may be too brutal and unchangeable for either states or external donors to support them, especially if such groups are involved in illegal activities.

Scheye (2009) acknowledges that the task of identifying policing assemblages and understanding their political dynamics and daily operations is enormous. Because of this, the role of local government or local NGOs in implementing his pragmatic realist agenda is critical. Such agencies possess the local knowledge required to understand how and why such groupings have formed within the post-colonial state context. Notwithstanding, the capacity and resources of such agencies to undertake the 'linking' function with non-state groupings is obviously limited, which is why donor support of such auspices is critical. Scheye (2009) argues that multiple agencies at the local level should be involved in implementing this agenda.

Scheye's position resonates with strands of thought connecting recent literatures on policing and pluralism with what is termed 'left realism' in British criminology. In the policing literature, David Thacher (2009: 59) has proposed the idea of police being conceived as society's 'or else' institution, which means that police would only intervene when their specialist capacities are required to exercise force, investigate crimes and restore order in situations of unrest, significant social conflict or turmoil. This conception echoes Brogden and Shearing's (1993) work on the South African context, which calls for a core state police role that both approves and augments non-state policing arrangements. British criminologists Kinsey, Lea and Young (1986) have described this emphasis on core policing as 'minimal' policing, based on the premise that the police should be called upon when their special skills, authority and expertise are needed. Active involvement of non-state actors in the delivery of security is encouraged by these core and minimal perspectives, while advocates of minimalism stress that policing providers should be co-ordinated and regulated by local authorities, such as municipal agencies, and that a punitive and coercion-based approach to policing should be avoided.

Our case studies indicate that both the police and community safety groups agree with this minimalist view which stresses, as Reiner (1992: 145) puts it, that "police intervention should be confined to cases where there is clear evidence of law-breaking, and should take the form of the invocation of legal powers and criminal process". This approach would translate into several key components in practice. The first component is the promotion of accountability within the state police, which is Scheye's (2009) first reform pillar discussed above. This component would have two key dimensions: (1) improving the democratic character of police core functions - the exercise of force and the use of legal authority; (2) strengthening the accountability of police to the communities they serve by acting on citizens' requests for their services when these core capacities are needed. Overall, this accountability pillar is aimed at improving state police effectiveness within a plural system. This means that once the police are clear about their own role, and feel less pressured to respond to situations not requiring their core capacities, a space will be created for them to actively encourage and support non-state policing arrangements.

By relating to non-state policing actors in this way (being an 'enabler' of non-coercive policing from the bottom-up), the police would contribute to a larger project of building a consensus-based policing system in South Africa. A consensus-based system is one where there is a continuous and reciprocal flow of information between the public and the police (Kinsey et al. 1986: 192).

The second component involves the 'anchoring' of non-state policing systems in local state systems of oversight and regulation. Without a doubt, the legitimacy of groupings such as the ones we discussed is open to question because they mostly have no formal mandate or systems of accountability and they rely on the spirit of voluntarism. In poor communities, they have few material resources, with little chance of direct government assistance even though they carry out important public safety functions. Accordingly, we need to consider the recognition, resourcing, and accountability mechanisms or 'anchorage' (Loader and Walker, 2007) of such groups. As we discuss below, one possibility for such an anchor is a local state coordinating body for safety and security within local government.

Implications for external donor support

Recognising African states as hybrid or plural political orders opens up a range of possibilities for donor assistance. This is important "as alternative sources of finance are hard to come by" (Oya and Pons-Vignon 2010: 190), especially in economies reliant on extractive production subject to rapid and sometimes crushing fluctuations in price and demand. Forward-thinking donors in the field of development have already begun to embrace the plural governance perspective, and resources are increasingly (though still slowly) being channelled towards non-state bodies that are often the real providers of public goods and services. This donor funding perspective is based on the view that closeness to the ground, and flexibility in adapting their response mechanisms to basic needs, gives civil society organisations and 'non-traditional' actors' legitimacy to challenge the state where it fails. Donor organisations now speak of 'light touch' and 'long-arm' approaches to donor funding, which translates into channelling funds to both established civil-society groups such as NGOs as well more organic civil society groupings such as the community safety groupings in Durban (Tembo and Wells 2007).

One objective in this kind of funding is to prevent government and established NGOs from overshadowing small-scale operations that have limited human and technical resources. Redirecting funding away from central government, with appropriate regulatory safeguards, encourages long-term, strategic programmes of "state building through civic engagement" (Tembo and Wells 2007: 23).

This approach to donor funding gives credit to community resilience and also to the role that more traditional institutions and newer kinds of organic civil society groups can play in service delivery. With this approach, a range of civil society entities (like community safety groups) become "assets and sources of solutions that can be drawn upon [...] to forge constructive relationships between communities and governments, and between customary and introduced political and social institutions" (Boege et al. 2008: 16). For this donor approach to work, it needs to be accompanied by state policy that focuses on actively forging partnerships "between the formal and informal that seeks gradual and incremental change based on local realities" (Stephens 2009: 153). For this what is required is a developmental state perspective that embraces hybridity in principle and in practice.

For the model to work, particularly with groups that are not as established as recognised NGOs, intermediary 'anchors' need to be identified (see Tembo and Wells 2007) which ensure that civil society entities operate accountably and in line with broader developmental programmes, and that government policy and practice supports plurality. In the case of plural policing initiatives, we suggest that the most appropriate intermediary and anchor is local government.

The need in developing countries is not for a centralized policing apparatus driven from the top down, but rather for a horizontal assemblage of policing actors that is anchored locally and shaped by local research, planning and oversight. Building on Scheye's (2009) argument for the importance of linking state and non-state actors in the delivery of security and justice, we suggest the establishment of local co-ordinating bodies that can identify existing policing actors as well as establish and implement a process of identifying security deficits in order to give all sectors equal assurance of security. Where deficits are found, resources to deal with them can be augmented by using donor funding to support the development of bottom-up schemes that link with and complement local state police services.

This arrangement for local anchorage resonates with Loader's (2000) idea for 'policing commissions' (see also Loader and Walker 2007). Implementation, backed by the authority of local government, could fall under the auspices of an existing local government department or be undertaken on its own. Donor contributions could then be channelled through relevant local government departments for the benefit of locally-based initiatives. The value of this approach lies in the capacity for local government to "(i) mediate where relations between civil society and the [central] state may be especially conflictive; (ii) make the link between civic engagement and efforts to strengthen the capabilities and responsiveness of state institutions; and (iii) absorb the inherent risks where they do not have the diplomatic weight that donors enjoy" (Tembo and Wells 2007: 6). This could have the dual effect of building capacity in local government while at the same time empowering non-state actors within a regulated, accountable and legitimate framework.

A local government safety body could then play an oversight and co-ordinating function, and help to develop models for 'safe-environment' neighbourhood associations that could outline how patrols are done, how security-related problems are identified, who they are reported to, at what point the police must be called in, and what to expect of the police. But perhaps most importantly, the local government safety body should help in evolving principles that will guide the activity of all policing actors. It is to local government departments that problems with community safety groups or the police should be reported. These bodies would become, in a sense, hubs of accountability and knowledge-sharing.

Volunteer efforts also need some kind of formal recognition, which is best conceived through creative input from all actors. This could be factored into donor funding programmes and budgets. But recognition need not be monetary; it could include giving volunteers an honorary police medal or certificates of good community service. We think these might be warmly received by many, but they could also help a productive citizen who needs a leg-up to enter training or the formal economy. Incentive planning such as this could also include the creation of block grants designed to link neighbourhood associations with the police (see Bayley and Shearing 1996).

What we are proposing in this article may all seem to be fantastical. However, governments across the African continent recognise the centrality of localised non-state policing groupings to achieving broader safety objectives. In some African countries the state directly sponsors such groupings (see for example Baker 2010). In South Africa, government has called upon communities to form street committees so as to facilitate direct involvement in the governance of security at the most local level. Yet programmes for organising and implementing this remain *ad-hoc* and tenuous.

Donors may still have to be convinced of the worth of such funding 'experiments', and this is only likely to occur if grounded research is undertaken that demonstrates the value and significance of plural policing arrangements, and if (academic) researchers work collaboratively with government actors. National governments need to be supportive of these funding arrangements, which they should be if they are committed to bolstering existing and new hybrid governance arrangements.

Conclusion

There is general acceptance now that policing governance in Africa can best be described as hybrid, or nodal, or pluralized. Indeed, in the criminological literature policing governance is now seldom presented as something that states *can* or *should* do on their own (Zedner 2009). As our Durban studies illustrate, the state police in Africa do not monopolise policing nor, in many cases, even particularly claim to. Fresh thinking about the state in Africa and the active role of non-state actors in everyday governance encourages new approaches to policing dilemmas: finding practical solutions that simultaneously promote an active citizenry and a minimal state police body able and ready to respond when called upon.

Practical solutions must take account of the finite resources of both the state and the citizenry and capitalise on all existing capacities, mandates and skills. Donor agencies have an important role in ensuring the workability of plural policing. We share the emergent, yet still marginal, international donor view that external donor funding is needed where resources are limited, but should be directed primarily at local government and non-state bodies that are contributing to localised security outcomes. Neither improved security nor significant developmental agendas have been achieved through focusing on the central state exclusively as the rightful beneficiary.

We leave the modalities of the requisite co-ordinating donor and its relationship to other donors as an issue for future exploration. Suffice it to say that the co-ordinating organ would itself require oversight and that those dissatisfied with its decisions should have superior structures to which to appeal. Their character must equally be left to future discussion. What cannot be compromised, however, is the need to move beyond western ideals and state-centric solutions to the interwoven problems of development and insecurity in South Africa.

References

APPIAH, Kwame Anthony
1992 *In My Father's House: Africa in the Philosophy of Culture*. Oxford: Oxford University Press.
BAKER, Bruce
2002 'Living with non-state policing in South Africa: the issues and dilemmas.' *Journal of Modern African Studies* 40(1): 29 -53.
2009 'Hybrid policing in sub-Saharan Africa'. Paper presented at the USIP, GWU and WB conference on *Customary justice and legal pluralism in post-conflict and fragile states*, November 17-19. The George Washington University, Washington D.C.
2010 'Linking state and non-state security and justice'. *Development Policy Review* 28(5): 597-616.
BAYLEY, David H.
2011 'The Morphing of Peacekeeping: Competing Approaches to Public Safety'. *International Peacekeeping* 18(1): 52-63.
BAYLEY, David H. and Clifford D. SHEARING
1996 'The Future of Policing'. *Law and Society Review* 30(3): 585–606.

BERG, Julie
2004 'Private Policing in South Africa: The Cape Town City Improvement District - Pluralisation in Practice'. *Society in Transition* 35(2): 224-250.
BOEGE, Volker, Anne BROWN, Kevin CLEMENTS and Anna NOLAN
2008 'On hybrid political orders and emerging states: State formation in the context of 'fragility'. Berghof Research Center for Constructive Conflict Management, Berghof Handbook Dialogue, Paper No. 8.
BRAITHWAITE, John
2006 'Peacemaking networks and restorative justice'. Pp. 195-217 in J Fleming and J Wood (eds.), *Fighting Crime Together: The Challenge of Policing and Security Networks*. Sydney: University of New South Wales Press.
BROGDEN, Mike
2004 'Commentary: Community policing: A panacea from the West'. *African Affairs* 103(413): 635-649.
BROGDEN, Mike and Clifford D. SHEARING
1993 *Policing for a New South Africa*. London: Routledge.
BRUCE, David AND Rachel NEILD
2005 *The police that we want: A handbook for oversight of police in South Africa*. Johannesburg: Centre for the Study of Violence and Reconciliation in association with the Open Society Foundation for South Africa and the Open Society Justice Initiative. Available at http://www.csvr.org.za/papers/papdbrn.pdf
BUTTON, Mark
2008 *Doing Security: Critical Reflections and an Agenda for Change*. Houndmills: Palgrave Macmillan.
CARLEN, Pat
1992 'Criminal Women and Criminal Justice: The Limits to, and Potential of, Feminist and Left Realist Perspectives'. Pp. 51-69 in J. Young and B. Matthews (eds.), *Issues in Realist Criminology*. London: Sage.
CHABAL, Patrick and Jean-Pascal DALOZ
1999 *Africa Works: Disorder as Political Instrument*. London: James Currey, London.
CHANG, Ha-Joon
1999 'The economic theory of the developmental state.' Pp. 182-199 in Meredith Woo-Cumings (ed.), *The Developmental State*. Ithaca, NY: Cornall University Press.
CRONIN, Jeremy
2005 'The people shall govern: class struggles and the post-1994 state in South Africa'.http://amadlandawonye.wikispaces.com/2005-11-05,+Cronin,+The+People+Shall+Govern [accessed 9 March, 2012).

DEVEREUX, Stephen and Francie LUND
2010 'Democratising social welfare in Africa'. Pp. 152-171 in V, Padayachee (ed.), *The Political Economy of Africa*. London: Routledge.
DIXON, Bill
2007 'Globalising the local: A genealogy of sector policing in South Africa.' *International Relations* 21(2): 163-182.
EDIGHEJI, Omano
2006 'The discourse of the developmental state and a "Peoples Contract" in South Africa'. Paper written for the Centre for Policy Studies Seminar Series. Johannesburg. August.
ELLIS, Stephen
2009 'South Africa and the decolonisation of the mind'. Inaugural lecture, Faculty of Social Sciences at Vrije Universiteit Amsterdam, 23 September.
HART, Keith, and Vishnu PADAYACHEE
2010 'South Africa in Africa: from national capitalism to regional integration'. Pp. 410-428 in V. Padayachee (ed.), *The Political Economy of Africa*. London: Routledge.
JOHNSTON, Les, and Clifford D. SHEARING
2003 *Governing Security: Explorations in Policing and Justice*. London: Routledge.
JONES, Trevor and Tim NEWBURN (eds.)
2006 *Plural Policing: A Comparative Perspective*. London: Routledge.
KINSEY, Richard, John LEA and Jock YOUNG
1986 *Losing the Fight Against Crime*. Oxford: Basil Blackwell.
KYED, Helene Maria, and Lars BUUR
2006 'New Sites of Citizenship: Recognition of Traditional Authority and Group-based Citizenship in Mozambique'. *Journal of Southern African Studies* 32(3): 563-581.
LOADER, Ian
2000 'Plural Policing and Democratic Governance'. *Social and Legal Studies* 9(3): 323–45.
LOADER, Ian, and Neil WALKER
2007 *Civilizing Security*. Cambridge: Cambridge University Press.
LUKHELE, Andrew Khelha
1990 *Stokvels in South Africa: Informal Saving Schemes by Blacks for the Black Community*. Johannesburg: Amagi Press.
MANGCU, Xolela
2006 'Why SA needs local democracy more than local government'. *Business Day*. Thursday, 17 February.

MARKS, Monique, and Sean TAIT
2011 'You strike a gathering, you strike a rock: Current debates in the policing of public order in South Africa'. *South African Crime Quarterly* 38: 15-22.
MENKHAUS, Ken
2007 'Governance without Government in Somalia: Spoilers, state building, and the politics of coping'. *International Security* 31(3): 74-106.
2001b 'Thinking about developmental states in Africa'. *The Cambridge Journal of Economics* 25: 289-313.
MTHEMBU, Bongani
2008 'Street Committees Target Crime'. *Daily News*, 11 August. http://www.iol.co.za/index.php?click id=13&set id=1&art id=vn2008 0811112912248C771834#more [accessed 9 March, 2012].
OLAYODE, Kehinde
2005 'Reinventing the African State: Issues and challenges for building a developmental state'. *African Journal of International Affairs* 8(1 & 2): 23-43.
OLOWU, Dele
1994 *'The nature and character of the African state'.* Paper presented at the AAPM 15th Roundtable in Banjul, Gambia, 24-29 January.
OLOWU, Dele, and James WUNSCH
2004 *Local Governance in Africa: The Challenges of Democratic Decentralization.* Boulder, CO: Lynne Rienner Press.
OYA, Carlos, and Nicolas PONS-VIGNON
2010 'Aids, development and the state in Africa'. Pp.172-198 in V, Padayachee (ed.), *The Political Economy of Africa*. London: Routledge.
PADAYACHEE, Vishnu and Keith HART
2010 Introducing the African economy. Pp 1-17, in Vishnu Padayachee (ed.), *The Political Economy of Africa.* London: Routledge.
REINER, Robert
1992 *The Politics of the Police (2nd Edition).* New York: Harvester Wheatsheaf.
ROBBINS, G., and C. SKINNER
2009 'Public Debate Needed on Warwick Triangle'. *Mercury Newspaper* 9 June, letter to editors page.
ROCHE, Declan
2002 'Restorative justice and the regulatory state in South African Townships'. *British Journal of Criminology* 42(3): 567-577.

SCHÄRF, Wilfried

2000 'Community justice and community policing in post-apartheid South Africa: How appropriate are the justice systems of Africa?' *IDS Bulletin* 34: 74-82.

SCHÄRF, Wilfried, and Daniel NINA

2001 *The Other Law: Non-State Forms of Ordering in South Africa*. Johannesburg: Juta.

SCHEYE, Eric

2009 'Pragmatic Realism in Justice and Security Development: Supporting Improvement in the Performance of Non-State/Local Justice and Security Networks'. Netherlands Institute of International Relations. http://www.clingendael.nl/publications/2009/20090707 cru local justice scheye.pdf [accessed 8.31.2011].

SHEARING, Clifford D.

1994 'Reinventing policing: Policing as governance'. *Imbizo: Rethinking Policing* 1: 12.

2001 'A Nodal Conception of Governance: Thoughts on a Policing Commission'. *Policing and Society* 11: 259–72.

SINGH, Anne-Marie

2008 *Policing and Crime Control in Post-Apartheid South Africa*. Ashgate: Aldeshot.

SOUTH AFRICAN POLICE SERVICE ACT

1995 (Act No. 68 of 1995), 4 October, Pretoria.

STEINBERG, Jonny

2008 *Thin Blue: The Unwritten Rules of Policing in South Africa*. Cape Town: Jonathan Ball Publishers.

STEPHENS, Matt

2009 'Typologies and benefits of interaction between state and non-state justice systems.' Paper presented at the USIP, GWU and WB conference on Customary justice and legal pluralism in post-conflict and fragile states, November 17-19. George Washington University, Washington D.C.

TEMBO, Fletcher, and Adrian WELLS

2007 'Multi-donor support to civil society and engaging with 'non-traditional' civil society: A light-touch review of DFID's portfolio', June. ODI, London. www.odi.org.uk (Accessed 31.08.2010)

THACHER, David

2009 'Community Policing and Accountability.' Pp 57-70 in P. Grabosky (ed.), *Community Policing and Peacekeeping*. Boca Raton: CRC Press.

VAN DER SPUY, Elerena
2000 'Foreign donor assistance and policing reform in South Africa'. *Policing and Society* 10: 342-366.
WADE, Robert Hunter
2003 'What strategies are viable for developing countries today? The World Trade Organization and the shrinking of 'development space'.' *Review of International Political Economy* 10(4): 621–644.
WOOD, Jennifer, and Clifford D. SHEARING
2007 *Imagining Security*. Collumpton: Willan.
WORLD BANK
1998 'Assessing Aid: What Works, What Doesn't, and Why'. Washington: Policy Research Report No 18295.
WUYTS, Marc
1996 'Foreign aid, structural adjustment, and public management: the Mozambique experience.' *Development and Change* 27: 717-749.
ZEDNER, LUCIA
2009 *Security*. London: Routledge.

NEITHER STATE NOR CUSTOM – JUST NAKED POWER: THE CONSEQUENCES OF IDEALS-ORIENTED RULE OF LAW POLICY-MAKING IN LIBERIA

Stephen Lubkemann, Deborah Isser and Peter Chapman

Introduction

Eight years ago Liberia emerged from a ravaging civil war that had raged for fourteen years and that had been preceded by a decade of political coups and coup attempts, violent governance, and unrest. In 2012, as the country recently held a hotly contested second round of national elections, Liberia is regarded as a tentatively successful, but fragile, case of post-conflict peace-building and democratization. There are many encouraging signs that the current democratically elected government is striving to break with the predatory and repressive practices of previous administrations such as those of Liberia's recent warlord Presidents—Samuel Doe (1979-1990) and Charles Taylor (1997-2003). At the same time, Liberia still confronts significant challenges in its effort to secure peace, consolidate democracy, and jumpstart reconstruction and development. High levels of unemployment, continuing land disputes that often map onto wartime ethnic divisions, the continuing ruminations of ex-combatants, and the charged atmosphere surrounding the pronouncements of the Truth and Reconciliation Commission all provide potent reminders that volatile forms of social and political antagonism continue to lurk perilously near the surface of Liberia's fragile polity.

In this article we examine the effort to rebuild and reform the justice system in Liberia, which has been one of the cornerstones of peace-building policy. Our key argument is that while the approach that is being used to reform the justice system aims to correct a historical legacy of discrimination that had been embodied and implemented through a pluralist legal system, it is failing to address and in fact may actually be accentuating the 'justice vacuum' faced by most Liberians. Moreover, in characterizing customary justice and other informal dispute resolution mechanisms primarily as sources of inequality and discrimination, while simultaneously neglecting to explore how the formal justice system works in actual practice, this approach at best misses the rationale behind popular preferences for customary over formal forms of legal recourse and at worst simply dismisses it as a form of unreasoned adherence to "tradition" that should and can be 'educated away". As this article will explore, these preferences do not channel any form of blind or reflexive adherence to culture but rather are based upon an empirically well-founded suspicion that the state justice system privileges the powerful while ignoring many of the concerns that average Liberians believe justice should address as well as the principles they believe should prevail in order to produce results that can effectively modify undesirable behavior and safeguard the interests of victims and society—or in other words, deliver "satisfactory" justice.

We further explore the consequences of this "policy ignorance" by examining how— somewhat paradoxically—justice reform measures that are intended to be a pillar that supports Liberia's post-war peace-building strategy are in fact doing little to contain mounting perceptions that power and resources are the only true determinants of justice outcomes. These sentiments underwrite growing dissatisfaction with all forms of justice, though particularly with the state system. Perhaps most ironically, these reform efforts that aim to address a historical legacy of discrimination are being interpreted by many rural Liberians as a process of political subjugation rather than of civil emancipation. Thus rather than contributing to the legitimation of Liberia's incipient democratic state and to a sense of participation in the political process, these policies are in fact fomenting resentment against the state by contributing to a view that sees it as an intrusive mechanism for promoting the interest of Monrovia-based elites. The argument we present in this article is based on an extensive collaborative field study conducted under the supervision of Deborah Isser and Stephen Lubkemann in 2008-09.[1]

[1] Isser, Lubkemann and N'Tow, (2009). This study was based on 10 months of fieldwork conducted by teams in four counties (Lofa, Nimba, Grand Gedeh, Montserrado) involving in-depth case interviews with over 130 disputants, 39 local customary justice practitioners, and 35 focus groups (disaggregated by gender and age).

Conducted primarily in the three most war affected rural counties in Liberia (Nimba, Lofa and Grand Gedeh)—and to a more limited extent amongst residents of the capital city of Monrovia—this study extensively documented how average Liberians perceived and navigated the topography of post-war options for seeking justice and how they reacted to specific justice reform policies.

Simultaneously with this field study, Isser and Lubkemann collaborated with our third co-author, Peter Chapman in the supervision of a legal review of the history and current status of Liberian legislation on legal pluralism, and the co-coordination (with partners from the United Nations Mission in Liberia and the Carter Center) a multi-year high-level dialogue that brought senior Liberian policy-makers together with legal and sociological specialists and international partners to discuss the policy implications of the findings of both studies. Involving extensive one-on-one consultations with senior level officials, in addition to several group meetings, and culminating in a *National Conference on Enhancing Access to Justice* in early 2010 this process afforded us a great deal of insight into the imperatives, constraints and (often divergent) interests that inform the community of policy-makers who are shaping justice reform efforts in post-conflict Liberia.[2]

The article is divided into four sections. First we provide a brief review of Liberia's turbulent political past that highlights how the dual justice system developed historically and how a specific configuration of state (formal courts), state-linked (customary chiefs), and non-state institutions (e.g. churches, voluntary associations, other community-based institutions) interacted in the past. In the second section we explore how the international community largely dismissed all but the state-specific institutions in their justice reform vision and efforts during the immediate post-war period and as a consequence have yet to develop contextualized, empirically-based strategies for justice reform that effectively respond to the needs and demands of the majority of Liberia's population. In the third section we discuss what our field study reveals about how Liberians view the performance of the customary and formal justice systems, what they believe satisfactory justice should entail, and how they are coping with what is by and large an unmet need for justice. We highlight how local preferences for customary justice options often contrast with international efforts to curtail and constrain these same institutions. We also explore how redress is being pursued in the justice vacuum that has resulted.

[2] This article builds on Lubkemann, Isser and Banks (2011).

In the fourth section we conclude by exploring some of the implications of popular perceptions and reactions to post-war justice reform for rule of law and peace building objectives in Liberia and reflect more on how this case suggests the need to reframe the questions that guide justice reform in comparable contexts. Our approach in this article mirrors the approach that informed our field study; to empirically ascertain the real alternatives and choices that Liberians perceive and react to on the ground, rather than attempt to compare idealized alternatives that exist only on the paper on which they are written. This approach is an analytical reaction to both policy debates about and academic analysis of customary justice institutions that juxtapose a rather oversimplified—and sometimes grossly caricaturized—portrayal of customary systems against an idealized portrayal of a western-style formal justice system.

Justice and Internal Colonialism in Liberian History

Liberia's origin as an independent nation traces its roots to the founding in 1816 of the American Colonization Society (ACS), which was started in the United States by a coalition of Quaker abolitionists and slave owners in order to repatriate freed slaves back to Africa. The first group of freeborn blacks and freed slaves arrived in 1822 and established a permanent settlement at Cape Mensurado (Monrovia). These first settlers were augmented by large numbers of captives who were rescued from slave ships bound to the Americas but interdicted by British and later US naval vessels. Just a quarter century later, in 1847, Liberia declared itself an independent nation.

The country's first Constitution in 1847 laid out civil rights and a plan of government based on the American model, but these laws and rights were reserved exclusively for the Americo-Liberian settlers and did not apply to the various ethnic groups who were gradually and violently brought under the sovereign control of the Liberian state throughout the late 19th and early 20th centuries. The origins of a dual justice system can be traced back to this historical project of conquest. Thus, as early as 1869 the Interior Department was granted broad powers to govern all aspects of the 'hinterland', including the exercise of judicial power over the native subjects "with due regard to native customary law and native institutions."[3] This form of indirect rule evolved into a dual legal system

[3] January 23, 1869 Act of the Legislature; Gray v. Beverly (1 LLR: 500; 1907).

whereby the hinterland was governed by customary law and institutions under the purview of the executive branch, while Americo-Liberians were subject to statutory law and courts of the judiciary.

This system received its highest form of official elaboration in the Rules and Regulations Governing the Hinterland of Liberia (1948) (commonly known as the 'Hinterland Regulations'), which were ostensibly revised, although substantively unchanged, in 2000.[4] The Hinterland Regulations remain, in large part, an archaic blueprint for nineteenth century colonial style rule. With regard to the administration of justice, they lay out the jurisdiction and appellate hierarchy through the establishment of customary courts, which essentially comprise a five-tiered system of courts: Clan Chiefs Courts, Paramount Chiefs Courts, District Commissioner, Provincial Commissioner (County Superintendent), the Provincial Court of Assize (now the statutory Circuit Court). The jurisdiction of the chiefs covers circumscribed geographic areas (i.e. the town or clan).

The Hinterland Regulations also lay out certain substantive rules regarding, for example, customary marriage, the use of corporal punishment, and the use of trial by ordeal. It thus created a system of state-sponsored customary justice that was distinct from the statutory system that serviced the Americo-Liberian elite, but also from the systems that had been historically practiced by local populations. As in many colonial societies, this manufactured hybrid system enabled the native population to retain at least some semblance of their existing practices and laws even as it enshrined forms of exclusion that protected the political power of the Americo-Liberian elite and transformed native leaders and institutions into agents of the state. The relegation of the overwhelming majority of Liberians to a state-backed form of customary justice and their exclusion from the formal system was emblematic of the more general policies of governance that also excluded the 'indigenous' population from meaningful participation in the political process, from most economic benefits, and from access to education.

For those with access to the formal justice system, it proved to be largely a tool of elite domination. While the justice system was directly modeled on the common law and legal principles of the United States, it never lived up to the structure prescribed by law, nor to the ideals of a rights-based justice system it was purported to be modeled after. Liberian history is replete with frequent episodes of

[4] There is some debate as to whether the Hinterland Regulations are still in effect. See, e.g., Barbu 2009.

executive interference in the judiciary and manipulation of the courts to serve political aims (Sawyer 1992; Banks III 2006). The power struggles, coups, and wars waged over the last quarter century only accentuated and aggravated these historical tendencies. At the time of the 1980 coup the formal system was believed by most Liberians to cater to the wealthy and political elite whose criminal conduct went largely unpunished, even while poor people lingered in jail for extensive periods without trial. Open and unchecked corruption tainted public confidence in the formal judicial system and played a significant role in undermining the legitimacy of the Americo-Liberian state and ultimately in underwriting its violent overthrow in 1980.

Following the coup, the Liberian Constitution was suspended, the branches of government were dissolved, the functions of the Legislative and Executive Branches were consolidated in a new military People's Redemption Council, led by Master Sergeant Samuel K. Doe, and the entire core of judges of the formal Liberian court system were dismissed (except for the Chief Justice of the Supreme Court who was publicly executed). Throughout his decade-long rule Doe used the judiciary to consolidate power, eliminate opponents of the regime, silence dissent, suppress basic fundamental and human rights, and curtail freedom of thought and the press. These measures together with his campaign of ethnic cleansing played major roles in fostering popular resentment that others would capitalize upon to ignite the Liberian civil war. Between 1989 and 1997, the first stage of Liberia's civil war, the country experienced the effective dissolution of the national government, the re-collapse of what remained of its formal legal and judicial system and institutions, and the reign of anarchy.[5] The war appeared to finally end in July 1997, with the election of Charles Taylor as President of Liberia. However, those elections failed to resolve the political crisis and within three years Liberia was once again engulfed in civil war. Under pressure from the international community and effectively losing the war, Charles Taylor resigned the presidency on August 11, 2003. Shortly thereafter a National Transitional Government of Liberia (NTGL) was established with significant United Nations support.

[5] It is estimated that during the fourteen years of armed conflict at least 100,000 Liberians were killed (Ellis 2006: 312-16). Moran suggests up to 200,000 were killed during the conflict (Moran 2006: 5), while thousands more died from causes associated with or accentuated by the war. At least 300,000 inhabitants fled the country and a much larger number were internally displaced. Liberia became one of the poorest countries in the world.

By the end of the war the formal justice system retained virtually no capacity and enjoyed no legitimacy amongst the populace or the international community. Its condition was described as follows by a team from the International Legal Assistance Consortium (ILAC) that visited Liberia in 2003:

> There is an almost unanimous distrust of Liberia's courts and a corresponding collapse of the rule of law. Liberia's Constitution provides for an Anglo-American legal system, but in reality, there is no effective separation of powers, a limited understanding of the principles of transparency and accountability, little knowledge of contemporary notions of human rights, limited access to legal advice and defense counsel, and unconscionable delays. Taylor's government withheld salaries from judges, prosecutors, court staff, police, and prison officers for 2.5 years. Judgment, freedom, and even life itself, were often sold to the highest bidder (ILAC 2003: viii).

Customary Justice and Authority in the Aftermath of War

The civil war also had an effect on customary justice systems. While there was some evidence that internal and refugee displacement and the intervention by warlords and military commanders had prevented many customary justice institutions from working effectively, or distorted their function in at least some parts of the country, almost nothing was known (though much was assumed) about the status of these institutions prior to our field study. In fact, empirical ascertainment of the extent of this system's post-war existence and the manner in which it might be functioning—or not–was the first question that animated the field study from which this analysis is drawn (Isser, Lubkemann and N'tow 2009).

One of the key - and somewhat surprising - findings of our study was that customary justice institutions continued to function in virtually all rural communities and at all levels down to the most local.[6] Our findings in this respect

[6] We argue that if our research has found strong evidence of the survival and continuity of customary justice institutions in Liberia's most conflict devastated and socially-disrupted counties – Lofa, Nimba, and Grand Gedeh– it is likely that customary institutions remain at least as relevant throughout the rest of the country's rural counties.

dovetail with a survey conducted by the Oxford Centre for the Study of African Economies in 2008-9 ("CSAE Survey"), which found that some form of customary justice accounts for almost ninety percent of dispute resolution (Sandefur and Siddiqi 2011). Our field study also indicated that the post-war customary justice system was structured more or less as set out in the Hinterland Regulations, involving a hierarchy from senior members of a household or a family, extending through a succession of chiefs: in ascendant order, quarter chiefs, town chiefs, clan chiefs, and paramount chiefs. Beyond the paramount chiefs the customary system's chain of referral continues first to the District Commissioner, and then to the County Superintendent. Decisions that fail to satisfy one or both parties in a dispute at lower levels are appealed through this chain of referral. The Liberian state itself—and more specifically the Ministry of Internal Affairs, which has taken the lead in re-constituting the administrative system of chiefs that was disrupted during the war—thus remains an important source of authority and legitimacy invoked by the chiefs much as it had been prior to the conflict.[7] At the same time our interviews ascertained a strong articulation of preference for the chiefly system, which underwrites the expressed belief of many chiefs that they are the best equipped to understand and deal with most justice issues in their communities. Government of Liberia consultations on the dual justice system, in late 2009 and early 2010, revealed similar opinions.

The 'ritual officers' (masters, zoes) of the secret societies, such as the Poro and Sande in central and western Liberia[8] or others[9] in Southeastern Liberia, comprise

---

[7] The Ministry of Internal Affairs remains responsible for liaising with chiefs. Nearly all of the chiefs in Liberia we interviewed view themselves as government officials and agents of the state in their communities. The "National Traditional Council of Liberia" is a part of the Ministry of Internal Affairs (MIA), which has a Deputy Minister for Cultural Affairs who is responsible for liaising with chiefs. Even with Liberia's weak bureaucratic capacity, the Government of Liberia keeps many chiefs on payroll. While traditional leaders note that they are not regularly paid, there is often an understanding between chiefs and the MIA that they should be. Furthermore, an (unpublished) study produced by Saah N'Tow for the United Nations Mission in Liberia revealed that of the nearly 80 Tribal Governors interviewed in six counties, nearly all reported they were officials of the Liberian government and more than 60% reported being on Government of Liberia payroll (United Nations Mission in Liberia 2011).

[8] Poro is a male sodality [secret society] found among several groups in central and western Liberia, including the Vai, Gola,

another category of customary justice practitioners who survived the war and who continue to exercise considerable influence now in the post-war period. Having no form of official articulation with the state their basis of legitimacy is derived solely from local communities.

Much as family heads and elders are expected to serve as the first line of customary resolution for disputes that arise within immediate and extended families, society officials are expected to be the first - and often ultimate - authorities to deal with disputes that arise among members of their constituent groups. This expectation includes even significant crimes that the law stipulates should be referred to the formal court system (such as cases of rape and violence that result in blood). In this second category of solely community-based authority an important role is also played by religious leaders such as Imams and some church leaders, in particular of Pentecostal and charismatic sects, by professional association officials, such as market associations, and by minority chiefs, such as local Fula chiefs. As with the Poro and other societies, these authorities often act as the first line of recourse for disputes amongst their constituent members.

Post-War Donor-Supported Reform Efforts (2003-2009)

The establishment of rule of law was highlighted by the international community and its first elected government as a core objective and task for post-conflict

---

> Dei, Mende, Bandi, Loma, Kpelle and part of the Ma [Mano]. The society serves two primary functions. It is the main institution to enculturate young males and to formally carry them through the rite of passage from child to adult. In addition, the elders of the Poro serve as the intermediaries between the ancestors and the living, and thus act as the ultimate arbiters of asocial actions which affect the society. The female counterpart of this organization is the Sande Society. (Gibbs 1962: 349).

For more detailed discussion of these and comparable institutions in Liberia and in West Africa—including their roles in dispute resolution see (historically): Little 1949; Bellman 1984; (and contemporary) Fanthorpe 2001, 2007.

[9] One example is the kui societies of the Grebo in Southeastern Liberia. (Olukoju 2006: 25).

peace-building. Throughout this first five-year post-war period (2003-2009) international donors and those in leadership roles in the Liberian government coalesced around a series of orienting principles that in effect have provided a general approach to justice reform. Thus despite differences in emphasis and perspective amongst actors who on occasion had disagreements they largely shared an overall approach that will be explored below. This approach may be characterized as:

1) 'Dismissive of Non-State Justice Actors' (in the sense that it has either ignored or sought to reduce the power and minimize the role of customary institutions in the provision of justice);

2) 'Legalist' (in the sense of placing a primary emphasis on legislation and legal forms, as opposed to taking a functionalist approach to justice);

3) 'Formalist' (in the sense of privileging investment in and capacity building of the formal justice institutions in the image of western ideals);

4) 'Centralist' (in the sense of pursuing a top-down model for effecting legal and institutional reform that emphasizes and invests in change at higher institutional echelons first and foremost).

Dismissing non-state actors

During the post-war period justice reform efforts took two approaches to legal pluralism and to non-state justice providers more specifically. One approach simply dismissed Liberia's historical model of legal pluralism as well as any ongoing role played by non-state justice providers as largely inconsequential to future reform efforts. The other approach viewed the dual justice system as emblematic of the fundamental and historically constituted forms of structural socio-political inequality that underwrote social discontent and fueled violent conflict over the previous three decades, and therefore needing to be 'fixed' (Sawyer 1992; Banks 2006; ICG 2006). Consequently, most justice reform efforts have focused on building the infrastructure and professional capacity of formal institutions, often with an underlying belief that as the formal system becomes reestablished Liberians will simply choose to engage with the formal system. When mainstream justice reform efforts have engaged with the dual justice system they have often been driven by a well-meaning and 'progressive' intent to remove what they see as the discriminatory dichotomy between the formal and customary justice systems in order to establish a single system that conforms to international legal and human rights standards and that equally applies to all Liberians.

One overarching assumption embedded in this approach to justice reform is that this objective will be accomplished by ensuring that the formal legal system eventually becomes the primary - or even sole - forum of recourse for Liberians who seek justice. This assumption is buttressed by two paradigms that dominate state-building and peace-building as conceived by the United Nations and other members of the international development community: the concept of the Weberian state (and its notions of sovereignty) and the doctrine of the universality of human rights. To some, legal pluralism violates both of these precepts and is therefore incompatible with the modern state-building and/or human rights proliferation project. By early 2006, for example, the International Crisis Group reported that some officials within the University of Liberia were discussing elimination of the dual justice system (ICG 2006).

The operationalization of this approach to pluralism has typically involved three primary types of action: (1) an effort to constrain the scope of jurisdiction of customary courts to minor disputes; (2) reaffirmations of prohibition of specific customary justice practices (such as trial by ordeal) that are viewed as inherently at odds with international human rights norms; and (3) the drafting of a number of 'exemplary' laws that aim to address either high profile human rights violations (e.g. the so-called 'Rape Law') or that correct gendered forms of inequality that previously enjoyed legal protection (e.g. the 'Inheritance Law').

This approach has largely been pursued through a two-pronged strategy that couples civic education with more coercive forms of action. Civic education has largely consisted of a barrage of programs that aim to 'sensitize' the Liberian public about human rights and the rule of law and that inform chiefs that all but the most trivial civil cases—and certainly all criminal cases including rape, murder, and any case that draws blood—are to be the sole purview of the formal courts.[10] There has also been an effort to make it known that chiefs who accept such cases

[10] The Government of Liberia, in collaboration with their international partners, has pursued this through radio messaging. The joint Ministry of Justice and Judiciary Pre-Trial Detention Taskforce has established a Public Education Subcommittee which is tasked with finding ways to educate the population and community leaders on due process guarantees and the Liberian constitution.

are liable for prosecution. This also included a campaign of public media denouncement of all forms of trial by ordeal as illegal and the allocation of scarce prosecutorial resources to go after a particular brutal incident of trial by ordeal in order to serve as a warning to others.

Form over Function: a legalist and formalist belief in the transformative effect of law

Policy-makers have diagnosed the problem of justice primarily as a matter of flawed laws. The solution that follows therefore, is to reform these laws so that they meet international 'best practice' standards. Once such exemplary laws and policies are drafted, reformers contend that the Liberian public simply needs to be educated about the benefits, after which their behavior will be modified. Accordingly, resources have been prioritized to improve the law and the legal knowledge of lawyers—through regular County Attorney and Public Defender trainings, through the establishment of the Judicial Institute, and by providing support to the only law school in Liberia. Additional resources have been allocated to educate the public about their rights and about the formal law—through measures such as the ubiquitous signs along the roads leading into Monrovia that exhort motorists to avoid paying bribes to police officers, to pay their taxes, or refuse to 'compromise rape' cases and instead report these to the police. Other visible measures include public notices in court houses that inform the public about what fees are legitimate–in an effort to curtail bribery and the charging of all manner of 'informal fees'. Resources have also been allocated to NGOs and civil society organizations tasked with carrying out public dissemination campaigns about new laws and regulations. In short, this approach conceptualizes the transformation of the justice system as a task that can be accomplished primarily by drafting the right laws and then addressing knowledge deficits about those new laws.

This approach fails in the Liberian context for two primary reasons: First, it ignores the fact that law and justice are always deeply implicated in social and political relations and informed by culturally-differentiated concepts and hierarchies of value. Change in behavior and belief cannot be simply legislated or taught but rather must be socially and politically negotiated. The relationship between laws and behavior is thus always mediated by those factors that underwrite the extent of law's social endorsement. Notably, conformity to international standards is not usually a factor that matters much in securing local social endorsement. Factors that are much more influential include local perceptions of both the relevance and moral legitimacy of the laws, and of the power and political legitimacy of those who promulgate and attempt to enforce them[11].

This last point highlights the second primary fallacy of an approach that places its faith in the law as a primary mechanism for transformation–namely: it ignores what Pritchett et al. (2010) term 'state capability traps.' Pritchett et al. (2010) seek to understand how state capabilities expand and why some (or many) projects fail. After demonstrating that development, even under the best circumstances, takes significant time, they suggest there are two primary reasons for consistent underperformance of development agendas: (1) the adoption of 'best practice', leading to what they term as 'isomorphic mimicry,' where state institutions try to emulate successful models in more developed states and (2) 'premature load bearing,' where, often encouraged by the development community, a state's bureaucracy can become 'unhinged' due to wishful thinking and overloading institutions with unrealistic demands.

The belief that the institutional mechanism that is supposed to deliver and enforce these laws can be relatively rapidly and dramatically transformed through inputs such as trainings and the rebuilding of infrastructure is unrealistic—particularly in a post-conflict context such as Liberia. As Pritchett et al make clear, bureaucratic transformation under even the best of circumstances always takes significant time. Moreover it is also always a political process and not merely a technical one—all the more so when the institutional apparatus itself is a branch of government in a country where political power has been violently contested and the legitimacy of government is still itself being re-established (Brinkerhoff 2005; Pugh 2000).

Thus, even with a core group of dedicated personnel in the Ministry of Justice, Judiciary, and other government agencies, Liberia is decades away from, say, the United States, or even Ghana—a system frequently cited as a 'best practice model' to which Liberia might aspire. Failing to take into account the long-term nature of reform can be problematic as—especially in a post-conflict environment like Liberia—it is critical to develop mechanisms capable of addressing grievance and building public trust in legitimate institutions, be they formal, informal or hybrid.

[11] For a discussion of analytical models of social change and the factors that affect social endorsement see Lubkemann 2008.

Missing the User: a centralist strategy of building formal institutions from the top-down

Justice reform efforts have further focused on the highest levels of the Liberian justice system—the capacity and resources of the Supreme Court; formal legal training (e.g., training lawyers, rebuilding the University of Liberia's law school); public defenders for circuit courts and magisterial courts in Monrovia. However, with limited resources, the lower levels of the formal system—the interface at which the average citizen is most likely to engage—were entirely neglected after the war and remain secondary in emphasis even now.

The lack of capacity within the formal system is most acutely visible at the local level. Thus, of over 400 Magistrates in Liberia 2008, only 5 had a law degree as required by statute and many were not even high school graduates (Lubkemann, Isser and Banks 2010. In the post-war period most courts in the counties were not functioning due to widespread absenteeism of judicial personnel reluctant to take up remote posts. While Public Defenders and County Attorneys have been hired and resourced in recent years, there continue to be reports that they are not present for entire terms of court. In general, police throughout the country continue to lack the most basic equipment necessary to do their jobs, such as vehicles to transport those arrested or carry out investigation; handcuffs; or even typewriters and simple stationary supplies (Lubkemann, Isser and Banks 2010. Moreover, 'capacity' itself has typically been cast as a matter of providing formal institutions with training and equipment and thus that requires a 'technical fix' -without necessarily addressing far more fundamental sociological, political, and economic factors that play a fundamental role in the *quality* of the services these institutions provide. Thus, as we will discuss at greater length below improving the 'capacity' of these institutions—in the sense of empowering them with tools that facilitate their action—without addressing 'capacity' in the sense of *how* they act is likely to be seen as particularly problematic by the vast majority of the Liberian public.

This approach has also typically placed relatively little emphasis on institutions that are not part of the formal justice system. When existing informal institutions have been engaged by donors and policy-makers, they are often seen either as mechanisms through which to provide civic education about the formal system or as the targets for that education itself. Many policy-makers still express the need to 'sensitize' traditional leaders as to the tenets of formal law and international human rights law and there is a continued focus on the need to expand the capacity of state institutions (in the Weberian sense) at the local level. The Zero Draft of the

United Nations Peacebuilding Priority Plan for 2011-2013, envisioned measuring success in "Enhanc[ing] access to justice and community security at regional and county level" by, among other indicators, monitoring the number "of cases referred from traditional/customary mechanisms to the formal system." (United Nations Peacebuilding Commission 2011). Instead efforts have focused on expanding access to a formal system, for example, through the James A. A. Pierre Judicial Institute's Professional Magistrate Training Program which educated a class of non-lawyer Magistrates to be deployed in rural areas. While there is no doubt that the formal justice system is in dire need of increased capacity, research demonstrates that these top-down approaches have largely failed to address the justice concerns of the majority of the Liberian population (Schia and Carvalho 2009; Sandefur and Siddiqi 2011.

The Formal and Customary Systems in Comparative Perspective: Local Liberian Views

The Liberians interviewed in the course of our study very clearly expressed an overwhelming preference for the customary system over formal court alternatives, that is, when they seek a third party of any sort to resolve a dispute. The CSAE Survey shows that resort to a customary authority for purposes of dispute resolution was over ten times more likely to be the case than resort to a formal court (Sandefur and Siddiqi 2011). This survey found that formal courts were approached in 3% of the civil disputes reported and 2% of the criminal disputes reported, whereas over 30% of the time (civil) and 24% of the time (criminal) disputes were taken to customary authorities.

Calculating the costs of formal and customary justice: accessibility, opacity, and corruption in comparison

The marked preference of Liberians for customary justice forums over formal ones relates—in part—to differences between the two in their accessibility (especially for rural inhabitants) as well as in costs, perceived transparency, and their perceived susceptibility to undue influence (for all Liberians). Costs refer not only to fees, but to the significant indirect costs associated with the distance traveled, the number of such trips and the duration required, which mean time spent away from livelihoods—whether it is subsistence farming or wage-based work.

The cost of hiring a lawyer remains another financial obstacle faced by any

Liberian who opts for recourse through the formal system. Many of our respondents abandoned plans to pursue cases in the formal justice system, or they simply never considered this option in the first place. Many rural respondents could not even afford the cost of travel to Monrovia to find a lawyer, much less the lawyer's fees. Since our field study was completed, Public Defenders were hired to reach rural areas, and while they are responsible for serious criminal cases, we would argue that they have resulted in little gains in the sorts of disputes that most Liberians face. Such lawyers typically charge for civil representation and, again, are typically not present at the interface between average citizens and the state and in most counties instead focus efforts on cases at the Circuit Court.

A further significant cost that all Liberians invariably take into account is that of corruption. Outright bribery is assumed to play a far more determining role in most formal court outcomes than the substantive merits of the case. It is simply taken as a matter of fact that bribery is indispensable if one wants to win a case, and consequently that there is little point in pursuing a case in court if one cannot or is unwilling to assume such 'costs.' In fact, our study found that the expectation that officials in the formal court system will find some way to illegitimately extort money is sometimes so strong that it affects the willingness of litigants to reveal exactly what wrong they have suffered because they fear it may be further compounded by official extortion:

> One funny thing that I thought of about the court was, when I carried the complaint, I did not mention about the planks. I only told the judge that 'E' and his brothers beat me on my land because if I have mentioned about the planks, the court could have definitely demanded to have a share in it. And so I felt for my nephew and never exposed it out. (Man interviewed in Nimba County who had been beaten and robbed by his nephews, as quoted in Isser, Lubkemann and N'tow 2009: 41).

The menu of dubious costs that Liberians expect to confront in a typical formal court proceeding are likely to include: 'sponsorships' to pay for police transportation costs and perhaps time to take someone into custody, or fuel to investigate a case; a variety of ad-hoc 'writ', 'filing', 'bond fee', 'referral' and 'case registration' fees (with police and courts alike); the financial responsibility on the part of the accuser/presumed victim to provide food for an accused who is imprisoned (or else that person will be set free); and even money to pay for the paper on which depositions are taken. Time after time, Liberians report that even the most egregious crimes fall by the wayside within the state courts unless money for such 'fees' keeps flowing.

Second, Liberians cite concerns with the opacity of formal court proceedings. To most Liberians the formal legal process is profoundly bewildering and consequently disempowering. Victims / plaintiffs and perpetrators / defendants alike express frustration at being bounced around from official to official, court date to court date, or detention cell to detention cell - all without ever understanding the reason why. In even the most egregious cases, such as the following one documented in our USIP/GWU Study, the formal system seems incapable of addressing the plight of victims—even as it disempowers and re-victimizes them in other ways:

> A man raped an eighty-three-year-old woman. The woman was taken to the hospital where the rape was confirmed, and the suspect was arrested and jailed. The victim's daughter went to the magistrate court to pursue the case, but she was told that she had to pay five hundred Liberian dollars. After she did, she was told to get a second medical report. The case was then referred to the circuit court. After traveling a second time to the circuit court in Voinjama, they were told that it was the end of the term and they would need to come back the next term. The next term, there was no transportation available and it was the rainy season. The victim was put in a wheelbarrow for transport, but as her health was failing, her daughter decided to bring her mother home and to go to the court herself. Once there she was told that unless her mother was present the court would not hear the case. The next day she was told by the court that the suspect had broken out of jail. In the meantime, while she was at the court, her mother died. (Isser, Lubkemann and N'Tow 2009: 40)

The opacity of formal court proceedings is a second factor that underwrites the widespread suspicion that formal courts are inevitably biased, subject to undue influence, and to the whims and interest of presiding officials. For instance, we collected evidence of cases in which the 'laws' that were invoked by the officials in the formal justice system seem to be simply invented outright so as to further their self-interest. Some of the starkest examples include legally unfounded invocations of impunity—exemplified by a statement such as: "a state official cannot be charged or imprisoned if he is standing/working under the flag of the nation" (Isser, Lubkemann and N'Tow 2009: 43-4)—and made-up laws, as for instance stated by a judge in one case: "if you go to someone's house and afterwards something is found missing you are responsible according to Liberian civil law." (Isser, Lubkemann and N'Tow 2009: 44) Even in instances where court officials do follow the letter of Liberian law, limited understanding of normative and procedural features of the law often leads aggrieved parties to believe they were in fact taken advantage of. Our evidence also suggests that it is not uncommon for women litigants in a variety of types of cases to report being victims of sexual harassment and sometimes even violence at the hands of the very state justice officials to whom they turn for assistance.

Liberians are also deeply frustrated by the ease with which detainees secure release, which may happen by bribing officials, because the police will release a detainee unless the accuser agrees to pay for that individual's food and lodging in prison, or because the detainee has been held for the constitutionally mandated period and there is not sufficient evidence to hold him or her further. The 'privatization' of the responsibility for sustaining detainees ultimately means that the detention of a suspect has been transformed into a responsibility that victims are forced to assume in practice. The sentiment of injustice and outrage that this imposition engenders is obviously considerable.

All of these factors in combination lead many Liberians to conclude that the formal justice system is overwhelmingly governed by three dominant factors: the personal power and interests of state officials, the monetary wealth of individuals that allows them to pay bribes; and, the capacity to mobilize forms of social and political power in order to influence court officials. We collected numerous accounts of Liberians reporting that a decision to resort to the formal system was made not to secure a just or fair outcome but rather to leverage personal resources that could provide an unfair advantage in the resolution of a case. In short, the formal court system is actually seen as an effective mechanism by which an individual who has more resources (personal connections, political power, money) can gain an unfair advantage against someone who cannot mobilize such resources. Thus rather than a remedy for injustice the formal system is viewed by many as *a mechanism by which the rich and powerful very effectively perpetrate injustice.* From this perspective, the social ubiquity of this refrain by a female interviewee is unsurprising: "there is no justice for the poor." (Isser, Lubkemann and N'Tow 2009: 42) Ultimately—and notwithstanding the resources poured into the reform of the formal justice system by the international community since 2005—our research demonstrates that the formal justice system has continued to suffer from an extreme deficit of popular credibility.

In contrast to the formal courts most rural Liberians have ready access to customary justice institutions, in particular to the chiefly courts.[12] Customary justice institutions were also consistently reported to involve far lower direct costs than formal courts and to reach resolutions much more rapidly, which reduces many indirect costs associated with the loss of time. The costs in customary forums are also viewed as far more consistent, predictable, and fair than in the formal system. Most chiefs use a publicly known standard set of fees for most offenses. Fees collected by a chief tend to be used to cover transportation or other administrative costs, including the cost of stationary. Many chiefs even report foregoing fees for parties who cannot afford them, accepting chickens or rice in lieu of money, or substituting fees with work for the chief or the community.

The procedures involved in customary justice proceedings are generally described as far more understandable and transparent than those in the formal courts. Particularly, Liberians feel that because they can understand customary proceedings they are more readily able to identify situations of partiality. The transparency also allows them to take measures that can counterbalance such partiality, which may involve appeal within the customary system itself. Our research established that rulings pronounced in customary justice settings are not viewed by either customary justice providers or local users as terminally binding– in the sense that they can be, and often are, appealed to higher authorities in the customary system, local Ministry of Internal Affairs officials, and even on occasion to the state justice system itself. Arguably, it is the particular way in

[12] Customs, and by extension customary law, vary significantly amongst Liberia's major ethno-linguistic groups, but also to a considerable extent within them (Moran 2006). Thus, for example, religious professions while being highly varied, including a broad continuum of Christianities (assorted zionisms, various mainstream denominations, Roman Catholicism), Islam, and a variety of indigenous animist religious beliefs often vary within ethnic groups and local communities alike. Throughout different parts of the country there is also significant variation in the extent to which power and authority is centralized at even the most elementary levels of social organization including families, kinship networks, and local communities. Nevertheless, the broad principles that we discuss below are largely shared by Liberia's customary legal systems at least to an extent that clearly differentiates them from the principles that inform the formal justice system, historically derived directly from the US system.

which Liberian customary systems allow for an extensive and relatively rapid appeal process that absolves it of the accusations of generalized and inherent partiality that Liberians associate with the formal system.

Customary and formal justice principles: local views of fundamental differences

Entirely aside from factors such as cost, ease of access, and transparency, our interviewees also preferred the customary justice forums because they provided a service that embodies values and priorities that are different to those of the formal system. Liberians draw a strong contrast between the fundamental principles and values that define 'justice' and govern its application in how they perceive the formal court system and those that are applied in customary justice resolution. For instance, one of the most consistent complaints levied against the formal court system is that it is overly narrow in how it defines the case at hand, consequently failing to address the full range of social factors and relationships that ultimately inform any specific instance of conflict or dispute. Customary mechanisms by contrast focus on what lies 'behind' the immediate dispute, and which is seen to powerfully inform it:

> So actually looking at the [formal] court, they only focus on the nature of your complaint and care less to know what transpired in the past. So in short, the court does not satisfy the both parties when cases are resolved by them. But for our traditional people they look at the nature of the case and also dig out the past to know what happened, and based upon that they peacefully resolved the matter. And at the climax the both parties leave with smile. And so to conclude, I prefer the Customary System (Isser, Lubkemann and N'Tow 2009: 47).

> [...] what I like about the customary system is, it is not expensive and our elders and chief focus on how to reunite the disputing parties. Above all, they gave the both parties the opportunity to explain the underlying cause that resulted in the current dispute.... In court the judge only focus on the existing current matter at hand, leaving the underlying causes. So I solely prefer our traditional people to handle our matters. (ibid: 47)

Thus, when resolving a case, chiefs strive to do more than to merely ascertain which immediate party is at fault and who is innocent. Instead they probe more deeply in search of a form of 'truth' that goes beyond the narrow dispute at hand

and beyond the two immediate disputing parties to identify and address the more fundamental root issues and broader social factors that inform and are affected by the dispute. Liberians evaluate the adequacy of justice in terms of its ability to address such deeper social maladies of which any particular dispute is viewed as merely symptomatic. The formal system defines the scope of action for 'justice' in almost exactly the opposite way: as limited to the immediate disputants and demonstrable violations in a specific instance of wrong-doing.[13]

In order to adequately address the deeper truth of the matter, chiefs do not usually make determinations alone. Instead, most of the time they rely extensively on the counsel and participation of community elders and, where deemed relevant, on representatives of specific social constituencies such as youth, women elders, or even the elder members of the families of the contending parties. Chiefs and elders also specifically seek out the counsel of what might be termed 'expert witnesses' who can provide insight into either the deeper social dynamics that underwrite the root truth of a matter (such as in the case of elders from the families of aggrieved parties), or on the substantive issue in question (such as in cases where elders knowledgeable about customary land boundaries are asked to testify). Liberians' interest in seeing root 'truths' addressed rests on a deeply held assumption that incorrect or injurious behavior ultimately stems from damaged and acrimonious social relations. In order to be seen as adequate, justice must work to repair those relations, which are the ultimate and more fundamental causal determinants, rather than merely treat the behavioral expressions that are viewed as their symptoms. Redress is therefore considered inadequate if it does not attempt to produce reconciliation among the parties.

Thus although the specific balance struck among different priorities may vary from case to case and across individual customary justice practitioners, most descriptions of procedures and of actual case proceedings that we collected suggest that after ascertaining the truth of the matter, achieving social reconciliation is the overriding concern. Chiefs often speak about 'compromising' a case, which means finding a resolution that satisfies both parties and allows them "to go with smiles on their faces." (Isser, Lubkemann and N'Tow 2009: 48)

The customary approach takes up the mitigation of adversarialism as an inherent

[13] For similar findings elsewhere see for example Benda-Beckman 1984; Huyse and Salter 2008; West 2005.

objective of justice and a key factor in determining the quality of the outcome achieved. In stark contrast the formal justice system takes adversarialism as the given point of departure—and the core driving mechanism—of the justice process. Following the western model, the formal system's legal proceedings are thus supposed to determine winners and losers among adversaries--but have no business addressing adversarialism per se. In fact, in the formal system, the resolution of a case that clearly determines guilt and innocence (and that punishes the offender) is considered to have fully satisfied the requirements of 'justice', even if the resolution also happened to increase adversarialism and social friction among the contending parties.

The formal system also tends to emphasize punitive forms of redress against perpetrators, while paying little if any attention to the restoration of a victim's condition. While most Liberians do believe that punishment has a role in the process of redressing injustice, most believe it should generally be subsumed under other priorities that are viewed as more important. While there are cases in which behavior is judged to be so horrific that perpetrators are viewed as entirely beyond social repair, in the vast majority of situations (even including many cases of murder and rape), the repair of the victim's condition and social reconciliation are viewed as more important objectives than punishment per se. In fact punishment that inflicts some form of pain or loss (including imprisonment) upon a perpetrator in a manner that does not directly contribute to reconciliation or that overlooks or even hinders the repair of a victim's condition is seen as augmenting adversarialism in undesirable ways that impede, rather than contribute to, true justice. When comparing the solutions meted out by the two systems most Liberians tend to agree with the following assessment by one of their compatriots:

> Our traditional laws help us to handle our dispute very easily and after the settlement of these disputes, the disputants go with smiles in their faces . . . In fact, the statutory law brings separation among our people. After the [formal] court ruling we observe that the guilty one is either put in prison or heavily charged to pay cost of court, bond fee, etc. So I prefer the customary system (Town Chief from Nimba County as quoted in Isser, Lubkemann and N'tow 2009: 54).

Compensation that attempts to restore the condition of a victim is also a very high priority, and one that most Liberians accused the formal system of neglecting. At the same time it is interesting that compensation is still often viewed as secondary to the objective of reconciliation. Thus we found a number of cases in which victims chose, or were convinced to forgo compensation entirely when it was a hindrance to reconciliation, for example where the perpetrator did not have the means to pay. In some cases victims actually chose to incur additional costs in order to resolve the case peacefully through customary means. In one instance, we encountered that the victim even voluntarily covered the fees of the perpetrator associated with hearing the case in customary court. Such an instance of compensation differs from experiences in the state justice system where victims and perpetrators are forced to pay by police and such monetary exchange is not driven by a restorative or conciliatory purpose.

Ultimately preference for the values that govern customary justice reflects the interest of most Liberians in deploying practical and proven measures that can realistically minimize the chances that undesirable behavior will be repeated in the future in the particular socio-economic and political context in which they live. Preference for measures that provide for the social reinstatement and redemption of a perpetrator rather than merely his or her punishment, that attempt to address the underlying grievances that may inform immediate behavior, that prioritize repair to victims, and that ensure that disputants and their extended relatives can continue to 'get along' do not merely reflect some sort of reflexive and unconsidered 'cultural preference' that is subscribed to simply because 'that is what we have always done in the past.' Rather such priorities represent an astute reading of the realities, constraints, and possibilities of social survival in the context in which they live. Given that there is a large body of legal anthropological work spanning decades that has underscored precisely this point[14], what is perhaps most remarkable—and bears further investigation—is why legal reform programs in places like Liberia still remain so thoroughly unaware of and/or disinclined to account for these well established facts.

It must be highlighted that this is a context in which the formal legal system and the police are more likely to be a source of predation than of normative enforcement and thus in which local communities must rely heavily on their own mechanisms for norm enforcement rather than on state officials who have little capacity and are not trusted. Similarly those mechanisms must account for forms

[14] See for example: Middleton and Winter 1963; Evans-Pritchard 1976; Douglas 1970; Fisiy and Geschiere 1990; Comaroff and Comaroff 1993; Geschiere 1997; Ashforth 2005; West 2005).

of local economic and social interdependency - embodied in and enacted through social relationships—upon which daily survival may quite literally depend. Moreover, in this context there are no 'social service backstops' that can attend to the condition and plight of victims—and thus justice must include mechanisms for attending to these problems.

Liberians covered by our study also prefer the customary system because they believe it is far more capable of and willing to address the full range of offenses, problems and crimes that they believe they confront. Some of the issues that Liberians want to see addressed as justice include forms of behavior such as public insults that might be considered offensive but not worthy of treatment, or even admissible, in the formal justice system. Again the practical importance of maintaining workable social relations in a particular socio-economic and institutional context goes a long way to explain why behavior that puts those relations at risk is viewed as a problem that needs to be addressed.

A large majority of Liberians also hold a deep-seated and pervasive belief that mechanisms and practices exist by which some individuals deploy supernatural means to hurt or even kill others, most often in order to augment their own power (Ellis 1999). As we discuss in greater detail below, and has been found to be the case elsewhere as well (e.g. Douglas 1970; Evans-Pritchard 1976; Ciekawy and Geschiere 1998; Fisiy 1998; West 2005; Ashforth 2005; Lubkemann 2008) the formal system's refusal to recognize or address witchcraft does nothing to diminish beliefs and concerns that it exists and poses a serious threat to society. The formal system's refusal to address these issues undermines public confidence in its capacity to address the root of many crimes and civil offenses, while policies to suppress the tools used to identify witches increase popular recrimination against and suspicions about the officials and institutions driving this effort.

Finally, in contrast to the formal system, Liberians for the most part also report that resolutions reached through customary processes are more likely to be carried out. As we have already noted a key feature of customary law is that it aims for a solution agreed upon by both parties. When achieved such consensus assures a relatively high degree of 'enforcement success'. Indeed much of the work of customary dispute resolution is sitting down with both parties and their family members and other people of influence to bring them to agreement and acceptance of the resolution. Of course a party that does not accept the resolution of a customary court is free to reject it and appeal to the next level. However, our research indicates that ultimately the decisions of customary courts are not usually coercively enforced.[15] Rather, in the absence of mutual agreement, it is social pressure that is the factor of last resort in ensuring that the parties accept and comply with the decision in the case.

No Justice in Sight: Popular Perceptions and Reactions to the Justice Vacuum-and their Implications

If the popular preference for customary over formal justice is a stark one it is also to some degree a relative one that fails to fully capture the options—or lack of options—that shape local approaches to justice as a whole in post-war Liberia. In fact most Liberians are so frustrated and disillusioned with all their justice options that they are opting against taking their disputes to either formal or customary justice institutions. The aforementioned CSAE Survey thus found that despite a marked preference for customary over formal forums when a third party was sought, on average, over 59% of the time Liberians chose not to approach either formal courts or to use customary mechanisms at all. (Isser, Lubkemann and N'tow 2009: 75). It is in this space that we locate Liberia's current 'justice gap'.

Mounting skepticism about the effectiveness of both formal and informal justice forums are rooted in somewhat different reasons and rationales. Thus, while the authority of customary law was buttressed before the war by the weighty role that kinship-based and gerontocratic forms of authority played in the organization of Liberian societies, those very forms of authority became the source of grievances that underwrote the armed mobilization of youth (Richards 1996; Hoffman 2011a; Utas 2005). An entire generation of Liberian child-soldiers has thus been socialized with reference to other logics of social authority (Hoffman 2011b). In this sense the social basis of authority that underwrites customary systems may be less stable in certain contexts—particularly urban ones—than it once was. Massive

[15] A handful of the chiefs we interviewed did refer to the use of prisons and corporal punishment (usually lashes or 'country hand-cuffs', referring to the process of restricting the movement of a detainee by tying him or her in a set location), as something that they used in the past, and in some cases, as something they would like to have at their disposal again. Our data indicates only that the use of such measures is currently a rarity, although there remains a somewhat greater tendency to use force in the process of detaining and investigating reluctant perpetrators.

urbanization and displacement may have also contributed to the erosion of these former underpinnings of customary authority in rural areas as well. While some chiefs bemoan the war's effect on inter-generational relations, the evidence we collected on how youth view the legitimacy of customary authorities and practices was somewhat mixed. This leads us to conclude that this is still an open question that requires more focused empirical research.

Another significant limitation of customary forums recognized by many chiefs themselves is that their intervention only works when litigants share an interest in, or are at least open to, the goal of reconciliation. For the practical reasons already discussed previously, interest in reconciliation is likely to increase to the extent that litigants are part of the same local community. This adds a further limit to customary justice: it is far less effective in dealing with cases when one of the litigants is an outsider. It may also be less effective in contexts where different forms of socio-cultural heterogeneity underwrite different sources of 'legitimate custom', such as those of mixed ethnic communities or in which religious pluralism is significant.[16]

The chiefs, disputants, and focus group participants in our study tended to attribute the most significant limitations on the effectiveness of the customary justice system to the new post-war government and donor-supported policies that effectively restrict the jurisdiction of chiefs and the methods they can deploy, as outlined earlier. Chiefs claimed, for the most part, to be adhering to these policies and refusing to take cases that involve death, rape, violence that induces blood, and, less consistently, major theft, and referring these cases to state officials.

The most general and overarching of these is the policy that limits the jurisdiction of customary mechanisms to minor crime, requiring that all cases of bodily injury and serious theft be handled exclusively by the formal system. While this is not necessarily new - the Hinterland Regulations set out a limited criminal jurisdiction for chiefs courts' - it was historically honored more in the breach. However, under the new post-conflict dispensation chiefs are being pressured to respect the

[16] Ongoing research led by Lubkemann on the topography of urban justice that is documenting the range of informal justice forums, their interactions with each other and with formal institutions, and the justice choices made by Liberians in urban Monrovia may provide additional empirical evidence that speaks to these questions.

limits set by the new policies, sometimes under threat of prosecution.

Chiefs and local community members do not find that the limits placed on the jurisdiction of chiefs are legitimate or constructive. There was a fairly broad consensus that chiefs are generally better-equipped and customary principles far more appropriate, to the task of bringing justice to all but the most heinous forms of murder, rape, and violence. Manslaughter (involving accidental killing) and cases of alleged rape between young lovers in particular were two examples that respondents felt the customary system could resolve more effectively and for which it would produce rulings that would be fairer than those afforded by the formal court system. Chiefs reported that they are frequently pressured by members of their community to consider cases they are officially forbidden from taking. Some admitted that in practice they did so, provided both parties requested it.

Another finding of our study is that the majority of Liberians interviewed feel that the government's blanket prohibition on the use of trial by ordeal (TBO) is further crippling the effectiveness of customary justice resolution. Perhaps no other practice has received as much attention from the United Nations and human rights community. A recent Solicitor-General, with strong backing from the international community, spearheaded a widely publicized campaign to end this practice with a blanket prohibition and the showcasing of exemplary prosecutions.

There is also perhaps no practice that is more caricaturized and whose local meanings, social uses, and nuances of practice are less well understood—to great consequence—by rule of law reformers. As we have argued elsewhere there are in fact a wide variety of types of practices and reasons for their use that are lumped under the terms TBO and/or 'sassywood'. The differences among these practices are immensely important to consider for purposes of formulating legislation and a justice reform policy that adequately attends to local concerns (see Lubkemann, Isser and Banks 2010 and uses for TBO). First, TBO can be used as a means of identifying the guilty party when an admission is not forthcoming. In such cases, some form of TBO is administered to the suspect or suspects, and it is believed that only the guilty party will suffer some form of harm. Second, TBO can be used to ensure that truth is spoken by suspects, witnesses, or others. Here, it is believed that those who undergo the TBO will suffer some form of harm if they do not tell the truth. TBO in this way is used most commonly as part of the fact finding in a customary proceeding, but was also cited as an important way for men to determine if their wives committed adultery. In a variation on the first and second uses, suspects themselves may ask to undergo TBO in order to prove their innocence. Third, TBO can be used to 'get rid of the witch.' This is most commonly used to enable suspected members of witch societies (known variously as snake societies, 'Bambah' societies, Korsaw-Korsaw, among other names) to 'swear off the witch' and become mainstream members of the community.

Indeed most rural Liberians that we interviewed called for some form of TBO to be reinstated because they firmly believed the ban was causing considerable harm in their communities by depriving them of a reliable and effective tool for solving crime and keeping order. TBO was also seen as the only tool for solving certain types of particularly pernicious and feared problems, such as witchcraft. The ban on TBO is blamed for a litany of problems: the inability to resolve crime because the guilty cannot be identified; the inability of the innocent to clear their name; for reducing the incentive for parties to admit their guilt (given the lack of alternative means of proving it); for a general increase in criminality and sense of impunity; and most significantly, for a drastic increase in the most lethal forms of witchcraft, coupled with the growing strength of the 'snake societies', which promote and are believed to benefit from witchcraft. While Liberian discourse is marked by allegations of increasing strength of 'snake societies' and 'heart men', measures are being read by local populations as mere 'naysaying' which suppresses what is regarded as 'known and proven' solutions to genuinely feared problems while failing to offer any viable alternative solutions, and often inadvertently creating new problems altogether.

We also found evidence that the struggle to find alternatives to TBO for dealing with witchcraft may actually be strengthening other purely community-based customary justice institutions, in particular so called 'secret societies', whose legitimacy is grounded in local socio-cultural precepts, such as the Poro society. Unable to deal directly with witchcraft themselves because of the prohibition against TBO, several chiefs report that they now rely even more heavily on the ritual specialists of the Poro society to produce solutions. As a result social pressure to join these societies is increasing in some communities. Such pressures can have markedly negative effects in mixed communities. In Lofa County, for example, throughout 2010 and 2011 there were reports of a Guinean ritual specialist moving from town-to-town investigating witchcraft. Lorma community members were typically prepared to pay for the specialist's services while Mandingo community members were not. This lead to numerous allegations of witchcraft and further fractured community relationships.

Policy makers implementing the Rule of Law agenda have surely intended to both improve access to and the quality of justice for average Liberians, to cultivate popular knowledge of and subscription to international human rights norms, and to strengthen and assert the legitimacy of the state. However, contra these intentions we have found significant evidence that most Liberians believe the current approach is merely undermining the effectiveness of the customary system without providing any alternative mechanisms that improves security and justice or effectively copes with social antagonisms and disputes. The net result for most Liberians has been what we have termed elsewhere a 'justice vacuum' (Lubkemann, Isser and Banks 2010) where justice and accountability not improved and may even have declined despite millions spent on the justice system.

Liberians from across the social spectrum widely view this vacuum as a place in which the powerful, wealthy, and socially connected are able to secure unfair advantages in dispute resolution—often through the formal courts. In a context in which formal courts and police are believed to be guided by self-interest and as highly susceptible to undue influence, litigants are most likely to appeal to the formal system if and when they believe they will be able to leverage money or social connections that will produce admittedly partial, and unjust rulings that are in their favor. Referral to the formal courts, or the threat of such a referral, was also recounted to us as a tactic that is used to advance contentious social agendas, for retaliatory purposes, or for gaining leverage in other matters that had nothing to do with the actual case in question. Thus in the opinion of one woman: "The new rape bill should be revisited because there are people here who are using it to attack one another." (Woman in a focus group as quoted in Isser, Lubkemann and N'tow, 2009: 54). This practice of 'making the case big' was mentioned in a number of our interviews as a typical way in which new laws, such as the rape law, were being deployed to nefarious ends never intended and with pernicious effects on the social legitimacy of that law and its legitimate users.

Under these circumstances the very meaning of formal law has been perversely distorted into a source of perceived injustice rather than a solution to it. The extension of the jurisdiction of formal courts is thus seen by many as reinforcing the mechanism through which the rich and the powerful -and justice officials themselves—can, and do, advance their own predatory interests. The current approach to justice reform is thus negatively affecting the legitimacy of formal justice institutions and human rights norms throughout Liberia.

Liberians confront this justice vacuum by seeking to mobilize extra-legal mechanisms that are neither part of the formal nor the customary justice systems per se, to influence formal and informal justice proceedings. As such, seeking justice is primarily an effort to identify someone you believe can effectively exert power over an opponent in order to achieve a partial outcome on your behalf, and to use money or some form of social capital to activate that power for your benefit. It is also an effort to monitor and prepare for (or even pre-empt) the possibility that an adversary in a case will manipulate similar social connections and use money to subvert justice. The only 'solution' is to make sure one is capable of playing this game with greater ultimate effect than one's opponent. In short, in the minds of most Liberians 'justice' is co-equal to the securing of influence.

Liberians thus decide how they will seek recourse based on a careful assessment of their own position (relative to that of other interested parties) within a single pool of institutional power, but which is embodied in particular persons. This single 'power pool' includes both customary and formal justice institutions, but is not limited to these sources alone. It also includes state officials who have no legal role in the statutory system but nevertheless may be called upon or chose to intervene in formal court or police proceedings. Our research identified a wide range of such officials including superintendents, national legislators, deputy ministers, immigration officers, and even diplomatic bodyguards, international NGO officials, UN personnel wealthy businessmen, and former military commanders.

Frustration with the perceived pervasiveness of the 'injustice of justice' also results in Liberians choosing to take matters into their own hands. To whit the conclusions of the brother of a murder victim whose inability to pay fees that would advance the case through the (statutory) courts led him to plan to: "take justice into our hands. We will take some boys and kill the perpetrator."

Such trends do not bode well for broader rule of law and peace-building objectives—including efforts to cultivate the legitimacy of the fledgling post-conflict state itself. Our research thus noted a disturbing tendency for ordinary Liberians to blame the government for the justice vacuum—both because its courts have proven incapable of providing justice, and because it has prevented other (customary) institutions believed to be capable of providing justice from doing so. Even more disturbing is the rise of a conspiratorial public discourse that imputes more nefarious motives and intentionality to government justice reform efforts. Thus some of our respondents went so far as to voice suspicions that the highest level government officials (e.g. Liberia's former Solicitor General being accused by name in at least two interviews) would surely only be suppressing TBO rituals that diagnose witchcraft if they themselves were members of the snake-type societies who performed and benefited from witchcraft.

In a social context in which the relationship between political power and socially subversive relationships to the supernatural have been extensively documented as potent sources for violent political mobilization (Ellis 1999; Richards 1996; Hoffman 2011b) the implications of such discourses for undermining the legitimacy of the government and re-invigorating conflict should not be taken lightly. Similarly, local suspicions that the extension of formal court authority over issues previously left to customary chiefs is a potential political incendiary that should not be ignored. This particularly regards the transfer of land dispute resolution to the formal courts, which could be seen as serving the land-grabbing ambitions of urban elites at the expense of the local rural citizens.

Finally, the anti-pluralist tendencies of the 'One Liberia' approach may be a source of political divisiveness that engenders stiff resistance from those whose very interests it is supposedly meant to serve. Our research found that customary justice institutions are not seen locally as merely the products — or mechanisms for reproducing - of historical discrimination, but also as a means by which local communities cope with both genuine challenges of order and practical concerns and historically served to resist the imposition of Americo-Liberian power. These mechanisms help express positive values that are deeply held and that differ in substantial ways from those that inform the formal justice system. As a consequence a 'One Liberia' justice policy that is all about extending the protections of the formal system (even in its ideal state) over all Liberians is greeted with considerable skepticism and resistance. In fact our research strongly suggests that a majority of rural Liberians view the current effort to constrain customary justice not as the eradication of discriminatory injustices that have harmed them but as yet another negative imposition by a central state that neither understands their social context nor favors their interests. While some blame foreign influence as the source of this intrusion, many also view recent government policies through a lens that emphasizes a specific interpretation of Liberian history in which a Monrovian elite is (again) seeking to impose its norms on those in the 'country', ultimately as a means to exploit them. This view brings rural Liberians directly into conflict with the 'progressive' assumptions that seem so self-evident to rule of law reformers who view the dual legal system as the embodiment of discrimination and inequality.

The Liberian Truth and Reconciliation Commission itself identified as an antecedent cause of the conflict the choice made by the early settlers to define Liberia as an Americo-Liberian state with a civilizing mission to be imposed upon the 'savage and barbaric' indigenous population, rather than to engage all of the Liberian people in the building of the emergent nation. It further warns that: "Liberia has yet to reconcile the two opposing ideas - the civilizing mission and the building of an African nationality" (Truth and Reconciliation Commission 2010: 240). Efforts to deal with this question of national identity will be further complicated by a range of political questions that extend far beyond the rule of law sector, including debates about the future role of the Ministry of Internal Affairs and the future of local governance. However, as we have argued elsewhere (Lubkemann, Isser, and Banks 2009) the crucial question of who gets to participate in making decisions about what that identity can and will be, is likely to be at least as critical to the success of Liberia's legal reform efforts -and to the broader task of building public confidence in democracy as a process that provides for genuine popular representation rather than the protection of elite privilege—as are concerns with eradicating past inequalities.

Conclusion

The process of post-war justice reform in Liberia is, in many ways, illustrative of broader ailments and quandaries that confront justice reform undertaken in societies with a history of legal pluralism. As the Liberian government, and their international partners, have entered a next phase of post-war rule of law reform there has been an increasing effort to engage with the multitude of actors active in dispute resolution—particularly at the local level. Forced to confront the fact that centralized reform has not lead to significant efficiency gains or improvements in access to or quality of justice, the rule of law community now generally recognizes that dispute resolution actors at the local level may have to play significant roles in the process of reform (even if this is viewed as an 'interim' role by more orthodox rule of law actors).

The *National Conference on Enhancing Access to Justic*e held in April 2010 is an example of this recognition (Republic of Liberia 2010). The conference brought together traditional leaders, community leaders, and members of the formal legal community to discuss how different dispute resolution systems could work together to expand access to justice. This cooperation, to date, has been largely conceptualized in similar ways to that of formal justice reform in Liberia.

Discussions have been centralist and formalistic, with the belief that modified behavior will flow from new legislation or new policies. 'Cooperation' between the two systems can be facilitated through new policy frameworks; trial by ordeal can be 'addressed' by reauthorizing those forms that are determined to be 'non-harmful' and then disseminated to traditional communities; problems with the performance of magistrate judges can be improved by making the public aware of the appropriate statutory fees.

Experience of the government's Pre-Trial Detention Taskforce in many ways mirrors the discussion of the *National Conference on Enhancing Access to Justice*. With limited reductions in the overall numbers of pretrial detention, government and international partners began to discuss how traditional and community leaders may work to solidify reductions in instances of prolonged pretrial detention. Such discussion, however, seeks to 'harness' these actors in support of the formal system. Traditional leaders may oversee bail and probation from the formal system; they may relieve the stress on the formal system by mediating 'small-scale' disputes in an effort to free up the formal system for more significant cases; and communities simply need to be educated about the due process provisions of Liberian law to 'understand' why detainees are being released after they exceed the constitutional provisions for detention.

While both of these endeavors may realize some gains, improving justice in any substantial way for the average Liberian ultimately requires a far more dramatic and radical reconceptualization of the problem itself. New momentum for reform that reaches beyond central actors of the formal justice system must do more than educate communities and 'improve' community systems. The question itself must be recast from that of how to improve the formal system, or, for that matter even from how to define the relationship between the formal and customary systems. Instead, the question of how to improve outcomes for users should be the new point of departure for rule of law programming.

This is a significant shift in paradigm: rather than approaching justice reform as a means of bringing the laws and institutions up to a pre-determined structure and standard, it requires accepting that justice is not a technology or known formula, but a socially-embedded and contested concept. Legal pluralism is neither good nor bad; it simply describes a social fact. This requires an altogether different skill set and mandate for justice reform actors, one that allows them to focus on and engage with the idiosyncrasies of context, and to have the stomach for diverse, transitional and non-linear paths to change. This is also a much harder approach, with no clear blueprint for action. But a good starting place is to focus on a constructive process of community engagement to understand what people consider to be the greatest obstacles to justice and to encourage innovative means of addressing these in ways that are suitable to local particularities. This by no means excludes capacity building and reform of formal and informal justice institutions, but significantly it sees these as means to the end of improved justice rather than the end in themselves.

References

ASHFORTH, Adam
2005 *Witchcraft, Violence and Democracy in South Africa.* Chicago: University of Chicago Press.
BANKS III, Philip A.Z.
2006 *Liberia.* Unpublished Draft Study: United States Institute of Peace.
BARBU, Jallah
2009 An *Analysis of the Formal Legal Framework Governing Customary Law in the Republic of Liberia.* Unpublished: United States Institute of Peace.
BELLMAN, Beryl L.
1984 *The Language of Secrecy: Symbols and Metaphors in Poro Ritual.* New Brunswick, NJ: Rutgers University Press.
BENDA-BECKMAN, Keebet von
1984 *The Broken Stairways to Consensus: Village Justice and State Courts in Minangkabau.*Dordrecht: Foris Publications, 1984.
BRINKERHOFF, Derrick
2005 *Governance in Post-Conflict Societies: Rebuilding Fragile States.* London: Routledge.
CIEKAWY, Diane and Peter GESCHIERE
1998 'Containing Witchcraft: Conflicting Scenarios in Postcolonial Africa.' *African Studies Review* 41(3): 1-14.
COMAROFF, Jean, and John COMAROFF (eds.)
1993 *Modernity and its Malcontents: Ritual and Power in Postcolonial Africa.* Chicago: University of Chicago Press.
DOUGLAS, Mary
1970 'Introduction: Thirty Years After Witchcraft, Oracles and Magic.' In Mary Douglas (ed.), *Witchcraft Confessions and Accusations.* London: Tavistock.

ELLIS, Stephen
1999 *The Mask of Anarchy: The Destruction of Liberia and the Religious Dimensions of an African Civil War* (2nd ed.). New York: New York University Press.
EVANS-PRITCHARD, Edward E.
1976 *Witchcraft, Magic and Oracles Among the Azande*. Oxford: Oxford University Press
FANTHORPE, Richard
2001 *Communities and formal/Informal Systems of Justice* (unpublished research report) Commonwealth Community Safety and Security Project, Sierra Leone, UK: DFID.
2007 *Sierra Leone: The Influence of the Secret Societies with Special reference to Female Genital Mutilation*. WRITENET/UNHCR-DIPS Report.
FISIY, Cyprian
1998 'Containing Occult Practices: Witchcraft Trials in Cameroon.' *African Studies Review* 41(3): 143-165.
FISIY, Cyprian, and Peter GESCHIERE
1990 'Judges and Witches, or How is the State to Deal with witchcraft? Examples from Southeastern Cameroon.' *Cahiers d'Études Africaines* 118: 135-156.
GESCHIERE, Peter
1997 *The Modernity of Witchcraft, Politics and the Occult in Postcolonial Africa*. Charlottesville: University Press of Virginia.
GIBBS, James
1962 'Poro Values and Courtroom Procedures in a Kpelle Chiefdom.' *Southwestern Journal of Anthropology* 17: 341-350.
HOFFMAN, Daniel
2011a 'Violence Just in Time: War and Work in Contemporary West Africa.' *Cultural Anthropology* 26(1): 34-57.
2011b *The War Machines: Young Men and Violence in Sierra Leone and Liberia*. Chicago: University of Chicago Press.
HUYSE, Luc and Marc SALTER (eds.)
2008 *Traditional Justice and Reconciliation After Violent Conflict: Learning from African Experiences,* Stockholm: International IDEA (Institute for Democracy and Electoral Assistance).
ICG (INTERNATIONAL CRISIS GROUP)
2006 *Liberia: Resurrecting the Justice System*. International Crisis Group: Africa Report (107).

ILAC (INTERNATIONAL LEGAL ASSISTANCE CONSORTIUM)
2003 *ILAC Report: Liberia*. Stockholm: ILAC.
ISSER, Deborah, Stephen LUBKEMANN and Saah N'TOW
2009 *Looking for Justice: Liberian Experiences and Perceptions of Local Justice Options*. Washington, DC: United States Institute for Peace: Peaceworks (63).
LIBERIA LAW REPORTS
1907 *Gray v. Beverly*. 1 LLR: 500.
LITTLE, Kenneth
1949 'The Role of the Secret Society in Cultural Specialization.' *American Anthropologist* 51 (1): 199-212.
LUBKEMANN, Stephen
2008 *Culture in Chaos: An Anthropology of the Social Condition in War*. Chicago: University of Chicago Press.
LUBKEMANN, Stephen, Deborah ISSER and Philip BANKS
2010 'Justice in a Vacuum: The Unintended Consequences of the Constraint of Customary Justice in Post-Conflict Liberia" in Deborah Isser (ed.), *Customary Justice and the Rule of Law in War-Torn Societies*. Washington DC: United States Institute for Peace Press.
MIDDLETON, John F. and E.H. WINTER (eds.)
1963 *Witchcraft and Sorcery in East Africa*. New York: Praeger.
MORAN, Mary
2006 *Liberia: The Violence of Democracy*. Philadelphia: University of Pennsylvania Press.
OLUKOJU, Ayodeji
2006 *Culture and customs of Liberia*. Westport: Greenwood Press.
PRITCHETT, Lant, Michael WOOLCOCK, and Matt ANDREWS
2010 *Capability Traps? The Mechanisms of Persistent Implementation Failure*, Center for Global Development: Working Paper (234).
PUGH, Michael
2000 *The Regeneration of War-torn Societies*. New York: Palgrave Macmillan
REPUBLIC OF LIBERIA
1869 *Act of the Legislature*.
1948 *Rules and Regulations Governing the Hinterland of Liberia*.
2010 *Record of Proceedings: A National Conference on Enhancing Access to Justice: A Review of the Traditional & Formal Justice Systems in Liberia*.
RICHARDS, Paul
1996 *Fighting for the Rainforest: War, Youth, & Resources in Sierra Leone*. Heinemann: African Issues Series.

SANDEFUR, Justin and Bilal SIDDIQI
2011 *Rights or Remedies? Shopping for Justice in Liberia's Dualistic Legal System.* Pp. 109-126 in Erica Harper (ed.), *Working with Customary Justice Systems: Post-Conflict and Fragile States.* Rome: International Development Law Organization.
SAWYER, Amos
1992 *The Emergence of Autocracy in Liberia.* San Francisco: Institute for Contemporary Studies.
SCHIA, Niels Nagelhus and Benjamin de CARVALHO
2009 '"Nobody Gets Justice Here!" Addressing Sexual and Gender-Based Violence and the Rule of Law in Liberia.' NUPI Working Paper 761.
TRUTH AND RECONCILIATON COMMISSION OF LIBERIA
2010 *Final Report.* Updated December 3, 2009.
UTAS, Mats
2005 'Victimcy, Girlfriending, Soldiering: Tactic Agency in a Young Woman's Social Navigation of the Liberian War Zone.' *Anthropological Quarterly* 78(2): 403-430.
UNITED NATIONS MISSION IN LIBERIA
2011 *Tribal Governors Assessment.* Unpublished: UNMIL.
UNITED NATIONS PEACEBUILDING COMMISSION
2011 *Peacebuilding Commission Priority Plan II (2011 - 2013)*, Zero Draft, 26 January 2011.
WEST, Harry
2005 *Kupilikula: Governance and the Invisible Realm in Mozambique.* Chicago: University of Chicago Press.

THE POLITICS OF CUSTOMARY LAW ASCERTAINMENT IN SOUTH SUDAN[1]

Cherry Leonardi, Deborah Isser,
Leben Moro and Martina Santschi

Introduction

Justice reform practitioners in both conflict-affected and developing countries are increasingly seeking ways to engage customary justice systems in their efforts.[2] This stems from the realization that formal justice systems are often inaccessible, unfamiliar and illegitimate for much of the population, and that the vast majority of dispute resolution occurs in customary forums. The approach taken by justice reform practitioners tends to entail recognition of the 'positive' aspects of customary justice, while seeking to minimize the 'negative' aspects. As these efforts generally occur under mandates that adhere to internationally-defined ideals of rule of law and human rights, this often translates programmatically into

---

[1] The authors would like to thank John Ryle and the Rift Valley Institute, and the various government officials, chiefs and other informants in Wau, Kajokeji and Aweil East who supported and enabled the original research for this paper, as acknowledged in Leonardi et al (2010). Thanks also to the two reviewers for their very helpful suggestions.

[2] In recent years guidance notes on how to engage customary justice systems have been issued and commissioned by the United Kingdom Department for International Development, the United Nations Development Program, the Organization for Economic Cooperation and Development and the International Development Law Organization. A wide range of NGOs and donors have invested in programming involving customary justice. (See Isser 2011, n.d.; Harper 2011).

attempts to preserve the accessibility and effectiveness of customary justice, while 'improving' its ability to meet rule of law notions of certainty, predictability, equality and due process. Moreover, justice reform practitioners - both international and national - tend to have as their goal the strengthening of a unified justice system under the regulation of the state. Thus, approaches to customary law often favour efforts to harmonize it with state law and to establish clear limits and hierarchical relations between the systems. This statist and legalistic emphasis, however, tends to focus on forms over functions and on ideal end states over practical strategies grounded in local realities and experiences. Consequently, efforts to 'fix' customary justice in line with Western notions of rule of law can serve to decrease, rather than increase, litigants' access to justice (Isser n.d.).

These international approaches to justice reform have been articulating with government policies and strategies in South Sudan, particularly since 2005. The 2005 Comprehensive Peace Agreement (CPA) brought to an end over two decades of civil war between the Khartoum-based Government of Sudan (GoS) and the Sudan People's Liberation Movement/Army (SPLM/A). The CPA created the semi-autonomous Government of Southern Sudan (GoSS), and established the right of the South Sudanese people to a popular referendum on self-determination, which would result in a vote for secession and the creation of the Republic of South Sudan in July 2011. Among the priorities of the GoSS during the interim period (2005-10) was the establishment of a justice system independent of the sharia-based system of the North, which would reflect the values and identity of the people of South Sudan. This in turn reflected the longstanding role and development of the SPLM/A's own judicial institutions from an early stage of the war in the 1980s, as well as its equally long - if frequently fraught - working relationship with chiefs, and increasing recognition of the latter's judicial and governmental role from the 1990s (Monyluak Alor Kuol 1997, 2000; Johnson 2003; Rolandsen 2005; Leonardi 2007; Mampilly 2011).

Customary law and chiefs' courts thus formed a key part of GoSS strategy in the interim period for both political and ideological reasons - customary law was asserted as key to the identity of South Sudan - as well as for practical reasons: given the very limited formal system, chiefs' courts in fact were resolving the vast majority of disputes. Policy discussions and interventions increasingly focused on the idea of customary law ascertainment, culminating in a GoSS-UNDP strategy proposal (Hinz 2009) whereby the customary laws of communities (usually defined as ethnic groups) would be identified and recorded in written form by the communities themselves, a process termed 'self-statement'. These statements would then become the basis for the direct application, harmonization, and modification of customary law, toward a unified system meant to comply with modern standards of equality and human rights.

This article analyzes the GoSS-UNDP strategy of customary law ascertainment and argues that it was driven by multiple political agendas more than by the needs of litigants at a local level. It is based on a more extensive report analyzing original field research conducted from November 2009 to January 2010 by a team of consultants for a joint project of the Rift Valley Institute and the United States Institute of Peace, in three locations in Southern Sudan: Aweil East, Wau and Kajokeji (Leonardi et al. 2010). Our point of departure was not ideal end-states, but rather empirical research aimed at understanding and contextualizing current practices and perceptions of justice.

The report describes a local justice system characterised by the amalgamation of multiple forms of law and judicial procedure, not distinct parallel customary and state systems. There was no clear line between formal and informal, state and non-state judicial institutions. Instead, our informants perceived these as part of a single hierarchical system, ranging from the occasional courts of headmen and elders, to the sub-chiefs' and chiefs' courts, and finally to the paralegal judges of sub-county *payam* courts, and the magistrates and judges of the county, state and regional courts. The composite nature of the law and justice provided in the local courts blurred the line between state and non-state. Rather there was a spectrum, from the settlement of minor disputes at the lowest level, largely through mediation and advice, to the handling of major crimes by magistrates and judges. But at all levels it was common for cases to be settled with a mixture of compensation and penalty, for reference to be made to the statutory codes of procedure and penalties, and for little if any distinction to be drawn between civil and criminal cases. As another report by Scheye and Baker (2007) makes clear, the so-called 'customary' courts in South Sudan were by no means 'non-state'.

This article argues that the multiple political agendas driving the goal of ascertainment produced inherent contradictions in the strategy itself. As Moore has long argued, law and justice are after all essentially political (e.g. Moore 1970). But the universalising discourse of international rule of law programming can mask the politics of interventions. And in the case of South Sudan, the politics of justice have intersected with broader debate over decentralisation of government and over ethnic and cultural rights. The article begins then by exploring the multiple motives for ascertainment and their political context, before examining the detailed proposals of the GoSS-UNDP strategy. It goes on to explore objections to these proposals that emerged in the course of the RVI-USIP research, and argues that here again discourse around law and justice at a more local level was also inherently political. Informants assessed the local courts in their wider political context, for example by comparing chiefs' courts favourably with higher judicial and government institutions that they characterised as alien or corrupt. And informants' views reflected their own place in local community politics and social hierarchies; it was often more difficult for the researchers to talk to those without a strong voice in the structures of local society. But this in itself produced another of our objections to the ascertainment strategy, namely that the process of self-statement would privilege certain elite discourses.

The article then explores the question of whether more certain or fixed laws - one of the goals of ascertainment - would strengthen or hinder access to justice for the weak or poor. While a more binding and impartial law might be considered a weapon for the marginalised (F. von Benda-Beckmann et al. 2009), we argue that it is important to start from the current context in South Sudan, where the justice system lacks the capacity to implement or enforce a binding law over powerful interests, even at its highest levels. In this context, our research suggests that the interests of poorer and weaker litigants were served more by the accessibility and flexibility of the law and justice currently provided by chiefs and by some county-level magistrates. The article explores the nature of this 'living law' as it was manifest in actual court cases, and argues that it differs from the normative assertions of customary law, which previous attempts at recording or ascertainment elsewhere have produced. Finally the article uses an example of recent tensions over customary law and justice in Rumbek to illustrate some of the potential pitfalls of trying to introduce greater certainty of judicial outcomes, and to reinforce our arguments for the politicised nature of law.

The Ascertainment Agenda: Motives for Recording Customary Law

The discourses of both the GoSS and its judiciary, and the international agencies working to support justice and legal sector reforms, have contained a number of tensions and contradictions in their focus on ascertaining customary law, which in turn reflect deeper political issues. These consist of tensions between visions of modernity and tradition that have endured in government discourse since the colonial era; tensions between centralising government tendencies and policies of decentralisation; and tensions between nation-building goals and the politics of ethnicity and cultural rights. All of these dichotomies relate to an underlying tension between the centralised state and local autonomy; it was revealing that when the RVI-USIP report was launched in Juba, the debate among the South Sudanese ministers, officials, judges and lawyers focused most intensely on the issue of judicial and legal decentralisation.[3] This section examines how such debates and tensions underlay the motives for the more specific project of ascertainment, producing fundamental contradictions for the strategy itself.

In the course of our research, positive expressions in favour of recording customary law were of two kinds: the desire of government judges to reference a written customary law to speed and strengthen their decisions, and a popular belief in some areas that each ethnic group should record its own set of laws to counterbalance the customary law of bigger or dominant groups. But the real drive to ascertain customary law was coming from the new government's desire to exercise greater control over the provision of local justice. It drew upon a Western state-building model that assumes that the state should be the main provider of justice (Baker and Scheye 2009). A further stated goal of some in GoSS and the judiciary was to 'harmonize' various customary law systems and statutory law, thus promoting 'national unity' (Madol 2009). During the report launch in Juba, a series of high-level GoSS officials recited a number of arguments in favour of recording and ultimately codifying customary law. These included ideological declarations that customary law was at the heart of national identity. Indeed the Interim Constitution of Southern Sudan had established customary law as a source of legislation (GoSS 2005).

The Chief Justice in 2010, John Wuol Makec, was leading arguments for customary law to form the basis of a common law system (Manyang Mayom 2010a), with obvious throwbacks to ideas of the late colonial period discussed by Moore (1992). She analyses a colonial memorandum circulated in Tanganyika in 1957 which contained remarkably similar discourse to that of the GoSS fifty years later. The memorandum praised African justice and likened customary law to the English common law. But it argued that this law needed to be recorded in order to establish 'certainty', and that it needed to be gradually reformed in line with British standards and legal norms: "Like fat rendered in cooking, the product was

[3] First author's notes taken during the RVI-USIP launch of *Local Justice in Southern Sudan* in the Home and Away Hotel, Juba, 22.10.10. See also Mabior Philip (2010).

to be altered even as it was being extracted" (Moore 1992: 22). And as Moore (ibid) argues, "[t]he pivotal notion is that there should be a rule-governed judiciary that dispenses justice uniformly".

In twenty-first century South Sudan, the goals have been almost identical. And these goals have also been produced and supported by international agencies, replacing the colonial 'repugnancy' proviso with universalising human rights criteria. In the process of recording customary law, 'harmful cultural practices' would be written out of it, reflecting a remarkable faith in the capacity of law to effect change.[4]

However, the launch of the RVI-USIP report produced debates which also demonstrated significant changes since the colonial policies of 1957 Tanganyika, and indeed since a more nationalist era of African legal policy. The 1957 memorandum made only passing mention of "local 'tribal' differences in customary law systems" (Moore 1992: 17). In the subsequent decades of African nationalism, tribes were supposed to give way to nations and tradition to modernity. But fifty years later, ethnic difference has been at the heart of political tension and debate in interim-period South Sudan, and has shaped the discussion of customary law ascertainment. It has also provided the main language in which to promote ascertainment at the local level, where some local and provincial political leaders were advocating recording laws in order to promote and protect tribal difference.

The prominence of the politics of ethnicity in debates over law reflects the wider international shift since the 1990s towards ideas of cultural rights and legal pluralism, in which cultural communities have the right to their own laws and legal systems (see Oomen 2005; Comaroff and Comaroff 2009). In South Sudan, defining cultural and legal difference could thus paradoxically be promoted as a means of guaranteeing rights and building the nation. Yet this could have the opposite effect on the ground, contributing to ethnic tensions and even conflicts.

At the core of the emphasis on ethnicity is really a deeper question about local autonomy and the central state. The RVI-USIP report launch event in Juba saw a heated debate between the GoSS vice-president, Dr Riak Machar, and members of

---

[4] For an example of the advocacy of a similar approach to customary law in Somalia, see Gundel (2006: 46-62).

the judiciary and ministry of legal affairs. Dr Riak challenged the latter to fulfil the GoSS commitment to decentralization, and complained that even Southern officials and politicians had been imbued with the long-standing centralizing tendencies and cultures of the Sudanese state (author notes; Mabior Philip 2010). At the heart of the often contradictory discourses around customary law and local justice we thus see fundamental disagreements over models of the state itself, between ethnic or regional federalism and unified, centralized government. Such debates fractured the old Sudanese state since the time of its independence, a legacy that is perhaps being inherited by the new state of South Sudan in its efforts to promote 'unity in diversity'.[5]

The challenge for the ascertainment strategy then was to somehow embrace all of these tensions. Like the various colonial and postcolonial attempts to state customary law in written form, the strategy resorts to a kind of doublespeak or 'double-think' (Moore 1992: 17). On the one hand it justifies ascertainment on the grounds of the need for greater consistency, certainty and predictability of judicial outcomes and the requirement for reform of local justice in line with national and international human rights law (Hinz 2009; Kuyang Logo 2009). Yet at the same time it aims at protecting cultural rights and legal diversity, by recording each 'community's' laws, and it promises to ensure flexibility and change rather than legal ossification. The proponents of ascertainment see no inherent contradiction in these goals, and employ euphemisms such as 'harmonisation' to express what would in effect be a hegemonic project of state legal and judicial control (e.g. SPLM 2004; Aleu Akechak Jok et al. 2004; Jones-Pauly 2006; Human Rights Watch 2009: 37).

On the ground the contradictions and tensions of similar state projects since the colonial era have tended to produce a disparity between policy and practice and sometimes between law and justice. In 2009-10, chiefs and other justice providers were interpreting and selectively employing statutory laws and state legal norms, primarily to authorise their penalties, but most of their procedures and decisions bore little resemblance to the official laws. In this way they were claiming to follow 'the law' but allowing considerable variation in practice. Yet in a sense this

[5] E.g. Jok Madut Jok (2011). The SPLM adopted 'unity in diversity' as part of its 'Vision, Programme and Constitution' in 1998 (Herzog 1998). The claim that diversity could be an asset rather than obstacle to a united Sudan has a long history; see e.g. Beshir (1979); Voll and Voll (1985).

is a product of the long history of government legal discourse, which has simultaneously promoted local culture and universal norms (e.g. Johnson 1986; Leonardi 2005). As we shall see, however, this has been a creative tension for litigants as well as for justice providers; disputants (even if inadvertently) have exploited the fractures of this composite legal and judicial system by employing its multiple, sometimes contradictory, logics and laws to argue their own cases and to engage in judicial forum-shopping (cf. K. von Benda-Beckmann 1981).

The 2009 GoSS-UNDP Strategy

The GoSS-UNDP strategy was drafted by Professor Manfred Hinz, who develops and modifies the demand among some GoSS officials and judges to codify customary law into a more subtle process of 'self-statement'. Hinz (2009) describes three main types of ascertainment: legally binding codification of customary law by statute; restatement (systematic written recording) of customary law,[6] and; 'self-statement' of customary law by 'traditional communities'. He proposes the last strategy for Southern Sudan. The key element in his account, applicable to all types of ascertainment, is the conversion of oral customary law into written form, a process that "contribute[s] to certainty in the application of customary law" (Hinz 2009: 40). "Self-statements come close to codification", he asserts, "codification not by the organs of state, but by organs of the traditional communities themselves ... [who] are also the ones to change their law when necessity arises" (ibid.: 40). It is this capacity to change and amend the law from below that is given as the key reason to favour self-statement over statutory codification. While this is an important acknowledgment of the flexibility and fluidity of customary law, we nevertheless argue that *any* attempt to define and record such laws misunderstands the nature of local justice, and is likely to encounter significant difficulties of implementation. In this section we examine the latter, before turning later in the paper to the more fundamental issue of the nature of law and justice at a local level.

The strategy's emphasis on community-based definitions and potential updating of laws, rather than state definitions or rigid codification, seeks to guarantee the

[6] The term 'restatement' was adopted in 1959 for the long-term project to record African customary law at the School of Oriental and African Studies at the University of London led by Antony Allott.

ownership of customary law by those who have developed and practice it, as well as recognising its changing nature. The actual process proposed for self-statement also considers the aim of preserving nuance, flexibility, and negotiability. However, the subtle but vital distinctions from other kinds of ascertainment lead us to raise some concerns about its implementation, in light of the findings of our research project. The strategy proposes a possible ten-step model, including defining and researching the 'target communities,' designing the ascertainment process with the agreement of these communities, training ascertainment assistants, conducting complementary research alongside the ascertainment exercise, and preparing the resulting publications in the vernacular and English (Hinz 2009: 72). This model would be adapted to the South Sudanese context, but nevertheless would clearly be a huge logistical exercise, raising questions of capacity and time. A particular concern would be whether the large number of ascertainment assistants would be capable of the level of sensitivity and understanding required to assist the recording of laws without influencing the process.

Once the process of self-statement was completed, there are also issues as to how the resulting documents would be used in practice. Observation of the courts suggests that chiefs and court members use any available written documents and legal codes selectively to add authority to their sentences. If written versions of customary law were available, it is highly probable that chiefs and perhaps judges would treat these as codes of law, even if that were not the intention. Written documents have an authority in themselves in South Sudan, making the distinction between code and statement largely irrelevant in practice. The desire of some leading figures in GoSS and the judiciary to formally codify customary law might also contribute to this tendency.[7]

Having said that, most chiefs and many judges currently refer to the penal code only selectively, and usually only to confirm a specific penalty awarded after a more complex discussion and resolution. Whatever written or unwritten rules or laws the chiefs refer to, they do so in flexible, contingent, and inconsistent ways. A recorded or codified customary law system would unlikely be applied rigidly,

[7] This has been the case in Kenya. Although the colonial government in Kenya specifically rejected the project of codification, they undertook a form of restatement. While not intended to be used as a code in a court of law, there is evidence that the written restatements are sometimes used as such even today (Harrington 2010).

particularly in the unsupervised rural courts. It would be absorbed back into local practice, leaving a question as to whether it had advanced the desired government goals of certainty and consistency. In either scenario then, the self-statements are unlikely to be used in ways that would advance the subtle goals of Hinz's strategy, to provide greater consistency without rigidity.

More significantly, Hinz's proposal leaves open the definition of the communities within which ascertainment would be conducted. Both government and international agencies have tended to associate customary law with specific ethnic groups, often assuming ethnicity to be a more rigid and bounded category than scholars have long argued.[8] There have been previous proposals to group tribes together for the purposes of ascertainment along the lines of outdated ethnolinguistic categories, such as that of Nilo-Hamites, a category that neither anthropologists nor linguists—much less the peoples themselves—employ any longer (Aleu Akechak Jok et al. 2004). Even the 'tribe' is a problematic unit to define; according to anthropologists, the Dinka, for instance, are not a single tribe but comprised of several tribal groups with multiple layers of sub-sections (e.g. Mawson 1989). In such segmentary societies it can be particularly difficult to distinguish between ethnic groups and sub-groups of an ethnic group; consequently ascertainment could trigger contestations over categories and contribute to the already heightened politicisation of ethnic units of administration and territory (Rolandsen 2009; Schomerus and Allen 2010). Most importantly, our research indicated considerable commonalities and shared values, norms and laws across the different research areas; the differences in 'customary law' most often cited were differences in the form or amount of compensation (and particularly between cattle and monetary payments) rather than in the definitions of the offence.

Perhaps the most dangerous potential result of ascertainment would therefore be its exacerbation of perceptions of ethnic difference. The GoSS-UNDP strategy does not stipulate that the ascertainment communities should be defined in ethnic terms,

[8] Aleu Akechak Jok et al. (2004:13): 'Each different tribal group in southern Sudan has its own discrete body of customary law... In effect there are fifty separate bodies of customary laws'. See also Jones-Pauly, cited in Santschi (2007: 6). Anthropologists and other scholars have of course long argued that ethnicity is a fluid, permeable and constructed form of identification (since, e.g., Barth 1969) but this scholarly view is frequently at odds with the notions of ethnicity instrumentalised by politicians in South Sudan and elsewhere.

but the language and process of defining customary law have already contributed to ethnically divisive concepts. Moreover, the proposed organization of customary law ascertainment seems likely to encourage the idea further that each ethnic group or category should have its own legal system and defend it against others. This notion was already trickling down to the local level: some people among the Fertit around Wau, for example, believed—and were being told by their judges and politicians—that they needed to protect their own customs in the face of laws said to be derived from Dinka traditions. The ethnicised discussion of law was only exacerbating the sense of division and political manipulation of tribalism in South Sudan. As this suggests, debates around ascertainment were thus shaped by local and regional as well as national politics.

The Local Political Context For Justice And Customary Law

There is a danger in the approaches of international rule of law programming that discussion of law is isolated from its political context, or that law is assumed to have the capacity in itself to alter or ameliorate structures of power. We found that our local informants were often much more aware of or explicit about both the limitations and the politics of law than some of the more ambitious policy-makers in the GoSS or the international organisations. This section examines how our informants contextualised the local justice system in both political and pragmatic realities.

Often people complained about corruption (bribery and deliberate delays), particularly in the courts of government magistrates and judges. They associated this with a general problem of government. A frequent target of criticism was the state police, whose ranks had been filled with former SPLA or militia soldiers; other reports too have identified the police as a major source of human rights abuses (Human Rights Watch 2009; Sebit Lokuji et al. 2009). And at every level from high court judges to elders, justice providers and a range of ordinary people emphasised the limited capacity of the courts to bring soldiers and powerful military or political leaders to justice; the courts frequently faced problems of intimidation and interference. It is important to understand the perspective of people living in this political and security context; criticisms of the courts were moderated by their perceived relative insignificance in comparison to the bigger problems people were experiencing in their post-conflict state. For many of our informants, it was not the details or recording of customary law that mattered, but the lack of judicial capacity to enforce laws of any kind against powerful political and military elites.

As well as this broader context, the courts were also of course situated in local political and social contexts. One of the problems with recent rule of law interventions in South Sudan has been the assumption that law can 'fix' social inequalities and end 'harmful' cultural practices. But when people leave the court they have to survive within surrounding societies, in which good relations with kin, patrons and neighbours have been a vital survival strategy during times of insecurity, displacement, hardship and war. Efforts to end the practice of Levirate marriage (inheritance of a widow by a male relative of her deceased husband), for example, would be welcomed by some women but might remove a vital source of support for others. Legal reform therefore needs to take into account the social and economic context in which litigants are pursuing their cases. Context is vital to court decisions, as one former SPLM lawyer, Dr. Peter Nyot Kok, explained in an interview with Francis Mading Deng about the pre-2005 SPLM judiciary:

> I have a feeling that what will have seemed to have been a shortcoming in research was not necessarily a shortcoming in the practice of the legal profession. I mean, documentation in terms of books, your [Mading Deng's] book and John Wuol Makec's book, were immensely helpful, but there was a lot of room for going out and finding what people were feeling and were living (Mading Deng 2010: 157).

The next section examines in more detail the capacity of the local courts to take into account what people were 'feeling' and 'living' - and indeed the capacity of law in itself to be 'living'. But firstly in the rest of this section, we argue that local justice in South Sudan both reflects social and political hierarchies, and yet also to some extent provides arenas in which to debate and contest such power structures.

There are important questions concerning the reinforcement of inequalities and discrimination in the local courts. Among our informants, there were some complaints at bribery and favouritism in the chiefs' courts, and many more at the general monetary costs of pursuing court cases. As perhaps in any judicial system, these costs might deter the poor from seeking justice. As one man, recently returned to Wau from Khartoum, complained of the town chiefs' court: "When you come to open a case they ask who you are and what you do, and if you have no job or look like a poor person, then you will find long delays, unless you can pay this bribe." His relative, a university lecturer, agreed that "for a poor man, there is no justice nowadays" (Leonardi et al. 2010: 42-3, 39). Poverty and low social status were more often cited as an obstacle to justice than the gender-based discrimination with which many international agencies are most concerned.

The local courts we witnessed clearly took into account the litigants' social standing, their reputation and the witnesses they could muster. It was often apparent that the outcome of a case was predictable in advance to those involved. The importance of social relations and social capital to the outcome of court cases meant that the local justice system was bound to primarily reinforce existing social structures and inequalities. Leading, respected families and clans were more likely to win court cases, while the chiefs were sometimes sneeringly and mockingly dismissive of those they perceived as 'troublemakers' or 'immoral', or who lacked strong ties to the local community.

But this did not preclude the sense of contest in court cases, which were often extremely adversarial in their style, in contrast to the sentimentalised descriptions outsiders sometimes give of customary justice. If young people or women were asked about customary law in other contexts, they often displayed reticence or shyness, claiming not to know the laws, and referring the enquirer to the chiefs and elders, who were seen to know the authoritative versions of customary law. Yet the same youth or women would appear in the court and argue vociferously for their versions of the laws governing property, marriage, or relations with co-wives, relatives, and neighbours. Court cases were a kind of stage on which people performed and orated in ways that many of them would never have done in any other context. Some chiefs' courts had women members, who gained and retained their position by demonstrating skills of logic and speech; female judges were also respected in this role.

The result was that the courts were arenas of intense debate and contestation, and their decisions tended to reflect wider social, economic and political change. There were particularly intense debates, for example, over how to deal with cases of impregnation of schoolgirls, as increasing numbers of girls were entering school; or how to manage relations and duties of cohabiting couples in the towns who had not legalised their marriage with the bridewealth payment, and often lacked any familial support; or whether the wives of long-absent soldiers had the right to remarry, and so on. Law was thus in continual process, and litigants were playing a part in arguing for change or constancy, albeit from varying positions of power and influence. Chiefs and court members of course had a privileged position in these debates, but in practice they were receptive to the individual context and performance of litigants, and to wider audience opinion - and they were subject to vocal criticism and boycotting of their court if they contravened public opinion too much.

Our research in itself reflected some of the inequalities of local societies underlying the justice system - we found it more difficult to access the views of women, or of the teenage thieves or drunk old man who were lashed in the court, or of those dissatisfied with the court decisions. Our positive assessments of local justice inevitably reflected the views of the more vocal justice providers, litigants and wider society. Yet this should also provide a further warning against ascertainment. The GoSS-UNDP strategy emphasizes that the ascertainment process should be representative: it should include 'normal' people, women, and youth in consultations and community meetings. But as Hinz (2009: 79-80) mentions, his own experience in such meetings is that women barely contribute (see also Koech et al. 1999: 41-2). Processes of recording customary law in other times and places invariably have privileged certain informants and elites within local society, whose version of law is then enshrined and perpetuated (Merry 1991; Oomen 2005). The danger then is that the written laws could become a resource for both litigants and court members who wish to assert authoritative definitions of customary law.

At present, the largely oral nature of local law ensures that it remains contestable. If male elders and chiefs dominate the process of recording it—which seems highly probable—the resulting recorded law is likely to represent a conservative version of contested, changing norms, and its application could have an unwelcome or retrogressive effect. Certain elders and chiefs already have a privileged position in the judicial system, but to record their version of law would strengthen their hand against internal challenges from younger people, returnees, or urban or educated people.[9] In theory, according to the GoSS-UNDP strategy, intra-community debates over customary law would be channelled into the process of ascertainment and into regular updating of the recorded laws. But evidence from similar attempts to record and update customary law in other countries suggests that these processes remain likely to be dominated by elders and chiefs; regular updating requires considerable long-term commitment and resources from government or other

[9] This has been the case in both Tanzania and South Africa (Natal and Kwazulu), where codified versions of customary law trumped more progressive practices in court (Harrington 2010).

sources.[10] Our argument is that individual court cases generate greater debate and more vocal participation than the kind of community meeting advocated in the ascertainment strategy.

The extent to which social inequalities can be mitigated by legal reform is a debated one. A recent discussion by F. von Benda-Beckmann et al. (2009) suggests that legal pluralism can reinforce inequality by decreasing the binding power of the law over the more powerful or wealthy; greater flexibility can work against the weaker parties because the strong tend to determine the choice of forum or rules. Previous research in South Sudan revealed some arguments for recording customary law on such grounds - people believed that if the chiefs were bound by written law, their decisions would be fairer, particularly to youth (Leonardi 2009; Leonardi et al. 2005). But on the other hand, F. von Benda-Beckmann et al. (2009: 12) also suggest that weaker parties may be able to manipulate and exploit the contradictions in the rules to pursue 'creative strategies'. Our research for the RVI-USIP report certainly suggested that the flexibilities and multiple norms and rules of the composite local court system provided opportunities for litigants to exploit the gaps and contradictions, and thus sometimes to get around the obstacles of social hierarchy and poverty.

Living Law?

While Hinz's ascertainment strategy aims to change and reform aspects of customary law to better protect individual rights, we argue that - if its vision were fully achieved - it would conversely restrict the extent of change already occurring in and through local judicial arenas. In this section we argue that the notion of recording customary law fundamentally misunderstands the meaning and function of law in local contexts, particularly in terms of its plurality and its capacity to adapt and change, and to transcend ethnic categories.

An expanding body of scholarship has increasingly argued that customary law is not simply a set of rules and sanctions, but a contextually defined process, involving flexibility, negotiation and reinterpretation of a dynamic body of

[10] For example, Tanzania's policy on codification envisioned the need for regular updates, but this was never carried out. Similarly, the Natal codes in South Africa failed to reflect updates in practice (Harrington 2010).

knowledge to reflect what is considered reasonable under the circumstances (e.g. Comaroff and Roberts 1981; Oomen 2005). The research for the RVI-USIP report supported this view. There were common, normative rules evident in and usually across the research areas, primarily concerning rights in property and persons: for example it was everywhere considered an offense for a man to have intercourse with a married woman, or to impregnate an unmarried woman without paying bridewealth for her. But while rules or normative principles in these areas were inscribed into social practice, most of the same rules were also being regularly transgressed in everyday life, as (particularly young) people defied them or as changing contexts required modifications. These rules were not simply applied in the courts as rigid laws. As one study of local law in South Africa puts it, "Rules might be the language in which disputes are argued, but they do not determine their outcome" (Oomen 2005: 210). Indeed language might be taken further as a metaphor for local law: language-speakers habitually follow linguistic rules without necessarily being able to explain or articulate these rules; at the same time they contravene other rules of grammar or pronunciation, and borrow from other languages, so that the vernacular is always changing and never entirely rule-bound.

In South Sudan, local justice providers were accounting for a complex range of factors in deciding the outcomes to cases, which might include the characters and oratorical performance of the litigants and their witnesses, their family's status and reputation, and the wider, changing socioeconomic context, including the effects of war. The rules of marriage and widow inheritance were being questioned in the context of the prolonged absence or death of soldier husbands. Each case was negotiated, argued, and bargained out to come to a conclusion that was by no means predictable on the basis of the bare bones of the case, as a high court judge in Juba explained: "Customary law means procedures as well as laws, like the way that the audience participates in the judgment. It is all about logic and what is reasonable" (Ladu 2007).

The contested nature of customary law is exemplified by the following summary of an SPLM Court of Appeal Case at Rumbek on May 11 2004:

> The appellant in this case had cohabited with a lady for seventeen years, and had five children with her. The lady, however, had previously been married and had one child. Her husband had been killed fighting for the SPLA, but in the Dinka custom of widow inheritance, she was still considered to be married to his

> family, and so her relationship with the appellant constituted adultery. Her first husband's brother had therefore successfully sued for the return of the widow and all her children, in a series of local courts, and eventually the high court in Rumbek. The appeal court judges decided to reverse these judgments in favour of the appellant by formally divorcing the widow from her first husband and granting paternity rights to her second husband for all but the eldest of their children (their first child was still considered to be born out of adultery and hence to belong to the first husband's family). Their recorded justifications were somewhat varied, however. One judge declared that in Dinka custom, if a wife had been left without care for two years or more, her legal husband's family could no longer claim rights over a child she produced with someone else; also, the length of an adulterous relationship validated it in terms of paternity rights. The other judge argued that in Dinka law the first marriage would never be invalidated unless formally divorced (by returning bridewealth), but that in this case the customary law should be set aside in order to consider the best interests of the woman and children. As recorded in the court verdicts, "In any case, Dinka customary law could not have taken into account the impact of the national duty on the family of a soldier who goes to the war-front to fight the enemy." (South Sudan Law Society 2004)

Although these Dinka judges reached the same conclusions, their deliberations—and overturning of a previous decision by another Dinka judge—reveal the differing interpretations of customary law even among judges within what might be considered a single ethnic group. The second judge also assumed that customary law was a fixed body of law that could not accommodate the effects of modern wars. Yet the court system has been a key arena for debating and negotiating the socioeconomic effects of war in recent decades, and customary law has been changing as a result. Cases such as this reached the highest courts specifically because the laws were ambiguous and contingent, requiring the individual circumstances and timing of events to be considered.

That plaintiffs rather than government or police prosecutors nearly always opened cases also meant that the litigants contributed to defining which rules were to be considered relevant to the case (cf. Comaroff and Roberts 1981: 130). For example, if a man opened a case against another man for impregnating his daughter, the rules regarding parental rights over daughters would be invoked—though there would still be considerable room for negotiation as to whether marriage or compensation should be the outcome, and, if the former, what the bridewealth should be. But if a young unmarried woman working in a town independently opened a case against a man for failing to provide for her after impregnating her, she would argue a different set of obligations and responsibilities, though she might also point out the man's failure to marry her legally (i.e. by paying bridewealth).

Our informants expressed a strong belief in the *idea* of 'the law' - 'the law is one' as some put it - as a resource or power to which they might appeal in defence of their rights in property and persons. The law in this sense is both abstract and singular. When people were asked to define laws in the plural, they invariably described penalties. Once a court had ruled on the fault or guilt of a party in a case and determined the desired solution, the chief or judge would probably refer more explicitly to 'laws' to assign a penalty and restitution. The scales of fines or punishments were commonly understood to be set by the government; indeed, the Arabic word widely used for any court penalty is *hukm,* which is closely related to the word for government, *hakuma.*[11] When any of our informants were asked what the laws were, they usually referred to the amounts of these penalties, rather than to the underlying principles and definitions of wrongs. And when local people advocated recording customary law, they tended to mean specifying the amount and form of compensation. To varying degrees, governments have set court penalties and compensation amounts, albeit in consultation with chiefs. For offenses that appear in the penal code, the statutory penalties formed a guide, though they were not always adhered to in practice. Fixed compensation scales tended to have been worked out more on a local or individual basis; one town quarter chief in Wau, for example, produced his own annual 'codes' listing compensation and fines for various types of cases.

The major exception to this - and an important precedent for the current ascertainment strategy - was the set of pan-Dinka laws for the whole Bahr el Ghazal region agreed by chiefs' conferences at Wanh Alel and codified in 1975 and 1984 (the latter led by the current Chief Justice in 2011, John Wuol Makec).

[11] For a historical discussion of the meaning of *hukm* in northern Sudan as 'the ability to punish through a government-recognized court', see Willis (2005).

Most Dinka would say that the government 'made' the Wanh Alel laws, though their enduring use reflects an apparent consensus over the amounts of the penalties and compensation for the most universal offenses: murder (compensation of thirty cows, plus one as a court fine), adultery (seven cows) and impregnation or elopement of an unmarried girl or woman (one pregnant heifer plus a minimum bridewealth of thirty-six cows). But these fixed penalties acted as a minimum bottom line, above which there was often still considerable room for negotiated settlements, particularly of elopement and marriage. A court decision to impose Wanh Alel penalties was often only the beginning of the complex part of the case, in which the court might have to allocate the individual contributions of cattle from specific members of the family, frequently sparking off further internal disputes over debts and obligations. And in practice, Wanh Alel was irrelevant for the great number of complex disputes over cattle and family obligation that came to the courts in its area of application. Only the penalties for murder, adultery, and premarital impregnation and elopement remained in common use, and in the case of the latter, plaintiffs usually preferred the court to push for a marriage rather than enforce the rather small Wanh Alel compensation. The endurance of the Wanh Alel penalties suggests that there was value in having established bottom-line scales of compensation, but this did not remove the need to negotiate the decisions and wider implications in the courts. In the recent economic context, even the basic compensation amounts of Wanh Alel were being criticized as outdated.[12]

Most cases were much more complex disputes, within as well as between families, over debts, obligations, and offenses that might go back generations. To give just one example observed by Leonardi in a Rumbek town chiefs' court in 2006, a case of the elopement of a girl by the defendant evolved into a complex internal dispute among his relatives over their willingness to contribute to his (cattle) bridewealth in order that he might marry the girl concerned and satisfy the plaintiff, her male relative. The defendant's paternal uncles claimed that it was not yet his turn to marry in the proper sibling order and that they did not have enough cattle to pay the bridewealth, particularly as he was also trying to marry another girl from a wealthy family who were demanding high bridewealth. The defendant's sister then spoke up for him, accusing their uncles of mistreatment because their father had

[12] The former governor of Lakes State raised the compensation and fine for homicide from thirty-one to fifty-one cows. Many other people have called for similar amendments as bride wealth has inflated from the 1970s and 1980s.

died:

> What our uncle said is wrong, because their sons had expensive marriages and when it comes to my brother they want to have a lesser marriage. Now is it because of the death of our father? If not, let them marry these two girls for my brother. I and my sisters have been married by rich families whereby each of us brought one hundred cows as bridewealth, and they have consumed it all on their different businesses. So if possible, Court, let these two girls be married for my brother to be equivalent to their sons' marriages.[13]

The court ordered the family to go away and arrange the marriage of at least one of the girls for the defendant. Young men who were in a junior position in their families often used elopement and resulting court cases to assert their right to marry and compel relatives to pay for their marriage outside the normal order. And the vocal participation by female relatives in this case underlines the point that individual court cases provide greater room for contesting gerontocracy and hierarchy than perhaps any other local arena.

As this kind of case reveals, families and communities were continually negotiating and contesting their 'rules', to maintain social relations, and to adjust to personal circumstance and changing contexts. The law against elopement was accepted as an underlying norm, but this law alone could not have satisfied the parties to the case.

While - as noted early in this paper - there was no sharp differentiation drawn by our informants between the courts of chiefs and of government magistrates, it was notable that the latter were more often criticised for relying too heavily on their 'books', rather than looking into the detailed circumstances of the case. It is not clear then that recorded customary laws would necessarily improve litigants' experience of justice, and indeed they might be seen to prevent satisfactory outcomes if applied rigidly; the defendant in the case above would presumably not have been enabled to marry if the court had stuck rigidly to the customary principles of the order of marriage within extended families. One former chief in Central Equatoria in 2005 claimed that the customary laws recorded there in the

[13] Notes on court cases in Rumbek Regional Town Court, 21.11.06.

1990s by Justice Deng Biong Mijak had proved unpopular when he tried to apply them:

> I worked as subchief and acting chief and was not bad. But some regulations were formulated for customary law, exactly defining the penalties. When I carried these out, people said I was a bad judge. So when I became unpopular I had to step down.[14]

The ongoing negotiation and contestation of rules and norms was also apparent in a common reticence in our research areas to take the lead in actually deciding and recording customary law, even among the chiefs themselves:

> We want to sit and make our laws, what is the fine and so on, so that we are one, together. The Dinka have laws but the Fertit do not. But people have been afraid to write them in case people say they made a mistake or something (Town quarter chief, 13.11.09, Wau, in English: Leonardi et al. 2010: 80).

A county judge inadvertently revealed the same reticence to fix compensation or bridewealth in her advocacy of recording customary law:

> It is good to record customary law. For example with the Fertit, in the case of compensation, say for spoiling a girl, you ask them what the amount should be. Amounts like 3,000 Sudanese Pounds have been agreed in the community, but then others say, 'no, it depends on the family sitting'. So the figures vary. But the Dinkas are uniform: seven cows for a married woman; or one pregnant cow for a girl. So it is very easy to settle. We need the Fertit to agree the same; then even a judge sitting alone will be able to apply it. Now we have to call the family members to say what the amount should be. In fact they usually make an agreement among themselves, so the law of contract comes in then (County judge, 25.11.09, Wau, in English: Leonardi et al. 2010: 76-7).

[14] Interview with elders and chiefs, Lasu Payam, Yei County, 2005 conducted by Leonardi as part of the SPLM-UNDP study of traditional authorities (Leonardi et al. 2005).

A number of chiefs and elders also claimed that their courts employed flexibility in sentencing in order to take into account the poverty of their people. This might have been self-propaganda, but there were pragmatic reasons for only demanding amounts that people were actually likely to be able to pay in the immediate future, given the limited capacity of the courts to follow up and enforce their decisions in the longer term. Even one young man praised the flexibility of the chiefs' courts in this regard:

> There are no written laws for the chiefs, only for the judge. It means for example that if there is a case of spoiling a girl, the chief will question the one who did it and ask if he wants to marry the girl. If he wants to marry, the fine will be smaller, to allow him to manage to pay for the marriage. But if he refuses to marry, the fine will be higher. So it is flexible; it is better than if the fine was just written (Young man, returnee, 2009: Leonardi et al. 2010: 76).

In Kajokeji, our research found considerable ongoing disputes over how to handle cases of impregnation of underage schoolgirls; in some of these cases the girls themselves vehemently protested at the punishment of their boyfriends or prohibition of their marriage by magistrates who imposed the statutory law on rape and the age of consent (Leonardi et al. 2010: 60-63).

The extent of contestation, negotiation and adjustment of the laws applied in the courts cannot be captured by legislation or by the written ascertainment of customary law. If the latter is recorded, it will represent idealised normative rules, which will no doubt be added to statutory law books as a means by which to add authority to decisions. But those decisions will continue to be made by chiefs and court members on the basis of individual cases and social context, just as in other local-level justice systems around the world, including lay magistrate courts (see Gordon and Meggitt 1985).

The extent of change going on in the courts was particularly apparent in urban areas of South Sudan. The findings of our research - and that of others - suggest that one of the strengths of the local justice system was its capacity to handle urban and interethnic cases, and thus to mediate among different groups and economic systems (see also Mennen 2007, 2008; Scheye and Baker 2007). Such capacity might be supported by continuing and extending the common existing practice of making court panels representative of their multiethnic jurisdictions, and by encouraging courts to consult chiefs and other expert witnesses in handling cases from ethnic groups with which the court members were less familiar.

Differences among local legal systems in Southern Sudan come down less to the offenses and laws themselves than to the specific amount and form of the compensation required. A 2004 World Vision report listed the basic customary laws and remedies for eight different ethnic groups from across Southern Sudan: The only significant differences were laws on incest, wife inheritance, and forced marriage (Aleu Akechak Jok et al. 2004). Rather than promoting the recording of customary laws by ethnic groups, the RVI-USIP report therefore recommended more opportunities and arenas for discussing legal norms and judicial practices among people of different ethnic groups. Chiefs and several older informants also claimed that regular cross-border meetings and courts in the colonial period had been an important means of building good relations between chiefs of neighbouring areas and of preventing and resolving conflicts across their borders. Forums that enable debate and improve interethnic communication and understanding would seem a more positive focus of support than interventions that encourage the formulation of discrete ethnic customary laws. But the emphasis on ethnicity in the GoSS-UNDP strategy and in much of the wider national discourse around customary law reveals the intensely political nature of law and the situation of the justice system in the wider context of political tribalism. This political context would also be apparent in disputes over customary law in Lakes State in 2010-11.

The Politics of Local Justice: An Example from Rumbek

In 2010, an ongoing debate about customary law erupted in the town of Rumbek, in Lakes State, which reveals some of the potential pitfalls and confusions of producing written laws, as well as the intensely politicised contexts in which legal and judicial reform is playing out. In 2010, the Lakes State Legislative Assembly produced the *Lakes State Customary Law Act*, with the stated purpose of 'Keeping security and peace' (in light of escalating local armed conflicts in the state during the interim period), and 'to provide the penalties which govern criminal acts' and prevent people 'from committing criminal offences'. The Act claimed to have been drafted in accordance with the interim constitutions of both Lakes State and Southern Sudan, and with the CPA, "as part of the effort to establish minimum Lakes state standards and uniform norms in relation to the existing penal laws currently in use in all judicial institutions in southern Sudan" (Government of Lakes State 2010).

The Act immediately demonstrates the composite nature of 'customary law' in South Sudan and the common amalgamation of civil and criminal law. Although it was not produced through anything like the kind of 'self-statement' process proposed by the GoSS-UNDP strategy, it does represent an attempt to make customary law accord with national constitutional law. Its provisions principally cover the perceived causes of conflict that were the primary concern of the Lakes legislators, detailing penalties for community leaders and cattle-keepers who committed actions that had been identified as provocative of conflict, such as moving into other community's grazing territories, allowing domestic animals to stray, performing rituals related to war or singing abusive songs. It also includes sections on adultery, rape and impregnation without marriage. The rape section (31) defines rape as "sexual or carnal intercourse with another person against his or her will or without his/her consent" and prescribes compensation of ten cows (or 10,000 Sudanese Pounds [SDG]) and imprisonment of up to ten years. The impregnation section (33) orders that a man who "rejects or jilts impregnated lady/girl commits an offence of destruction" and should pay three cows and a fine of 1000 SDG (plus seven cows to obtain paternity rights over the child).

In early March 2011, this Act came to wider attention when a series of convictions were reported in the South Sudanese media. The Lakes State High Court President sentenced over fifty young men to ten-year prison terms for 'defilement' of underage girls. The judge himself claimed to simply be enforcing the penal code which defines the age of consent as 18; he explained that the penalty for statutory rape was actually fourteen years and so he was showing leniency by reducing it to ten years (Manyang Mayom 2011). His verdicts led to protests in Rumbek, particularly by organised youth groups in the town, and to reports that the sentences were the result of the *Customary Law Act*. Media reports initially depicted the issue as one of generational conflict between youth and elders, with the latter held responsible for the Act. In December 2010, the chairman of the Rumbek Youth Union had already been cited in a news article as blaming the Act for bringing prostitution and death to society by prescribing ten-year prison sentences for impregnation. He attributed this to Article 33.1, which actually includes nothing about imprisonment. The same article cited a female youth leader who depicted the issue as a generational conflict, claiming that the law "was added by chiefs to try to stop girls falling in love with and marrying young men rather than older men" (Manyang Mayom 2010b).

Another explanation began to emerge, however, when one of the convicts told a reporter that the judge had "misinterpreted the law on Children's Act, Penal Code and Lakes State Customary Law" and had "defied Dinka cultures" by not recognizing that "[i]n our culture, if a girl is on her menstruation we consider her a mature woman" (Manyang Mayom 2011). This argument for a failure to understand Dinka culture became increasingly prominent, leading to the resignation of the judge and his transfer. Discussion by Leonardi with young men in Rumbek in June 2011 also revealed the continuing interpretation of the issue as ethnic rather than generational: the judge was from Kajokeji in Equatoria, and thus was accused of not understanding or respecting Dinka culture. Ironically, our previous research had recorded similar tensions in Kajokeji over the application of the statutory rape law for underage pregnancies by the county judge, who, in a direct inversion of the Rumbek cases, was blamed by the people of Kajokeji for not understanding Kuku culture because he was Dinka (Leonardi et al. 2010: 60-63).

Untangling the actual production of the Act and its perceived relation to the sentencing of young men for statutory rape requires further research. But its reporting indicates the intensely politicized nature and multiple interpretations of customary law that would be the context for any attempt to agree and record it, let alone to harmonise it with statutory law and the bill of rights. It reveals the potential for bitter contestation between generations or between people with different interests at stake in relation to any law. Perhaps most importantly, it reveals the potential for ethnicised interpretations of law and justice and the strengthening belief that even government judges should serve only in their home areas. Attempts to ascertain customary laws are likely to only cement the idea that law is ethnic, exposing the fundamental tensions between cultural rights and universal norms, and ultimately between ethnic or regional federalism and the centralized state.

Conclusion

The strategy for customary law ascertainment in South Sudan was the product of the articulation of longstanding government agendas with recent rule of law promotion efforts by international donors. Rule of law has shifted over the last two decades from a marginal issue to one recognized as a key pillar of development and stability. But, as many commentators have noted, the record of success is paltry (Samuels 2006; Jensen 2006). And the development of a virtual rule of law industry with a proliferation of guidance, prescribed end states and best practice are partly to blame (Isser forthcoming). Those promoting justice reform tend to do so from a fixed template based on idealized norms and institutional structures. Deviance from these ideals is then identified as the problem, and the task becomes to reform the laws and institutions to meet these ideals. In such circumstances, customary law and legal pluralism raise particular anxieties as they challenge the template. However, in the haste to 'get right' the laws and institutions, what gets overlooked is the question of *justice*, and its multiple and contextual meanings. The legalistic approach fails to understand justice as a manifestation of social and economic circumstances and as a dynamic process. It tends to essentialize legal orders into a customary-state dichotomy, or seeks to shoehorn 'living law' into fixed forms, rather than engaging with the more complex, hybrid and fluid system that prevails. This approach can also be used to mask or obscure the political motives and consequences of restructuring the legal order, and of shifting power from local, often semi-autonomous, actors to state institutions.[15]

An alternative approach that takes as its point of departure empirical realities concerning judicial practices, their local political, social and economic contexts, and their often flexible handling of laws has a far better chance of generating policy options that might deliver socially embedded and sustainable results. It helps us identify how well-intentioned policies may backfire and fail to achieve their goals when put into practice. The alternative approach also understands legal systems not as end-states that can be engineered by governments and international agencies, but as the product of internal processes of contestation, competing local interests, changing socio-economic circumstances and corresponding justice demands.

As the Rumbek example demonstrates, law is a political contest at all levels, from legislation to litigation. Attempts by governments and agencies to ensure greater certainty and consistency by defining laws are likely instead to become just one part of a body of resources that litigants and courts draw upon in arguing and settling cases - and a written law may be an asset for one litigant and an obstacle for another. Of course states are unlikely in principle to tolerate the notion of flexibility and living law that we have presented as positive aspects of the local justice system in South Sudan. But nor in the current context can the state extend full control over this system. In the gap between the legalistic ambitions of the state and the realities on the ground, litigants were exploiting any available

[15] See Moore (1973) on the 'semi-autonomous social field'.

resources with which to advance their cases. It is in this gap that people were themselves promoting 'rule of law' and generating change in the courts - and it is in this gap that interventions should be located. Between the ambitious goals of rule of law reform and the political constraints of a post-conflict context, there may be considerable opportunity to work with litigants and public to enhance the resources of information and knowledge that people were seeking to mobilise in their court cases. The *idea* of 'the law' has tremendous power and meaning in South Sudan, and is bound up very closely with the idea of the state. But if the goal of policy is to promote change, reform and participation, then there may be more to be gained from allowing this idea of law to be deployed and debated by individual litigants, than by enabling certain actors to define and restrict its meaning through a recorded ascertainment.

References

ALEU AKECHAK JOK, Robert A. LEITCH and Carrie VANDEWINT

2004 *A Study of Customary Law in Contemporary Southern Sudan.* Monrovia, CA: World Vision International and the SPLM Secretariat of Legal and Constitutional Affairs.

BAKER, Bruce and Eric SCHEYE

2009 'Access to justice in a post-conflict state: donor supported multi-dimensional peacekeeping in Southern Sudan.' *International Peacekeeping* 16/2: 171-185.

BARTH, Fredrik (ed.)

1969 *Ethnic Groups and Boundaries: the social organization of cultural difference*. London: George Allen & Unwin.

BENDA-BECKMANN, Keebet von

1981 'Forum shopping and shopping forums: dispute processing in a Minangkabau village in West Sumatra'. *Journal of Legal Pluralism* 19: 117-159.

BENDA-BECKMANN, Franz von, Keebet von BENDA-BECKMANN and Julia ECKERT

2009 'Rules of law and laws of ruling: law and governance between past and future'. Pp. 1-30 in Franz von Benda-Beckmann, Keebet von Benda-Beckmann and Julia Eckert (eds.), *Rules of Law and Laws of Ruling: on the governance of law*. Farnham: Ashgate.

BESHIR, Mohamed Omer
1979 *Diversity, Regionalism and National Unity*. Research Report no. 54. Uppsala: Nordiska Afrikainstitutet.
COMAROFF, John L. and Jean COMAROFF
2009 'Reflections on the anthropology of law, governance and sovereignty'. Pp. 31-59 in Franz von Benda-Beckmann, Keebet von Benda-Beckmann and Julia Eckert (eds.), *Rules of Law and Laws of Ruling: on the governance of law*. Farnham: Ashgate.
COMAROFF, John L. and Simon ROBERTS
1981 *Rules and processes: the cultural logic of dispute in an African context*. University of Chicago Press.
GoSS (GOVERNMENT OF SOUTHERN SUDAN)
2005 *Interim Constitution of Southern Sudan*. Juba: GoSS.
GORDON, Robert J. and Mervyn J. MEGGITT
1985 *Law and Order in the New Guinea Highlands*. Hanover, NH: University Press of New England.
GOVERNMENT OF LAKES STATE
2010 *Lakes State Customary Law Act 2010*. Rumbek: Government of Lakes State, South Sudan.
GUNDEL, Joakim
2006 *The Predicament of the 'Oday': The role of traditional structures in security, rights, law and development in Somalia*. Nairobi: Danish Refugee Council and Novib/Oxfam.
HARPER, Erica (ed.)
2011 *Working with Customary Justice Systems: Post-conflict and Fragile States*. Rome: International Development Law Organization.
HARRINGTON, Andrew
2010 'Key issues in customary justice: a comparative study'. Research report written for USIP: February. On file with the authors.
HERZOG, Herbert
1998 *Report: Mission on governance to Western Equatoria, Southern Sudan, 27/7 - 22/8/1998*. Liebefeld: Herzog Consult.
HINZ, Manfred
2009 '"To develop the customary laws into the common law of the Sudan..." Customary Law in Southern Sudan: a strategy to strengthen Southern Sudanese customary law as a source of law in an autonomous legal system.' Juba: draft final report for GoSS MoLACD and UNDP.
HUMAN RIGHTS WATCH
2009 *"There is No Protection": Insecurity and Human Rights in Southern*

Sudan. New York.

ISSER, Deborah (ed.)

2011 *Customary Justice and the Rule of Law in War Torn Societies*. Washington D.C.: USIP.

ISSER, Deborah

n.d. 'The problem with problematizing legal pluralism: lessons from the field'. In Brian Z. Tamanaha, Caroline Sage and Michael Woolcock (eds.), *Legal Pluralism and Development: scholars and practitioners in dialogue*. Cambridge: Cambridge University Press (forthcoming 2012)

JENSEN, Eric G.

2006 'The rule of law and judicial reform: the political economy of diverse institutional patterns and reformers' responses'. Pp. 336-81 in Eric G. Jensen and Thomas C. Heller (eds.), *Beyond Common Knowledge: Empirical Approaches to the Rule of Law*. Stanford: Stanford University Press.

JOHNSON, Douglas H.

1986 'Judicial Regulation and Administrative Control: Customary Law and the Nuer, 1898-1954'. *Journal of African History* 27: 59-78.

2003 *The Root Causes of Sudan's Civil Wars*. Oxford: James Currey.

JOK MADUT JOK

2011 'The new nation of South Sudan cannot afford cultural exclusion', *The New Sudan Vision* 7 June.

JONES-PAULY, Christina

2006 'Recommendations of the Workshop on Customary Law, Juba, Southern Sudan, 13-15 November, 2006: a commentary'. On file with the authors.

KOECH, Lazarus, Anne Laure GOINARD and Olaf WILLNAT

1999 'Community participation in the primary health care programme and the new system of governance: West bank, Equatoria Region, New Sudan'. Aktion Afrika Hilfe e.V.

KUYANG LOGO, Harriet

2009 'Legal Pluralism in Southern Sudan': paper presented at the Conference on Customary Justice and Legal Pluralism in Post-conflict and Fragile Societies, hosted by the US Institute of Peace, George Washington University and the World Bank, Washington D.C. Nov 17-18.

LADU, George (Justice)

2007 Interview by Leonardi, High Court, Juba: 8 January.

LEONARDI, Cherry

2005 'Knowing Authority: Colonial Governance and Local Community in Equatoria, Sudan, 1900-56'. PhD thesis: Durham University.

2007 'Violence, sacrifice and chiefship in Central Equatoria, Southern Sudan'. *Africa* 77/4: 535-558.

2009 'La justicia local y el poder de la oficialidad en el Sudán Meridional', *Revista CIDOB Afers Internacionals* 87: 65-93.

LEONARDI, Cherry, DENG BIONG MIJAK, and Eli ACHOL DENG

2005 *Traditional Authorities in Western and Central Equatoria, Southern Sudan*. Juba/Nairobi: UNDP.

LEONARDI, Cherry, Leben Nelson MORO, Martina SANTSCHI and Deborah H. ISSER

2010 *Local Justice in Southern Sudan*. USIP Peaceworks No. 66. Washington D.C.: USIP.

MABIOR PHILIP

2010 'Decentralized justice is lucrative, says Machar'. *The Citizen* 23 October: 1-2.

MADING DENG, Francis

2010 *Customary Law in the Modern World: the crossfire of Sudan's war of identities*. New York: Routledge.

MADOL, Reuben (Justice)

2009 Speech at the Strategy Workshop on Strengthening of Southern Sudanese Customary Law as a Source of Law. Juba: 7 October. Notes on file with the authors.

MAMPILLY, Zachariah C.

2011 *Rebel Rulers: insurgent governance and civilian life during war*. Ithaca NY: Cornell University Press.

MANYANG MAYOM

2010a 'Interview: Avoid taking law in own hands, says S. Sudan chief justice'. *Sudan Tribune* 10 January.

2010b 'Lakes State: Law against impregnating girls "useless" says youth leader', *Sudan Tribune* 12 December.

2011 '50 youths to be charged with defilement in Rumbek', *Gurtong* 8 March.

MAWSON, Andrew N. M.

1989 'The triumph of life: political dispute and religious ceremonial among the Agar Dinka of the Southern Sudan'. PhD thesis: Cambridge.

MENNEN, Tiernan

2007 'Legal pluralism in Southern Sudan: can the rest of Africa show the way?' *Africa Policy Journal* 3: 49-73.

2008 *Adapting Restorative Justice Principles to Reform Customary Courts in Dealing with Gender-Based Violence in Southern Sudan*. DPK Consulting for UNFPA, San Francisco, CA.

MERRY, Sally E.
1991 'Law and colonialism: review essay.' *Law and Society Review* 25/4: 889-922.
MONYLUAK ALOR KUOL
1997 *Administration of justice in the (SPLA/M) liberated areas: court cases in war-torn Southern Sudan*. Oxford: Refugee Studies Programme.
2000 'The Anthropology of Law and Issues of Justice in the Southern Sudan Today'. MPhil thesis: University of Oxford.
MOORE, Sally Falk
1970 'Politics, Procedures, and Norms in Changing Chagga Law.' *Africa* 40/4: 321–344.
1973 'Law and Social Change: the semi-autonomous social field as an appropriate subject of study'. *Law and Society Review* 7/4: 719-746.
1992 'Treating Law as Knowledge: telling colonial officers what to say to Africans about running "their own" native courts'. *Law and Society Review* 26/1: 11-46.
OOMEN, Barbara
2005 *Chiefs in South Africa: law, power and culture in the post-apartheid era*. Oxford: James Currey.
ROLANDSEN, Øystein
2005 *Guerrilla Government: political changes in the Southern Sudan during the 1990s*. Uppsala: Nordiska Afrikainstitutet.
2009 *Land, Security and Peacebuilding in the Southern Sudan*. Oslo: PRIO
SAMUELS, Kirsti
2006 *Rule of law Reform in Post-Conflict Countries: Operational Initiatives and Lessons Learnt*. World Bank Social Development Paper No. 37.
SANTSCHI, Martina
2007 *Report on the Traditional Leaders Conference 9th-13th August 2007, Torit, Eastern Equatoria State*. Swiss Peace.
SCHEYE, Eric and Bruce BAKER
2007 *The Multi-Layered Approach: Supporting Local Justice and Security Systems in southern Sudan*. Draft report for DFID Strategic Development Fund.
SCHOMERUS, Mareike and Tim ALLEN
2010 *Southern Sudan at Odds with Itself: dynamics of conflict and predicaments of peace*. London: Development Studies Institute, LSE.
SEBIT LOKUJI, Alfred, Abraham Sewonet ABATNEH and Chaplain KENYI WANI
2009 *Police Reform in Southern Sudan*. Ottawa: North-South Institute and

Centre for Peace and Development Studies, University of Juba.

SOUTH SUDAN LAW SOCIETY

2004 *New Sudan Law Reports, March-Sept 2004*. Yei (Copy in author's possession).

SPLM (SUDAN PEOPLES' LIBERATION MOVEMENT: SECRETARIAT FOR LEGAL AFFAIRS AND CONSTITUTIONAL DEVELOPMENT, CUSTOMARY LAW STEERING COMMITTEE)

2004 *Report on the First Customary Law Work Plan Workshop*. Nairobi.

VOLL, John Obert and Sarah Potts VOLL

1985 *The Sudan: Unity and diversity in a multicultural state*. London: Croom Helm.

WILLIS, Justin

2005 '*Hukm*. The Creolization of Authority in Condominium Sudan.' *Journal of African History* 46: 29-50.

HYBRID AND 'EVERYDAY' POLITICAL ORDERING: CONSTRUCTING AND CONTESTING LEGITIMACY IN SOMALILAND

Louise Wiuff Moe

Introduction

Consensus is growing, within academia as well as within policy circles, that prevailing western and liberal peace and state building frameworks have not had the desired effects in terms of creating legitimate state institutions, development and peace in post-conflict settings in Africa, and more broadly in the Global South.[1]

[1] The 'liberal peace' refers to the prevailing practise of peace building, which is supported and promoted by the most powerful states, together with leading international organisations, including monetary organisations. The strategies and aims underlying these interventions are justified with reference to liberal-democratic governance ideals, and ideals of market-led economic growth. As noted by MacGinty:

> the concept of the liberal peace is a broad umbrella, as it takes account of the ideology of peacemaking, the socio-cultural norms of peacemaking, the structural factors that enable and constrain it, its principal actors and clients, and its manifestations (MacGinty 2010: 393).

The explanations of the limitations are divided. Yet, a number of scholars and policy observers have pointed to two major, and closely related, problems of the international project of implementing and advancing liberal democratic statehood and peace in Africa. First, the limited engagement of local populations and non-elites with state and peace building projects, and second, the considerable tensions between international fixed standards of state legitimacy and 'good governance', on the one hand, and local experiences and perceptions of what constitutes efficient and legitimate governance on the other hand (Andersen et al. 2007; Bellina et al. 2009; Boege et al. 2009a, 2009b; Brown et al. 2010; Chandler 2005; Debiel and Lambach 2010; Richmond 2010, 2011; Taylor 2009).

Current policy discourse has moved away from previous optimistic democratization scenarios, and instead emphasises 'difference'. A recent OECD report on legitimacy and state 'fragility', for example, notes that "state-society relations in non-Western states, *compared* to Western states, are more likely to be influenced by informal, unwritten rules (rooted in custom and traditional social practice) as *opposed* to formal, written, legal rules" (OECD 2010: 17, emphasis added), and that, "people's ideas about what constitutes legitimate political authority are *fundamentally different* in formal, rule-based Western states and non-Western states" (Ibid.: 3, emphasis added).

By way of solutions, some advocates of liberal state and peace suggest that "more of the same" will eventually have results (Roberts 2011: 410). From this perspective the challenges of post-conflict reconstruction are typically understood through the lens of 'state fragility'. A number of critics, on the other hand, seem to have arrived at the conclusion that liberal state and peace building is fundamentally unsuited, and illegitimate, in post-conflict communities in the Global South (Paris 2010).

The discrepancies between the 'image' (Migdal and Schlichte 2005) of the sovereign liberal-democratic state and the practices and de facto enactments of governance and political community on the ground in many so-called fragile post-conflict settings in the Global South are real enough. Legitimate state monopoly of violence is the exception rather than the norm and the appeal of rights and obligations associated with being a citizen of the state coexists with other, often stronger, ties of loyalty vis-à-vis local non-state groups (civic, ethnic, tribal, customary, religious, neo-patrimonial etc.).

Yet, despite these discrepancies, neither the challenges of political order and peace in Africa, nor the prospects for future developments (and possibilities for facilitating more inclusive governance), are necessarily best examined through invoking notions of sharp polarities or disjunctions between 'liberal/Western' versus 'communal/non western' political order – or, by extension, 'ideal type state' versus 'fragile state'. Rather than radical disjunction, historical developments testify to dense and intricate processes of exchange and shaping, even if far from equal, between Western-style state based practice and order, and forms of political community and ordering rooted in different regions in the Global South.

Post-colonial and post Cold War political ordering in the Global South has been characterized by powerful dynamics of both disintegration and reconfiguration of power and authority (Villalon 1998; Clapham 2000). In different contexts, local and domestic dynamics of ordering, security and conflict management present "real life alternatives" (Andersen et al. 2007: 5) to, or selective re-appropriation of, Western-liberal frameworks of governance and government and prevailing notions of order and disorder. Such reconfigurations can pose obstacles to peace and stability, but they can also be creative and generative.

In recent years a number of scholars have pointed out that the most promising, if contentious, forms of contemporary political ordering and peace building in fact take place exactly in the interstices, contestation and 'hybridization', between state-based and liberal practice, and local customs and 'everyday' life (Mac Ginty 2010; Richmond 2010, 2011; Boege et al. 2009a, 2009b; Brown et al. 2010; Clements et al. 2007; Darby 2009; Debiel and Lambach 2010; Kraushaar and Lambach 2009; Moe 2012; Roberts 2011). As argued by Richmond, analysis of the tensions and accommodations between these different sources of order and authority in the 'everyday' of post conflict settings, may reveal "a range of hitherto little understood local and contextual peace building agencies (...) which renegotiate both the local context and the liberal peace framework, leading to local-liberal hybrid forms of peace" (Richmond 2011:i).

The aim of this article is to examine the potential and limits of such a hybrid approach to advancing peace and political order, taking Somaliland as a case study.[2] The article in particular engages with the largely uncharted issue of how

[2] The analysis of the paper is shaped by my four months of fieldwork in Somaliland in 2008. During the fieldwork I was based at the Academy for Peace and Development (APD), as a visiting scholar. APD is a local action research institute driven by Somalis and based in Somaliland's capital Hargeisa. My colleagues at APD helped me to gain access and arrange interviews, and were of

political legitimacy is constructed or undermined, in the context of post-conflict hybrid political orders.[3]

So far post-colonial scholarship and critiques of liberal state and peace building have demonstrated conceptual appreciation and awareness of hybridity, and of the significance of 'everyday' practices and approaches to peace, but have shown limited empirical application of these concepts (Roberts 2011).[4] This article contributes to an empirical anchoring of the concepts of hybridity and the 'everyday' through the case study of Somaliland, and specifically through the exploration of issues of legitimacy. It also demonstrates how this speaks, more broadly, to the liberal peace critique and post-colonial appeals for new approaches to peace and political order that may succeed better in harnessing domestic legitimacy.

---

great help for my research in terms of discussing ideas and insights. The fieldwork comprised a number of key-informant interviews (individual interviews and focus group discussions), as well as participation observation and exploration of the challenges and achievements of ongoing local initiatives aimed at promoting complementary relations between different structures of governance and authority. Due to security precautions and limited funds the fieldwork was conducted only in the region of Woqooyi Galbeed/Maroodi Jeex, and mostly took place in the capital city of Hargeisa. Somalis from other regions and from the rural areas are therefore not represented in my interview sample. Moreover, the fact that I do not speak Somali was a limitation in the interview situations. As a former British protectorate and given a large diaspora-population many Somalilanders speak English. During interviews Somali colleagues, or friends/acquaintances of the interviewees, provided translation when necessary.

[3] In dominant state and peace building discourse, domestic political legitimacy has largely been seen as secondary to the issue of state capacity or, perhaps more precisely, as something that would automatically follow from state capacities and effectiveness through, for instance provision of services and public goods. This negates the highly political nature of state formation. Issues of legitimacy are directly linked to questions of power and authority, and hence are intrinsically political. Bringing legitimacy to the forefront therefore means to acknowledge the political character of state formation.

[4] The small number of existing empirical analyses of hybridity have, in turn, tended to focus on description of local order, while not engaging with broader post colonial discourses and the liberal peace critiques.

The article first introduces the concepts of hybridity and the 'everyday'. It discusses how these concepts have been applied and developed within post-colonial theory and liberal peace critiques. This provides for the theoretical footing and contextualization of the case study.

Drawing on my fieldwork in Somaliland, the subsequent sections focus on the developments in Somaliland from 1991 to the present. These sections examine how hybrid governance and government arrangements were constructed, and how they developed and transformed in the context of very low international intervention. The article demonstrates how the coupling of state authority, customary leadership and everyday practices of self-securing helped to legitimise and strengthen political order in Somaliland. It also attends to a number of tensions that have occurred as a result of such hybridization between different sources of legitimate authority.

This case study analysis represents legitimacy as an *issue* that entails ongoing contestations and adaptation between different forms of authority, rather than a *status* or a resource of state institutions that can be achieved simply through capacity building and elections (see also Roberts 2011). The concept of hybridity in this context helps to emphasize the significance of political process for crafting and maintaining political order.

Following the analysis of the largely unplanned process of internal hybridization of state authority and customary authority in Somaliland, the article proceeds to discuss how international actors are drawn into dynamics of hybridization.

Through an examination of a specific international-local initiative of peace dialogues and community policing in Somaliland, the article discusses possibilities for deliberately 'facilitating' and building upon hybridity - understood as positive mutual accommodation between different forms of (state and 'non state') legitimate authority and everyday agency – to advance local peace and security provisions, in the context of international intervention.

Hybridity and 'The Everyday'

Hybridity, and the significance of everyday life has long been the topic of anthropological and sociological research, but has only recently started to inform analysis of peace and state building interventions in post conflict settings (DIIS 2010; Mac Ginty 2010).

An emerging body of scholarship on hybridity in the context of peace and state building addresses a number of key issues and lines of critique of the liberal peace, and also provides an outlook on possible new pathways for peace building support. One strand of analysis within this body of scholarship focuses primarily on the internal dynamics of ordering in post-conflict settings, in particular the coexistence and interaction of state institutions and a multiplicity of 'non-state' actors and sources of legitimacy (see in particular Boege et al. 2009a, 2009b; Clements et al. 2007; Kraushaar and Lambach 2009). Another strand directs more attention to how external international donors and agendas interact, contest and merge with local actors and dynamics of ordering (see in particular Richmond 2010, 2011). These two strands of literature on hybridity overlap and supplement each other. They coalesce in a critical rethink of both the nature of post-conflict political orders and the role of international intervention in these contexts (see also Darby 2009; Mac Ginty 2010).

The concept of 'hybrid political orders' has been proposed as part of the critique of the label of 'fragile state' (Clements et al. 2007 - for later elaborations of the concept see Boege et al. 2009a, 2009b; Brown et al. 2010; Kraushaar and Lambach 2009). The concept of 'hybrid political orders' focuses on the nature of political ordering within post-conflict settings. It strives to move beyond definition through negation (non state, failed, illiberal etc) - that is, definitions that point to what is 'lacking'. Instead the concept of 'hybrid political orders' offers a starting point for comprehending the 'existing' - that is, the empirical, formative, processes behind political community within these so-called fragile settings. Boege et al. point out that "hybrid political orders is not an 'ambition'", not a goal to be reached and not a better alternative to the rational legal state model. Rather, they argue, "it is *what is the case* in many so-called fragile states and situations" (Boege et al. 2009c: 88).

In 'hybrid political orders' diverse and competing authority structures, sets of rules, logics of behaviour and claims to power co-exist, overlap, interact and intertwine. They combine elements of introduced western models of governance and elements stemming from local indigenous traditions of governance and politics, with further influences exerted by the forces of globalisation and related societal re-making or fragmentation (for example ethnic, tribal, religious) (Boege et al. 2009b: 24).

Concepts associated with the theme of 'fragility', such as informalization, clientelism, and neopatrimonialism also entail forms of hybridity, in terms of the merging of different spheres and governance logics. Yet, these phenomena are still evaluated against the yardstick of the formal 'ideal type' state. Recent analyses of hybridity in the context of peace and governance building seek to move beyond these juxtapositions so fundamental to political science, and instead make the blending of these spheres the explicit focus.[5] These accounts acknowledge that the coexistence of multiple structures of governance and authorities often imply contradicting logics and clashes. They flag, however, the need to also account for the more constructive features of socio-political arrangements beyond (or in interaction with) the state (Boege et al. 2009a, 2009b; Brown et al. 2010; Richmond 2010, 2011; Clements et al. 2007; Mac Ginty 2010). Mac Ginty argues there is a need for reassessing the negative interpretations of hybridity within International Relations theory (IR) and prevailing policy discourse to also note "the creative energies that hybridity often produces as well as the pacific and enduring results it produces" (Mac Ginty 2010: 407). Similarly, Boege et al. make the case that some structures of non-state power and customary authority can be viewed as "assets and sources of solutions that can be drawn on in order to forge constructive relationships between communities and governments" (Boege et al. 2009a: 20).

Such more encouraging traits of hybridity - and of political processes that allow for plurality - are displayed in the historical developments of political order in Somaliland, and also shape a number of experiences of political community elsewhere in Africa, and other regions in the Global South (see for example Boege 2008; Nyanmjoh 2004; Sawyer 2004).

The responsiveness to communal and indigenous approaches to peace and political community gets further articulated in the concept of the 'everyday' –a concept that has increasingly been taken up in a post-colonial analyses of peace and state building, and specifically in literature on hybridity (Richmond 2010, 2011; Darby 2009; Roberts 2011). The concept of the everyday dates back to Lefebvre (1971) and de Certeau's analyses (1984) of how everyday life is maintained by the numerous socially sanctioned practices and strategies people pursue and generate, in order to manage and secure their existence, and to appropriate social space (see

[5] In doing so, they stand on the shoulders of a number of scholars and concepts which have previously discussed the idea of 'hybridity'. These include for example: Bayart's 'Politics of the Belly' (1989); Homi Bhabha's 'in-between space' (Bhabha 1995) and the argument that hybridity may also reproduce external domination; Migdal's notion of 'State in Society' (Migdal 1998) and Cleaver's concept of 'Institutional Bricolage' (Cleaver 2002).

also Roberts 2011). In contemporary post-conflict settings concrete mechanisms of the everyday include, for example, small-scale patron-client exchanges, subsistence economies, family and kin protection networks, as well as customary law and authority that provide for social order, justice and security. Indeed, in many cases, including Somaliland, customary law and kinship relations, rather than state institutions, are the primary sources of local security and protection. These everyday mechanisms and practices represents what Darby (2009) defines strategies of 'self-securing'. Such practices are typically hidden to, and marginalized by, prevailing peace and state building discourse, which operates with a state based understanding of security. This lack of attention to hybridity (and the negative perceptions of hybridity) and to practices and priorities that derive from 'everyday life' is according to Roberts (2011) and Darby (2009) central to "the lack of local legitimacy that stigmatizes interventions" (Roberts 2011: 410; see also Darby 2009 and Boege et al. 2009a).

While hybridity and the everyday are left out of prevailing international intervention strategies, peace and order as ideas and as practice are, as noted by Mac Ginty (2010: 398), in reality "hybridized from the outset". They are formed through accommodation, cooperation, imposition and resistance in the historical encounters of Western and European rulers with people and communities in the Global South. A central analytical challenge is to dissect the various influences and modalities (local as well as international) that construct hybrid forms of peace, and seek to locate "the sources and direction of power and agency" (Mac Ginty 2010: 407; see also Richmond 2011).

While remaining apprehensive of the enormous power-imbalances shaping the encounters, recent post-colonial scholarship also draws attention to 'sites of resistance' in which "liberal and neoliberal forms of sovereignty and discursive power are mimicked, resisted and ultimately hybridised (...) in everyday contexts" (Richmond forthcoming: 18). Indeed, in conflict and post-conflict settings, including the Somali context, hybridity, resistance, local agency and ability to embark on alternative strategies often entail a significant moderation - or even undermining - of the practice, idea and legitimacy of liberal state and peace building (Richmond 2011). Through this analytical lens -which in particular has been employed in Richmond's liberal peace critique (2010, 2011, forthcoming) - the concept of the 'everyday' transcends description of the 'local' (as distinct territorially bound places) and instead refers to empirical, but not territorially fixed, relational sites of contestation, repulsion, reshaping and accommodation between international, liberal, state-based agendas and local agencies, customs and practices.

The accounts of hybridity and the everyday challenge the binary categories of 'non-Western local order' *versus* 'Western liberal order' that underpin prevailing Western academic and policy discourses. Notions of the 'local', 'informal', 'non-state', 'traditional' and 'communal' are all defined in terms of their difference and separation from the IR notions of 'state', 'formal' procedures, 'liberal rule' and 'liberal citizenship' (Baker 2010). Such understandings of 'difference' may be partly associated with a (commendable) recognition that transplanting liberal and rational-legal political institutions turned out not to work as smoothly as suggested by past optimistic democratization scenarios. Yet at the same time the drawing of strict boundaries between a 'local sphere' and a 'Western-liberal sphere', has also been instrumental in casting the 'local' as an undesirably 'divergent' and 'fragile' sphere, which can and should be managed by the Western-Liberal sphere.

Accounts of how post-colonial re-ordering in Africa – illustrated for example by the case of Somaliland – 'speaks back' to, and in some aspects overlaps and interact with, Western thought and practice may contribute to the reinsertion of Africa and of the 'local' into IR and policy discourses (Smith 2012).

A final observation is to note the revisionist aspirations (i.e. the aspiration to reform prevailing peace and state building support) in the literature on hybrid and 'everyday' peace and political order. While the 'everyday' represents a lens rather than an approach, and while 'hybrid political orders' may not be an 'ambition', the emphasis on the positive aspects of hybridity and plurality, and on the importance of 'everyday' strategies and interactions (as they play out locally, as well as in the 'local-international' encounters) does indicate a more prescriptive or revisionist undercurrent of the accounts discussed here. This is tied in with the post-colonial critique of the "diminution of the local in contemporary peacebuilding" and the "ontological narrowness" of the liberal peace (Roberts 2011: 410). The accounts on hybridity and the everyday, in other words, call for approaches to peace and governance that can better engage with the complexity and emergent nature of political community and political legitimacy, instead of relying on a projected ideal as the yardstick of 'what ought to be'.

Drawing on this conceptual groundwork, the remainder of the article examines the empirical manifestations of hybridity in Somaliland, the issue of legitimacy and political process in this context, and the possibilities for international actors to constructively engage with 'everyday' strategies of self-securing and hybrid conflict management to advance locally supported peace and security arrangements.[6]

Redefining the Pillars of Political Order in Somaliland

The disintegration of the central Somali state was followed by a wave of decentralized reconstruction of governance and government, which resulted in the emergence of sub-national political orders, of which Somaliland has proven particularly stable and peaceful. Somaliland declared independence in 1991, but has not been recognized by any other state or international organisation.[7]

The socio-political environment characterizing the Somaliland context immediately before the collapse of the Somali state in 1991, and in the aftermath of this state collapse, was an environment that necessitated and facilitated heterogeneous processes of bargaining, accommodation and cooperation between a range of different actors (Bradbury 2008; Renders and Terlinden 2010).

During the struggle against Siad Barre in the late 1980s a close cooperation developed between the northern customary leadership of the Isaaq-clan family, the largest clan-family in Somaliland, and the regionally based resistance force, the Somali National Movement (SNM). The SNM did not operate as a distinct guerrilla front, but rather as "an armed expression of the Isaaq people" (Prunier 1994: 62). This embeddedness of the SNM within the Isaaq-communities as well as the lack of any substantial external funding of the movement led it to rely upon customary authorities. The latter proved particularly invaluable as driving forces behind the mobilisation of support for the resistance amongst the northern Isaaq communities in general and amongst the business community and Diaspora in particular. In 1988 a council of customary authorities, a *Guurti,* was established in

[6] The article follows what Darby calls "a more hands on approach to the political in the post-colonial tradition" (Darby 2009: 700). There is a delicate balance between, on the one hand, drawing attention to the potentials and possibilities of international agencies deliberately and constructively engaging with hybridity (as a political process) and with the everyday (see Darby 2009) and, on the other hand, avoiding the risk of (mis)representing hybrid political orders as yet another ready made 'recipe' for implementation of order and peace.

[7] It claims its borders with reference to the territory of the former British Somaliland protectorate

order to make the mobilisation of resistance more effective and coordinated.[8] The nature of the northern 'resistance alliances' that developed, and the coordinating role of the customary authorities in this development, gave them substantial control over the SNM's economic resources and its politics (Jhazbhay 2009; Reno 2003; Bradbury 2008; Prunier 1994). Shortly after the defeat of Barre, Somaliland unilaterally declared independence, and the SNM formed the first Somaliland administration. This new administration was faced with the task of constructing a government from scratch, with very few resources, and minimal external support. Moreover, as noted by a former general in the SNM: "SNM was a liberation movement, not a political party. We had not prepared to make up a government" (Interview, 02.05.08 Hargeisa). In this context the defensive measures employed by local businessmen, traditional leaders and members of the Diaspora during the exploitative rule of Barre, proved important as tools for organizing and strengthening Somaliland's relations with the domestic productive groups and strong holders, as well as with the global economy and Somalis outside Somalia's borders. This strategy of exercising political authority through de-centralized 'space-spanning networks' (Agnew 2005) differ significantly from formulas that privilege clear distinctions between public and private activity and centralized bureaucracy (Reno 2003).

Within the domestic realm it soon became clear that local grievances, if left unaddressed, would have spill-over effects strong enough to undermine the broader project of re-establishing central institutions and governance structures (Bradbury 2008; WSP 2005). Peace and stability thus became the main objective from the early years of self-declared independence. Application of customary conflict resolution mechanisms became the means to reach this objective. On this backdrop the customary authorities in general, and the *Guurti* in particular, remained highly influential. They were now driving forces behind the peace and reconciliation process.

The regional clans, represented by customary authorities gathered in a series of local negotiations across the region. The achievements of these local processes paved the way for a number of huge Somaliland-wide clan conferences where broad peace agreements were reached and where the institutional framework for a new political order was created. The importance of controlling violence and reaching consensus at the local level as a precondition for reaching power-sharing

[8] The concept of Guurti originally refers to the highest political council of titled as well as non-titled elders in pastoral Somali society (Jhazbhay 2009).

agreements at the national level was emphasized by several of my interviewees.[9] By a Somali political analyst it was summed up as follows:

> Every clan had to accept the rebirth of Somaliland, and to accept Somaliland they had to deal with the 'next door' clan, to address all the grievances and to exchange *xeer.*[10] Only then could we start to agree on how to build a state. The local and regional conferences were handling conflicts of certain areas, and these conflicts would otherwise have destabilized the whole situation" (interview, Hargeisa, 17.04.08).

By pursuing a 'thin' government with only a minimum of authority and functions, while prioritizing local processes of reconciliation driven by customary authorities, the process of state formation was not turned into a zero-sum conflict-producing exercise (Bradbury 2008).

A huge clan-conference in the city of Boroma in 1993 was particularly noteworthy in terms of giving institutional substance to Somaliland's political order. The communities of Somaliland largely financed the conference. It lasted for approximately four months and an estimated 2000 people attended, including 150 voting delegates of customary authorities (Bradbury 2008).

The most important outcomes were:

- The adoption of a national charter defining a hybrid system of governance which formally institutionalized the 82-member *Guurti* council of clan elders in the upper house of parliament[11];

---

[9] The term 'national' here refers to Somaliland's de facto (albeit not de jure) statehood.

[10] Xeer is the Somali customary law consisting of unwritten 'social contracts' between the different clans.

[11] At a peace conference in Sheikh in 1992 the Guurti settled a large-scale intra-Isaaq conflict concerning the port of Berbera. This port is an important source of tax revenues. The mediation efforts were led mainly by traditional authorities from the Gadabursi clan, since they were perceived as a neutral third party by the combating Isaaq subclans. The Guurti was at this conference expanded from being mainly Isaaq-based, to incorporating all northern clans. It was this more inclusive

- The nomination of a lower house of parliament, based on clan representation;
- The formulation and adoption of a peace charter, which "elaborated a code of conduct for the people of Somaliland, in accordance with their traditions and Islamic values" (Bradbury 2008: 98). The charter formulated the responsibilities of the elders for settling conflicts and spearheading the demobilisation process. It also required all communities to make an oath to refrain from attacking any other clans. Altogether, the charter thus provided a 'national xeer', aimed at restoring the relationships among the northern clans and also providing the foundation for law and order (Menkhaus 2000; Bradbury 2008).
- The nomination of a new president, Mohamed Haji Ibrahim Egal, and vice-president Daahir Rayaale Kahiin (Menkhaus 2000; WSP 2005; Bradbury 2008).

As Menkhaus notes: "By any standard, this was an impressive accomplishment for a traditional peacemaking mechanism facing entirely new types of political challenges" (Menkhaus 2000: 189).

Institutionalizing a source of locally respected representational authority, the *Guurti*, was a way to redefine and legitimize the pillars of a new political order. It also broke with the form of centralized illegitimate power, which had constituted the state under the rule of Siad Barre. Moreover, whereas Barre had prohibited 'tribalism', the Somaliland system of governance, known as the *beel*-system (clan-based system), which was agreed upon at the Boroma conference, was based on the recognition of kinship as the basic mechanism for organizing social relations. Under the *beel* system both the *Guurti* and the House of Representatives were based on the principle that distribution of political seats should balance the centre with the periphery (Battera 2004) – i.e. secure national representation of all the northern clans.

After a more stable peace was finally established in the late half of the 1990s new political aspirations started to bourgeon. The *beel-system* was taken up to revision. In 1997 a new constitution was drafted, which spelled out the steps for a transition from a clan-based system to a multi-party system (Renders 2006). The proposal of

national Guurti council which was formalized as part of the system of governance at the Boroma national conference opening in January 1993 (Bradbury 2008).

the constitution, to start a transition from the *beel-system* to a restricted multiparty democracy, caused vigorous debate in Somaliland (interview with Somali political analyst, Hargeisa, 17.04.08). The *beel-system* proved both legitimate and viable in the early stages of post-conflict transformation. However, the proponents of discarding the *beel-system* argued that the disadvantages were that the system had an inherent risk of encouraging the pursuit of narrow interests along clan lines and thus was less suitable as a framework for developing more ambitious political programmes. Moreover, the necessity of transition also became linked to the pursuit of international legitimacy in the form of recognition.[12] In 2001 the final draft of the new constitution, which explicated a commitment to multi-party politics as well as to an independent Somaliland, was sent to referendum and endorsed.[13] Accordingly, the political system based on power-sharing along clan-lines was replaced with a system in which the head of state as well as the members of the House of Representatives and of the District Councils are elected through the ballot. Yet, the institution of the *Guurti* remained in place and the seats in this Upper House of Parliament are still distributed on the basis of clan representation. Since the adoption of the constitution Somaliland has completed four rounds of elections: local council elections in 2002, the first presidential election in 2003, parliamentary elections (only for the lower House of Representatives) in 2005 and, after multiple delays (see details next section) presidential election in 2010.

While Somaliland is known, first and foremost, for its relatively successful merging of 'tradition' and 'modern' institutions it is important to stress the

[12] Somaliland was perceived as having a better chance of becoming formally recognized if it adopted a political system based on multi-party politics (Renders 2006).

[13]Borrowing from the Nigerian model the constitution allows for a limited (three, in the case of Somaliland) number of official parties (ICG 2006). Although the constitution was endorsed by a significant majority within Somaliland, the referendum was boycotted in parts of the eastern regions of Sool and Sanaaq. Both Somaliland and Puntland lay claim to these regions, which fall within the territory of the former British Somaliland, but are inhabited primarily by the Harti clan, which is affiliated to Puntland. In the period between 1991 and 1998 Somaliland enjoyed significant support in these areas. However, over time many inhabitants in these regions have come to identify more with Puntland and with the commitment to a unified Somalia (Bradbury 2008).

significance of the *processes behind* this particular hybrid order. The legitimacy gains of the Somaliland political order lie with the processes through which this order emerged from – and became socially validated by – a plurality of existing social forces that represented domestic interests and clashes of interests, rather than from the merging of 'tradition' and 'modern' institutions as such.

This emphasis on process in relation to hybridity is present in for example Mac Ginty's (2010: 407) observations on "the creativity and pacific engagement that is often involved in constructing and maintaining a hybrid peace". This entails, he argues, "continuous processes of conflict management in which different interests and values coalesce, cooperate, conflict, re-coalesce and re-cooperate. Much of this process will be unplanned, and requires individuals and collectives to understand (and, if possible, reach an accommodation) each other's needs".

In line with this, I argue, that in Somaliland, the gradual legitimisation of the new political order was enabled exactly because the process was not 'planned', managed and sequenced by external actors or by a central state (see also Bradbury 2008). Peace and stability were not established because of the revival of state structures. Rather peace and stability were promoted through extensive local engagement and self-organisation, which became a *precondition* for reaching consensus on the pillars of a common political structure. This reveals how the domestic sphere is constitutive for the development of social and political relations, and hence for legitimacy.

This is particularly significant in the Somali context, on the backdrop of developments in the wider region where top-down attempts to 'manage' the domestic sphere and reviving central state institutions has resulted in radical de-legitimisation of external involvement as well as of domestic government representatives.

The integration of customary leadership and government authority was an inventive means of creating bonds between the emerging *de facto* state and a society in which several perceptions of what constitutes legitimate representation and governance co-exist. Yet, as will be indicated in the following section, this integration or hybridity does not per definition *maintain* legitimacy or secure ongoing engagement and participation of local people, which was critical in the formative period of the Somaliland political order.

Current Political Order in Somaliland

The bicameral legislature that alloys the *Guurti*, the clan based upper House of Elders, to the lower elected House of Representatives is the most explicit example of integrating customary principles with government in Somaliland.

On the one hand, this institutional arrangement was a way of tailor-making political order by promoting what Bellina et al. (2009: 21) refer to as "constructive interaction between diverse sources of legitimacy". As noted above, this was initially critical in legitimizing the emerging structure of state. On the other hand, the interaction between customary principles and government has not only adapted the structure of government to better match local expectations. It has also gradually reshaped the role and involvement of the members of the *Guurti*, and called into question their basis of legitimacy, as representatives of local communities.[14] In particular, the *Guurti* members' increasing involvement in shaping national politics has led to accusations that the members are more concerned about upward political loyalties vis-à-vis the executive branch of government than with downward accountability.[15] As noted by a local *aquil*: "It was clear that they were *from* the communities in the beginning. But they lost the link. What they want now is the political position and they have it" (group interview with customary leaders, Hargeisa, 15.04.08).[16]

Such public discontent was greatly accentuated when the *Guurti,* without broad

[14] For an elaborate discussion of how, in the Somali context, the involvement of customary authorities with 'high' politics can profoundly change their role and their basis for legitimacy, see Hoehne (2006).

[15] A number of incidents lend credence to this view: During the mid-90s when fighting between the government and the sub-clans of Idagalle and Haber Yunis broke out, the Guurti-members failed to negotiate. This can be seen as an early sign that their status as paid members of government compromise their legitimacy and make it difficult for them to mediate between the government and the local communities. More recently, in 2006 the term of the Guurti was extended for four years through a presidential decree that was issued without consultation with the House of Representatives (Bradbury 2008). In 2010 legislation was passed which extended both the term of both the Guurti and the House of representatives.

[16] The *Aquils* make up the category of traditional authorities most actively and directly involved in the everyday life of local people (Gundel 2006).

public or political consultation, consecutively extended the term of the previous president, and thus postponed the election date. For a period, the *Guurti* became a tool for the government of former president Rayaale to cling onto power and conduct increasingly centralist politics.[17] The fact that there is no agreed upon principle on how to select the members for the *Guurti* is another trigger for accusations that the incumbent *Guurti* members do not promote legitimate representation at the government level. The *Guurti* members were originally appointed by their clan at the Boroma conference, but as the older members have died their positions have been passed over without broader consultation. Some seats in the house are thus currently held by individuals who have inherited, rather than been appointed to, their position. This has created widespread popular criticism (WSP 2005; group interview with customary leaders, Hargeisa, 15.04.08; group interview with university graduates, Hargeisa, 09.05.08). This criticism indicates that customary authorities in Somaliland cannot, according to popular perceptions, legitimize their execution of power with reference to inheritance or other historical mechanisms of selection.

My interviewees indicated that the *Guurti*, as an institution, still has a significant role to play in maintaining security and stability. Maintaining the *Guurti* is also important for creating a space for party politics, based on majority vote, to develop further in the rest of the political system. It appears that what is being contested is not the legitimacy of the institution of the *Guurti* in itself, that is, as an institution for securing societal consensus. What is rather being contested is the way in which the *Guurti* for a period became part of a centralist power constellation.

These processes of legitimation and de-legitimation, and negotiated hybridity, illustrate the 'fluidity' of hybrid peace, and the dynamic nature of 'traditional' institutions (Mac Ginty 2010, see also Richmond 2011). At the same time these developments also indicate how the ability of customary institutions to connect with, and adapt to, state authority may entail a risk of undermining the former if their representative role vis-à-vis their communities are not actively maintained (see also Buur and Kyed 2007; Hoehne 2006).

---

[17] Dahir Rayaal Kahiin served as President Egal's Vice-President from 1993-2002. When Egal died during a private visit in South Africa in May 2002, Rayaale was in accordance with the constitution, sworn in as Egal's successor (WSP 2005).

Local Developments: Security and Justice

The institutionalization of the elders within the *Guurti* is but one way in which customary leadership is coupled to government in Somaliland. At the local level, especially within the domains of security and justice, the customary system and the Sharia courts are in different ways linked to the institutions and practices of government officials and institutions. While the bulk of everyday criminal cases and disputes are taken care of primarily by the customary system, the police at times assist in undertaking arrests.[18] However the police typically leave the subsequent process of arbitration to the customary authorities. Further, the settlements reached through the customary system are in some cases registered and filed, and thus 'formalized', by the formal judges as well as the police (group interview with customary authorities, Hargeisa, 28.03.08; see also Gundel 2006; Menkhaus 2007). This implies new hybrid forms of 'everyday' power and practices, different from modern bureaucratic authority, but also different from strictly 'traditional' authority.

In larger-scale conflicts the police and the military have a role to play in stopping the immediate fighting, yet the subsequent negotiations and the task of determining a settlement are usually taken care of by the customary authorities (interview with the head of the Burao outpost of Academy for Peace and Development (APD), Hargeisa, 20.03.08).[19] As stated by the head of the Burao outpost of APD: "actors from the government cannot do the negotiations, because they are not neutral" (interview, Hargeisa, 20.03.08).

The sanctions that underlie the customary system are, primarily, those of retaliation and conflict escalation. Government intervention remains a weak deterrent to the continuation of bloodshed. From a security perspective, this is a major reason why 'modern' governance is unable to stand alone (see for example Gundel 2006). Moreover, due to lack of resources the codified laws have not been reformed and developed. They are often ill-suited to address some of the contemporary forms of crimes, disputes and interests (interview with Somali professor in law, Hargeisa, 25.04.08; group interview with customary authorities, Hargeisa, 28.03.08). The non-codified customary system has proven highly

[18] Estimated 80-90 percentages of all crimes and disputes are handled through the customary system in Somaliland (Gundel 2006).

[19] APD is a local Hargeisa-based action research institute.

flexible. This system is together with the Sharia courts, largely perceived as more effective and legitimate than the formal courts (interview with Somali professor in law, Hargeisa, 25.04.08; Gundel 2006).

Even local business people often choose to consult the traditional system rather than the formal court system. It is therefore not only 'traditional' forms of conflict, which give the traditional system relevance.

In disputes about issues on which the traditional authorities lack knowledge, such as for instance business or technological matters, they at times call in people with specialized knowledge to clarify details (Gundel 2006). A local *Aqil* explained:

> The Aqils are in a position to use the resources, skills and knowledge from the communities. It is easy for us to call in a technical consultant, and therefore the traditional system is often effective also in disputes of a modern character. In fact the name 'traditional' gives a wrong impression. It is simply about using the resources and knowledge we have here (Group interview with traditional leaders, Hargeisa, 15.04.08).

These hybrid, locally crafted, security arrangements in Somaliland reveal alternative approaches to govern and to manage relationships with others. They illustrates how 'self-securing "challenges hierarchy, centralization, linearity and separation (borders)" and "unsettles the understanding that security is best handled from 'above'" (Darby 2009: 709).

Yet, while challenging prevailing understandings of security and peace, everyday strategies and practices of self-securing, do not per se stand in direct opposition to state practices and state formation. The creative merging of customary practices and state authority in Somaliland does indeed imply a revision of the concept of sovereignty and state monopoly on the use of force (Menkhaus 2006). However, at the same time it has enhanced *de facto* governance capacity and proven rather effective in keeping a high level of internal security. Provisions of security are, in turn, of critical importance for maintaining Somaliland as a functioning *de facto* state, since security is a precondition for the undertaking of several other activities necessary for the consolidation of political order. For example, the delivery of social services, the promotion of local businesses, and even the holding of elections are activities, which are not possible without basic security. In brief, the provision of security is vital for state legitimacy because it enables the very 'production' of state practices, functions and institutions (Bellina et al. 2009). At the same time, enhancing security is not, as shown, necessarily equal to building strong and fully sovereign state institutions. As argued by Menkhaus (2006), if state building is viewed as a means of enhancing governance rather than an exercise of strengthening state capacity for its own sake, then it is possible that pragmatic forms of 'shared sovereignty' can in fact promote the former by bypassing the latter. This challenges conventional state building approaches "which tend to conflate reviving formal state capacity with promotion of governance" (Menkhaus 2006: 11).

Also evident in Somaliland, however, is that when parallel coexistence of institutions (state and non-state) replaces mutually reinforcing interactions this can result in contradictions between the 'logic' of the state's constitutional and legal framework and the 'logic' of non-state systems of governance. For example, the application of customary law in some cases violates civil liberties and individual rights that are guaranteed in the constitution. This is because within the customary system collective responsibility is given priority over individual rights and in particular over women's and minority rights (Hargeisa, 28.03.08; interview with a staff-member of local human rights NGO, Hargeisa, 21.03.08).[20]

The dynamics of local justice and security thus illustrate that locally driven approaches to governance and security do operate within certain hierarchies and lines of inclusion and exclusion, and it warns against 'romanticising' custom (Richmond 2011) or viewing 'communities' as coherent collectives that represent all 'local' interests equally.

Expectations vis-à-vis the state have increased, and liberal discourses of individual human rights and gender equality have grown stronger within Somaliland. Additionally, the protection of these rights is seen as an important dimension of attaining international legitimacy in the form of recognition. At the same time the customary system continues to fulfil important functions in terms of conflict resolution and security in people's everyday life, both because it has proven highly adaptable and because kinship remains the basic social structure. Moreover, in many rural communities this system is the only system available. Also important to

[20] This is moreover linked to an issue of unequal access to justice between the urban areas, where people may choose between different justice systems, and the rural areas, where traditional authorities and religious leaders are the only actors to address disputes (APD 2002).

note, the customary system has not 'take over' functions from the state but is historically the main source of security and legitimate authority.

Hence, the context is characterized by delicate dynamics of push and pull between principles and practices of custom and tradition, and emerging liberal state institutions and practice. On the one hand, allowing customary authorities to apply the customary law *beyond*, and with no reference to, the constitutional laws can undermine the authority of the state as a protector of rights that are associated with citizenship. On the other hand, in the Somali context, attempting to *enforce* state authority and formal liberal laws upon local institutions, and aiming at replacing 'informal' systems and practices of governance is not only unfeasible due to lack of state enforcement capacities. It could also undermine popular legitimacy of the state. This is because in the Somali context centralized state power has a history of being predatory and unaccountable. Thus, the point is not that one system should 'trump' the other (Clements et al. 2007). Rather, it seems that constructing efficient and legitimate forms of governance will require explicit agreements on 'division of labour' between the different social forces and structures of authority, and developing consensus about procedures that can buttress these agreements. Moreover, and importantly, it will require that local people and communities can participate in and be part of shaping the processes of reaching such agreements.

The following section explores possibilities for international agencies supporting such multi-stakeholder processes, and plural arrangements.

Firstly, however, the section briefly attends to the general environment of international intervention in the Somali context. This provides the background for, secondly, examining alternatives to prevailing practices of intervention.

Local-International Dynamics in the Somali Context

Since 1991 many a high profile, internationally led, reconciliation and state building conference has been commemorated as a diplomatic breakthrough in Somalia, only to fail in the implementation phase. In these processes, state-building templates and standard diplomatic formulas have been "justified on the grounds that traditional Somali assemblies were unwieldy and far too time consuming, often lasting months rather than days or weeks" (Menkhaus 2000: 192). The problems of misconceived international intervention policies that focus narrowly on reviving a central state, and at the same time fail to learn from the successes of de-central community and customary processes of reconstruction, runs through as a recurrent theme in critical analyses of Somalia (see for example Hagmann and Hoehne 2007; Hagmann and Terlinden 2005; Menkhaus 2008; Moe 2012; de Wall 2012).

It has been extensively documented how, during the numerous internationally driven peace and state building conferences and reconstruction efforts, faction leaders and warlords have learned to perfection how to play the diplomatic game of the international community, to in this way gain access to internationally provided resources and 'state building' aid without having an actual interest in creating peace and inclusive government and governance (see for example Menkhaus 2000, 2008; Hagmann and Terlinden 2005; Samatar 2007).

The *dual track* strategy, recently announced by the US Department of State (US State Department 2011), indicates a willingness to move beyond an approach of 'state building' that engages merely with the Somali Transitional Federal Government (TFG) to also provide support to sub-state clan-based actors and semi-autonomous political entities, including Somaliland. Yet, as it stands, the United States launched strategy appears to be mostly driven by a self-serving anti-terror (anti Al Shabaab) incentive, rather than a broader vision of inclusive and representative governance, or security for local communities. Indeed, self-serving politics and double standards are longstanding and endemic not only amongst the Somali political elites but also amongst international actors, especially with regards to counter-terrorism. Menkhaus (2008: 189-90), for example, shows how Ethiopia and the United States, in particular, have publicly supported TFG, while simultaneously and covertly "empowering unaccountable and predatory local security forces" as part of 'counterterrorism' strategies.

In brief, international actors, allegedly in pursuit of state building, are part of a complex process of cooptation, subversion and alliance-making with a variety of local strongmen, elites and self-appointed 'clan representatives'. This generates its own forms of unintended local-international hybridity, which unfortunately seem to contribute more to the marginalization of the general population than to accountable governance and government. Boundaries of who are included and who are excluded in these processes tend to be shaped by geo-political interest, local-international power constellations and uncritical international insistence on establishing/supporting a central government, rather than by any common idea of legitimate political order or vision of how to bring on board the non-elite population and communities in reconstruction and reconciliation efforts. Turning to the specific case of Somaliland, the de facto state's relative stability has encouraged pragmatic inventiveness on the part of the United Nations

Development Program (UNDP), to pursue a development strategy that directly benefits Somaliland's process of state formation. The United Nations sticks to its position of non-recognition but engages with Somaliland by channelling aid and resources to the region by targeting funds for 'North-western Somalia'.

The United Nations launched 'Joint Program on Local Governance' (JPLG) specifically aims at supporting the development of representative and legitimate local governance (United Nations 2011). The support focuses on building technical and administrative capacities of the district councils. Such support is important for further consolidating local governance. Yet the program (along with similar international large scale programmes of governance support) suffers from insufficient participation of the Somaliland communities and their leaders in setting governance priorities, and from lack of attempts to strengthen and maintain linkages between local state institutions and existing traditional community institutions (see Gundel 2008).[21]

While Somaliland is the only region in Somalia that has elected district authorities in most districts, recent local research has shown that a majority of people and communities in Somaliland feel increasingly disconnected from these authorities and institutions, and have limited faith in their accountability (Yusuf and Bradbury 2011).

On this backdrop, and as argued by Gundel (2008: 1), approaches aimed at supporting local governance must reconsider the understanding of 'decentralisation' in the Somali context. There is a need for an engagement with a "*decentral* process of building governance institutions from bottom-up, and not a devolution or deconcentration of power from a government centre".

Previous developments in Somaliland (described in the first sections of this article) do lend credence to these points: they reveal how communities and the customary sphere are critical sites for peace and governance agency; how there is a direct link between peaceful relations on community level and possibilities for wider reconstruction; and; how actively building on plurality and combining customary

[21] This view was confirmed by interviews conducted during my recent, on-going, PhD field research. Interview with Abdullahi Mohammed Odowa, Director of Institute of Peace and Conflict Studies, Hargeisa University, Nov 2011. Interview with Dr. Adan Abokor, Somali political analyst, Oct 2011. Interview with Joakim Gundel, independent consultant and policy analyst, KATUNI, Nov 2011.

and introduced democratic institutions can give rise to new types of viable governance frameworks.

Examples of international programs aiding such processes, and providing support to already existing linkages between different forms of authority, so as to advance locally supported and legitimate governance, are scarce. They do exist, however, and some have been documented. They include for example: the participatory action research project on community peace building and development in Daraweyne (Somaliland), documented in the field guide 'Nabad iyo Caano' (Ford et al. 2002); Action Aid's program for supporting community peace building and the Council of Elders in Sanaag (Yusuf 2007); the peace and justice partnership between Somaliland traditional leaders and the Danish Refugee Council (Moe and Vargas Simojoki 2011).[22]

These initiatives indicate possibilities for 'facilitated hybridity' –i.e. approaches that conscientiously and deliberately facilitates and supports positive interaction and accommodation between different bases of locally legitimate authority and 'everyday' agency, to promote stronger and more inclusive governance.

The remainder of this section discusses the peace and justice project initiated by local traditional leaders from the Toghdeer region in Somaliland, in cooperation with the Danish Refugee Council, an international NGO.

Possibilities for Supporting Positive Hybridity

In 2003 a small group of traditional leaders in the Toghdeer region of Somaliland got together and discussed their concern over increasing insecurity and clan based revenge killings. They decided to approach the Danish Refugee Council (DRC) to ask for support in starting dialogues and experience sharing amongst the traditional leaders from the different regions, and amongst customary actors and security providers from the state (police officers, judges and representatives from the ministries of interior and justice). These traditional leaders were of the opinion that improved cooperation and stronger joint efforts between the different justice and

[22] The publication by Ford et al. (2002) proposes a practical approach to community driven peace and development in the Somali context. It could readily provide concrete guidance and inspiration for international agencies seeking to substantiate their proposed commitments to participatory approaches.

security providers were necessary in order to deal with this increasing insecurity (group interview with customary authorities, Hargeisa, 15.04.08).

Recognizing the significance of the traditional system as the key system for conflict resolution, and its role in the interface of state security and justice provisions and traditional law, the DRC agreed on supporting the initiative.[23] The DRC in addition took the opportunity to bring up the idea that the stake holders participating in the dialogues would not only to attend to issues of security and peace building, but also to the related issues of access to justice -and specifically the issue of co-existence of the three different justice systems (traditional law, state law and Sharia).

An accommodation between local and international priorities thus came to shape the aims and 'direction' of the project.

A few examples of outcomes from these ongoing dialogues are: the establishment of a mechanism to hand over offenders of serious crime - in particular intentional murder and rape - to the state authorities, instead of offering clan protection; commitments on the part of customary authorities to ensure the inclusion of vulnerable groups, such as Internally Displaced People and refugees, into the system of clan protection, and; the establishment of local 'Action Groups' (Somaliland's Traditional Leaders' Declaration 2006; Justiniani 2004; personal communication with customary authorities, Hargeisa, 30.03.08). The latter groups were a follow-up on the work towards augmenting the harmonization of the different legal systems in the three regions of Maroodi Jeex, Togdheer and Sanaag (Somaliland's Traditional Leaders' Declaration 2006; personal communication with customary authorities, Hargeisa, 30.03.08). The Danish Refugee Council's involvement in these projects took the form of facilitation of dialogues and support to the creation of small-scale networks between community actors and leaders and the local state officials. It also included support and funding for the logistics of the dialogue meetings (such as transportation, food, and planning) (DRC 2006a; Justiniani 2004; Personal communication with customary authorities, Hargeisa, 30.03.08). The dialogue and network-oriented approach allowed the Danish Refugee Council to support the flexibility, adaptability and hybridity, which have been key strengths in Somaliland's own pathway to reconstruction and peace.

[23] For an introduction to the underlying strategy of the DRC program supporting the traditional leaders in Somaliland and Puntland, see Joakim Gundel 2006.

A similar type of support was also provided in a number of community-based policing projects in the cities of Burao and Hargeisa, which were born out of the broader dialogue initiative.

These community-policing projects serve as remarkable examples of negotiations between a range of actors. One result has been constructive governance-alliances between government representatives and local communities (DRC 2006b). The projects have also helped enhance security and address the mutual mistrust between citizens and the state police, a mistrust rooted in years of predatory state police during the rule of Siad Barre. The community policing projects were economically assisted by local business people and spearheaded by local customary authorities who 'mediated' relations between the police and the local communities. They helped in reaching agreements of 'joint' patrolling and information sharing and supported the establishment of community policing committees (group interview with customary authorities, Hargeisa, 15.04.08.; DRC 2006b). This way of enhancing security and rule of law illustrates the close relation between the dimensions of capacity and legitimacy. One of the *Aquils* behind the community policing initiative explained to me that local mistrust, and the corresponding non-cooperative attitudes, towards the state police, had significantly reduced the police officers' capacity to guard the safety of the communities. Therefore in order for the police to be of any value for local people "attitudes and perceptions had to change. People had to understand that this police is from and for the communities. It is not a force" (group interview with customary authorities, Hargeisa, 15.04.08).

This particular example indicates that while a state that builds on non-state providers of security and stability may appear weak, institutionally as well as in terms of its enforcement capacities, "this very weakness may become a strength as the State gains legitimacy in the eyes of people because it does not attempt to impose its authority on local institutions" (Boege et al. 2009a: 20).

The example also illustrates 'hybridity' in the interface of local custom and international discourse. It indicates that hybridity can be deliberate, inclusive and responsive to community priorities, as opposed to the dynamics of local-international interactions that prevail in the South (briefly discussed above).

The peace and justice project built on mechanisms that are 'cultural intuitive' (Mac Ginty 2010), yet at the same time it was shaped by international support and input, and liberal notions of human rights and human security. Such hybrid approaches – drawing on multiple sources of ordering and legitimate authority – entails an adaptation and renegotiation of international discourse on security. They offer alternatives to the prevailing state-based (formal, legal, institutional) donor approaches to supporting peace, stability and justice. They do so by facilitating spaces for dialogue, supporting linkages between actors, and by building upon – rather than seeking to overcome – the diversity of socially sanctioned practices, including local people's everyday strategies of self-securing. In this context, liberal and international norms are revealed as facets of the 'everyday' diversity, rather than as universal positions located outside this diversity. This indicates how "'the everyday' may represent an opportunity to refocus peacebuilding in ways that address the lacunae in legitimacy" (Roberts 2011: 414).

Concluding Thoughts

The emergence and manifestation of a hybrid political order in Somaliland defies the modernist position that suggests an 'evolutionary' development from 'tradition' to 'modernity'. It also illustrates that the 'crisis of African statehood' is not merely a matter of a breakdown of old strategies of state control, and subsequent 'fragility' or 'failure' of political order, but also implies re-makings of order, beyond – but not necessarily in direct opposition to – the established Westphalian norm.

As for the issue of political legitimacy, Somaliland challenges the expediency of ideal-types of 'traditional' and 'rational legal/liberal' legitimate authority, as well as the notion of these types as inherently distinct and 'different'. Instead, the Somaliland case of hybridity re-casts these types as sources that contribute to wider processes of legitimisation and de-legitimisation of political order. The case indicates that it is not the quality of any *one* source of legitimacy that in and of itself provides a sustainable basis for political institutions and order, but rather a web of connected sources of legitimacy. Developments in Somaliland moreover illustrates that creating and maintaining such a 'web' requires a high degree of flexibility and pragmatism, not least because local expectations and perceptions of what constitutes legitimate and efficient governance are in flux. This resonates with Mac Ginty's (2010) point that hybridity and hybridization as an on-going, horizontal process that allows for negotiation, accommodation and contestation over diversity (i.e. of norms and beliefs and sources of authority) is worth embracing, as it can offer local acceptance and thus sustainability of peace. "Policy statements by many states and international institutions assert that peace is a 'strategic' goal. Yet, the evidence of the hybrid nature of the peace that prevails in many societies suggests that pragmatism rather than strategy plays a significant role in pacific outcomes" (Mac Ginty 2010:408).

It is noteworthy that the complex processes of negotiating peace and political order in Somaliland were not managed and sequenced by external agencies and agendas, but instead were allowed to emerge from within. This is a reminder that "'What works' sometimes works because of lack of international engagement" (DIIS 2010), or because of the reshaping or selective re-appropriation of prevailing peace building frameworks and introduced colonial models of peace and order. This also testifies to a "tense relationship between 'constructive engagement' with the old order and 'constructive disengagement from it'" (Cornelissen et al. 2012: 14).

Considering the issue of international intervention, the wider Somali context displays how local-international interactions and hybridity can take on complex dynamics in which international agendas are subverted and mimicked, in ways that draws energy and engagement away from common solutions and community priorities.

Yet, as illustrated with the example of peace dialogues and community policing projects, international donors and NGOs can potentially contribute to 'facilitating' constructive hybridity - in terms of supporting contestation and positive mutual accommodation between different socially sanctioned norms and sources of legitimate authority. These alternative NGO discourses may be part of re-focusing the practice and concept of peace support.

A refocus along these lines presents the challenge of creating spaces for working *with*, rather than *on*, clashes of interests and claims to legitimacy. It also entails deliberate engagement with local 'everyday' mechanisms and priorities in post-conflict settings, and explorations of possibilities for connecting complementary practices related to agency, self-determination, participation, security and social support networks. As noted by Richmond: "this everyday is not a benign space, but a tense episteme requiring understanding and translation (not mapping, explaining or essentialising)" (Richmond 2010: 690).

Analysis of such hybrid approaches to peace and political ordering may enable a reinsertion of 'the local' into IR and policy discourses. This would contest the liberal claim to universalism, and its search for state based unity. However, it would not entail a rejection of liberal principles and state practice per se - but rather disclose them as part of a multiplicity of sources of legitimacy within the everyday of political ordering. Notions of hybridity and the everyday aid such move beyond the primacy of *either* 'the local and communitarian' *or* the 'liberal and state based'. Questioning the "apparent naturalness" of this dichotomy, through the analysis of empirical experiences of hybrid and 'everyday' peace, does not erase differences but "shift them away from the zone of timeless oppositions" (Brown 2009: 80) into that of practical political issue.

References

AGNEW, John
2005 'Sovereignty Regimes: Territoriality and State Authority in Contemporary World Politics'. *Annals of the Association of American Geographers* 95(2): 437-461.

ANDERSEN, Louise, Bjørn MØLLER and Finn STEPPUTAT
2007 'Introduction: Security Arrangements in Fragile States'. Pp 3-21 in Louise Andersen, Bjørn Møller and Finn Stepputat (eds.), *Fragile States and Insecure People, Violence, Security and Statehood in the Twenty-First Century*. New York: Palgrave Macmillan.

APD (ACADEMY FOR PEACE AND DEVELOPMENT)
2002 *The Judicial System in Somaliland*. Workshop Report. Hargeisa: APD.

BAKER, Bruce
2010 *Justice and Security Architecture in Africa: The plans, the bricks, the purse and the builder*. Paper presented to Access to Justice and Security: Non-state Actors and the Local Dynamics of Ordering, International Conference, Eigtveds Pakhus and Danish Institute for International Studies, Copenhagen, November 1-3.

BATTERA, Federico
2004 'State- and democracy-building in Sub-Saharan Africa: the case of Somaliland - a comparative perspective'. *Global Jurist Frontiers* 4(1): 1-23.

BAYART, Jean-François
1989 *L'État en Afrique. La politique du ventre*. Paris: Fayard.

BELLINA, Severine, Dominique DARBON, Stein Sundstol ERIKSEN and Ole Jacob SENDING
2009 'The Legitimacy of the State in Fragile Situations'. *Report for the OECD DAC* International Network on Conflict and Fragility.

BHABHA, Homi
1995 'Freedom's Basis in the Indeterminate'. Pp. 47-61 in John Rajchman (ed.), *The Identity in Question*. New York: Routledge.

BOEGE, Volker
2008 'A promising liaison: kastom and state in Bougainville. *Occasional Paper no 12*, The Australian Centre for Peace and Conflict Studies, University of Queensland. http://www.issr.uq.edu.au/acpacs-publications (accessed 03.01.2012).

BOEGE, Volker, M. Anne BROWN, Kevin P. CLEMENTS and Anna NOLAN
2009a 'Hybrid Political Orders, Not Fragile States'. *Peace Review* 21(1): 13-21.
2009b 'On Hybrid Political Orders and Emerging States: What is Failing - States in the Global South or Research and Politics in the West?' In Martina Fisher and Beatrix Schmelzle (eds.), *Building Peace in the Absence of States: Challenging the Discourse on State Failure. Berghof Handbook Dialogue Series, No.8.* http://www.berghof-handbook.net/uploads/download/dialogue8_failingstates_complete.pdf (accessed 14.04.09).
2009c 'Undressing the Emperor: A reply to Our Discussants'. In Martina Fischer and Beatrix Schmelzle (eds.), *Building Peace in the Absence of States: Challenging the Discourse on State Failure. Berghof Handbook Dialogue Series, No.8.* http://www.berghof-handbook.net/uploads/download/dialogue8_failingstates_complete.pdf (accessed 14.04.09).

BRADBURY, Mark
2008 *Becoming Somaliland*. London: Progression.

BROWN, M. Anne
2009 'The pursuit of grounds'. Pp.55-90 in A. Brown (ed.), *Human rights and the borders of suffering*. Manchester: Manchester University Press.

BROWN, M. Anne, Volker BOEGE, Kevin P. CLEMENTS and Anna NOLAN
2010 'Challenging statebuilding as peacebuilding - working with hybrid political orders to build peace'. Pp. 99-116 in Richmond (ed.), *Palgrave Advances in Peacebuilding. Critical developments and approaches*. Basingtoke: Palgrave Macmillan.

BUUR, Lars and Helene Maria KYED
2007 *State recognition and democratization in Sub-Saharan Africa. A New Dawn for Traditional Authorities?* New York: Palgrave Macmillan.

CERTEAU, M. De
1984 *The Practice of Everyday Life*. Translated by Steven Rendall. Berkeley: University of California Press.

CHANDLER, David
2005 'Introduction: Peace without politics?' *International Peacekeeping* 12(3): 307-321.

CLAPHAM, Christopher
2000 'Failed States and Non-States in the Modern International Order'. Paper delivered on *Failed States III: Globalization and the Failed State*, Florence, Italy April 7-10.
CLEAVER, Frances
2002 'Reinventing Institutions: Bricolage and the Social Embeddedness of Natural Resource Management'. *European Journal of Development Research* 14(2): 11-30.
CLEMENTS, Kevin P., Volker BOEGE, M. Anne BROWN, Anna NOLAN and Wendy FOLEY
2007 'State Building Reconsidered: The Role of Hybridity in the Formation of Political Order'. *Political Science* 59(01): 45-56.
CORNELISSEN, Scarlett, Fantu CHERU and Timothy M. SHAW
2012 'Introduction: Africa and International Relations in the 21st Century: Still Challenging Theory?' Pp. 1-21 in Scarlett Cornelissen, Fantu Cheru and Timothy M. Shaw (eds.), *Africa and International Relations in the 21st Century*. New York: Palgrave Macmillan.
DIIS (DANISH INSTITUTE OF INTERNATIONAL STUDIES)
2010 'Justice and Security –when the state isn't the main provider'. *DIIS Policy Brief.* http://www.diis.dk/graphics/Publications/PolicyBriefs2010/PB-Justice-and-Security_web.pdf (accessed 01.02.2011)
(DRC) DANISH REFUGEE COUNCIL
2006 *Report of the Evaluation of Community Based Policing Project (CBP) in Somaliland.* Conducted by M. E. Muragu and Coalition for Peace in Africa (COPA). Hargeisa: DRC
2006a 'National Conference of Traditional Leaders in Somaliland', *Internal Concept Paper*
DARBY, Phillip
2009 'Rolling Back the Frontiers of Empire: Practicing the Postcolonial'. *Internationa Peacekeeping* 16(5): 699-716.
DE WALL, Alex
2012 'Getting Somalia right this time' in *New York Times*, the Opinion Pages, February 21, http://www.nytimes.com/2012/02/22/opinion/getting-somalia-right-this-time.html?pagewanted=all (visited 02. 26.2012)
DEBIEL, Tobias and Daniel LAMBACH
2010 *Global Governance meets Local Politics. On Western State-building and the Resilience of Hybrid Political Orders.* Paper presented at the IPRA 2010 conference (International Peace Research Association) in Sydney, Australia, 6-10 July.

FORD, Richard, Adan ABOKOR and Shukri ABDILLAHI
2002 *Nabad iyo Caano (Peace and Milk). Linking Peace Building and Development in a Decentralized Somaliland.* Worcester: Center for Community Based Development, Clark University.

GUNDEL, Joakim
2006 *The Predicament of 'Oday'.* Report for Danish Refugee Council and Novib / Oxfam (November 2006). Nairobi: Oxfam.
2008 *The District Based Peace Building and Reconciliation Project and The Community Based Peace Support Project*, Review Report for UNDP.

HAGMANN, Tobias and Ulf TERLINDEN
2005 'Faking a Government for Somalia'. *Sub-Saharan Informer* (Editorial and Commentary section), July 29, 2005.

HAGMANN, Tobias and Markus HOEHNE
2007 'Failed state or failed debate? Multiple Somali political orders within and beyond the nation-state'. *Politorbis* 42: 20-27

HOEHNE, Markus
2006 *Traditional Authorities in Northern Somalia: Transformation of positions and powers*. Working Paper no. 82. Halle/Saale: Max Planck Institute for Social Anthropology.

ICG (INTERNATIONAL CRISIS GROUP)
2006 'Somaliland: Time for African Union Leadership'. *Africa Report No.110.* Nairobi/Brussels: ICG.

JHAZBHAY, Iqbal
2009 *Somaliland. An African Struggle for nationhood and international recognition*. Midrand, South Africa: The Institute for Global Dialogue.

JUSTINIANI, Victoria
2004 'Human Rights and Peace Advocacy Impact on Somali Customary Law', *Evaluation Report for the Danish Refugee Council,* Hargeisa

LEFEBVRE, Henri
1971 *Everyday Life in the Modern World*. London, Allen Lane, The Penguin Press.

KRAUSHAAR, Maren and Daniel LAMBACH
2009 'Hybrid Political Orders: the Added Value of a New Concept'. *Occasional Paper*, Australian Center for Peace and Conflict Studies. http://www.issr.uq.edu.au/acpacs-publications (accessed 10.2010).

MAC GINTY, Roger
2010 'Hybrid Peace: The Interaction Between Top-Down and Bottom-Up Peace'. *Security Dialogue* 41(4): 391-412.

MENKHAUS, Ken

2000 'Traditional Conflict Management in Contemporary Somalia'. Pp 183-219 in W. I. Zartman (ed.), *Traditional Cures for Modern Conflict: African Conflict 'Medicine'*. Boulder: Lynne Rienner Publishers.

2006 *Governance in the Hinterlands of Africa's Weak States: Towards a Theory of the Mediated State*. Paper presented at the annual meeting of the American Political Science Association, Philadelphia. August 31.

2007 'Local Security Systems in Somali East Africa'. Pp. 67-99 in L. Andersen, B. Møller, and F. Stepputat (eds.), *Fragile States and Insecure People, Violence, Security and Statehood in the Twenty-First Century*. New York: Palgrave Macmillan.

2008 'Somalia: Governance vs. Statebuilding'. Pp. 187-214 in Charles T. Call and Vanessa Wyeth (eds.), *Building States to Build Peace*. Boulder: Lynne Rienner Publishers.

MIGDAL Joel and Klaus SCHLICHTE

2005 'Rethinking the State'. Pp. 1-41 in Klaus SCHLICHTE (ed.), *The Dynamics of States: the formation and crisis of state domination*. Burlington: Ashgate.

MIGDAL, Joel.

1998 *Strong Societies and Weak States. State-Society Relations and State Capabilities in the Third World*. New Yersey: Princeton university Press

MOE, Louise W.

2012 'Towards New Approaches to Statehood and Governance-Building in Africa: The Somali Crisis Reconsidered'. Pp. 87-106 in Scarlett Cornelissen, Fantu Cheru and Timothy M. Shaw (eds.), *Africa and International Relations in the 21st Century*. New York: Palgrave Macmillan.

MOE, Louise W. and Maria VARGAS SIMOJOKI

2011 'Supporting Access to Justice and Security. Traditional Leaders as Drivers for Change?' Paper prepared for the conference *Reflections on Somaliland Development: Lessons from two Decades of Sustained State Building, Local Institutional Development and Democratization*, Hargeisa November.

NYANMNJOH, Francis B.

2004 'Reconciling the 'rhetoric of rights' with competing notions of personhood and agency in Botswana'. Pp. 33-63 in H. Englund and F.B. Nyamnjoh (eds.), *Rights and the Politics of Recognition in Africa*. New York: Zed Books.

OECD (ORGANISATION FOR ECONOMIC COOPERATION AND DEVELOPMENT)

2010 'The State's Legitimacy in Fragile Situations. Unpacking complexity'. *OECD report*, http://www.oecd.org/dataoecd/45/6/44794487.pdf (accessed 10.2010).

PARIS, Roland

2010 'Saving Liberal Peacebuilding'. *Review of International Studies* 36: 227-365.

PRUNIER, Gerard

1994 'Somaliland: The Birth of a New Country?' Pp. 61-76 in Gurdon (ed.), *The Horn of Africa*. London: UCL Press.

RENDERS, Marlene

2006 *Traditional Leaders and Institutions in the Building of the Muslim Republic of Somaliland*. Ph.D. Thesis. University of Gent.

RENDERS, Marlene and Ulf TERLINDEN

2010 'Negotiating Statehood in a Hybrid Political Order: The Case of Somaliland'. *Development and Change* 41(4): 723-746.

RENO, William

2003 *Somalia and Survival in the Shadow of the Global Economy*. Queen Elizabeth House Working Paper No.100 (February 2003). Chicago: Northwestern University.

RICHMOND, Oliver P.

2010 'Resistance and the Post-liberal Peace'. *Millennium: Journal of International Studies* 38(3): 665-692.

2011 *A Post-Liberal Peace*. London, New York: Routledge

n.d. 'Beyond Local Ownership in the Architecture of International Peacebuilding'. *Ethnopolitics*. (Forthcoming)

ROBERTS, David

2011 'Post-Conflict Peacebuilding, Liberal Irrelevance and the Locus of Legitimacy'. *International Peacekeeping* 18(4): 410-424.

SAMATAR, Ahmed I.

2007 'The Porcupine Dilemma: Governance and Transition in Somalia'. *Bildhaan: An International Journal of Somali Studies* 7(1): 39-90.

SAWYER, Amos

2004 'Social Capital, Survival Strategies, and their Potential for Post-Conflict Governance in Liberia'. *Research Paper 15*, United Nations University, Paper presented at EGDI-WIDER Conference on Unlocking Human Potential - Linking the Informal and Formal Sectors, in Helsinki 17-18 September.

SMITH, Karen
2012 'Africa as an Agent of International Relations Knowledge'. Pp. 21-36 in Scarlett Cornelissen, Fantu Cheru and Timothy M. Shaw (eds.), *Africa and International Relations in the 21st Century*. New York: Palgrave Macmillan.
SOMALILAND TRADITIONAL LEADERS' DECLARATION
2006 Hargeisa, Somaliland.
TAYLOR, Ian.
2009 'What Fit for the Liberal Peace in Africa?' in Richmond, O. and R. Mac Ginty. 2009. The Liberal Peace and Post-War Reconstruction: Myth or Reality?, New York: Routledge.
UNITED NATIONS
2011 *UN Joint Program on Local Governance and Decentralised Service Delivery*. http://jplg.org/ (accessed 12.2011).
US STATE DEPARTMENT
2010 *A dual track approach to Somalia*. Podcast. http://csis.org/event/state-department-dual-track-somalia (accessed 27.05.2011).
VILLALON, Leonardo Alfonso
1998 'The African State at the Twentieth Century: Parameters of the Critical Juncture'. Pp 3-27 in Leonardo Alfonso Villalon and Phillip. A. Huxtable (eds.), *The African State at a Critical Juncture, Between Disintegration and Reconfiguration*. London: Lynne Rienner.
WSP (WAR-TORN SOCIETY PROJECT INTERNATIONAL SOMALI PROGRAMME)
2005 *Rebuilding Somaliland, Issues and Possibilities*. Eritrea: The Red Sea Press Inc.
YUSUF, Haroon
2007 *People Building Peace –The role of civil society in the prevention of armed conflict*. Research paper for Safer World.
YUSUF, Haroon and Mark BRADBURY
2011 'Public Perception of local councils in Somaliland'. Paper prepared for conference on *Reflections on Somaliland Development: Lessons from two Decades of Sustained State Building, Local Institutional Development and Democratization*, Hargeisa November.

SPINNING A CONFLICT MANAGEMENT WEB IN VANUATU: CREATING AND STRENGTHENING LINKS BETWEEN STATE AND NON-STATE LEGAL INSTITUTIONS

Miranda Forsyth

Introduction

Conflict management is done by both state and non-state institutions in Vanuatu, a small archipelago situated in the region known as Melanesia in the South Pacific. Each institution has a range of different resources available to it, for example, customary institutions in general are rich in human resources and legitimacy, while the state justice system has significantly greater financial and coercive resources. However, for a variety of reasons expounded upon below, both state and non-state institutions are failing to satisfactorily meet the conflict management needs of Vanuatu citizens (Forsyth 2009). The term conflict management is used in this article as it is broad enough to include processes which go beyond dealing merely with particular disputes, thus allowing a study "of the relationship of rule orders to behaviour" (Chanock 2000: xviii). The term 'justice' is avoided because it carries with it connotations associated with western 'justice' systems, such as the importance of individual rights, consistency in judgments, a fair and open trial, impartial judges and the right to present a defence. As discussed below, in countries such as Vanuatu, these may not be the priorities of conflict management; rather, concepts such as the re-establishment of peace and harmony in the community and the restoration of relationships are often prioritised. The use of the term 'justice' may mask these fundamental differences in agenda, creating the assumption that all systems are reading from the same page when there might be considerable divergence of opinion in what priorities to be pursued.

In Vanuatu, as in many developing countries, the resources necessary to manage disputes are spread across both state and non-state institutions,, and there is a lack of capacity for any one institution to monopolise these in the near future. Therefore any international donor interested in undertaking reform in this area must actively engage with both state and non-state institutions and actors. This reality of legal pluralism can provoke a number of responses. One is to attempt to harness the resources of the non-state system by bringing it within the apparatus of the state system (see for example Huyse and Salter 2008), and another is to create a new hybridized system that merges state and non-state orders (see for example Walker and Garu 2009, Boege et al. 2008). This article proposes a third approach: to create a conflict management web by building or reinforcing existing linkages between all state and non-state institutions and actors that are currently involved in conflict management (see also Baker 2010: 598). I argue that, regardless of the specific reform objectives involved, adopting an approach that focuses on strengthening linkages between the actors and institutions actually involved in a particular field will result in greater home-grown, legitimate and sustainable change in legally plural countries than an approach based on hybridization or subordination. Although the focus here is on conflict management, the general approach could be more widely applied, for example to other goals such as improving access to justice, compliance with international human rights, or building strong and legitimate institutions. The focus on linkages proposed here is thus in many ways more a philosophy about how to go about doing reform and development in pluralist countries, than a reform program with a particular goal.

The first section of the article briefly outlines the current legal environment in Vanuatu, focussing on the relationship between the state and non-state conflict management providers, and demonstrating the importance of better links between them in building more effective and legitimate conflict management. The second section demonstrates the potential of different sorts of links between the state justice system and customary actors and institutions. It reflects on a number of initiatives that have taken place in Vanuatu in the past five years at both national and local levels, which have been initiated by the state, non-state actors, international donors and academics.

Section three then introduces a new conceptual framework to assist international donors and state and non-state actors in creating such links, and also in developing, managing and aligning reform initiatives. The framework proposed is that of a 'conflict management web' that joins together different actors, institutions, systems and sub-systems through multiple linkages both within and outside a country. Such an approach requires a holistic view (Scott 2001: 332) to be taken of any reform project in this field. This entails prioritising co-ordination with other projects, and making strategic alignment of the reform agenda with the interests and needs of key stakeholders in both state and non-state sectors central to the project design. A conflict management web approach also emphasizes the importance of developing multiple linkages between state and non-state actors, donors and others: if one link breaks there are numerous others to bind the web together, and even if each link is individually weak, together they can be strong (Granovetter 1973, 1983; Braithwaite 2008: 201). Moreover, a conflict management web would support incremental reform projects, useful where there are not the financial resources or political will for large-scale institutional reform (Gupta 2002: 379). The conflict management web approach finds support in the arguments used by Baker (in this issue) to support a 'multi-layered' approach to policing and justice. It develops these ideas by positioning the creation of linkages between conflict management providers in-country and external sources of support (donors, academics, NGOs) at the heart of the analysis about how to improve conflict management. The final section of this article will more fully describe the web framework and discuss its implications for those involved in reform in legally plural countries.

The Vanuatu Legal Environment[1]

Conflict management in Vanuatu is mostly delivered by the state and the customary system of conflict management, referred to in Vanuatu as the *kastom* system.[2] Although the churches also play a role in conflict management, their role has not as yet been the subject of fieldwork, and so only state and *kastom* are

[1] This description is based upon fieldwork conducted in Vanuatu between 2002 and 2008. For a more detailed account see Forsyth (2009).

[2] Although the use of the term 'system' may be criticised in a number of respects including for being misleading because it implies a coherence and structure that the *kastom* system does not have, I have defended the use of the term elsewhere (Forsyth 2009: 95-96). Space does not permit a re-discussion of this point, save to note the concluding reason I gave for using it, namely that the "the *kastom* system is conceived of as such by many involved in its administration." (ibid.)

discussed in this article. The state system of conflict management is based on English and French models, introduced during colonial times (1901-1980), and comprises western-style laws and institutions. As a whole it currently faces a number of challenges, including chronic under-resourcing, slowness, limited geographical reach (particularly problematic given that the population is dispersed over numerous islands, some of which have no police post and many no court), human rights abuses and a lack of legitimacy as a result of being based upon a foreign system (Forsyth 2009: 166). As a result, the state alone is currently unable to provide its citizens with acceptable levels of conflict management, or personal security. For example, the Police Commissioner stated in 2011: "[the] Vanuatu Police Force has a limited budget and can only do a portion of its part in sustaining security in Vanuatu" (Marango 2011: 3).

The *kastom* system, in contrast, exists in one form or another throughout Vanuatu. It handles the vast majority of conflicts in every rural and urban community (Forsyth 2009: 97). The central idea of *kastom* is that the chief or chiefs of a community are responsible for managing disputes within their areas of authority.[3] They do so by holding public meetings with the parties involved in the disputes where the dispute is discussed, responsibility allocated and amends made through the payment of a fine, in the form of mats, kava, food, pigs, cows and increasingly cash, by one or both of the parties.

The *kastom* system throughout the country is incredibly diverse, but it is possible to identify several core principles. These allow ni-Vanuatu to distinguish 'their' system from the state system, even while separating their particular version of *kastom* from that of a different part of the country. For example, the Secretary of the National Council of Chiefs (NCC), in the context of a protest about prison conditions in which the prisoners had fled to the NCC for protection, stated on the radio:

> We made a ceremony and then the Chiefs handed the prisoners over to the other system of governance, that's the police again. So, it was really *from one system to the other and making sure*

[3] Chiefs are the heads of particular communities and gain their positions through a variety of mechanisms including blood line, election and ability (Forsyth 2009: 61). Generally an individual chief will deal with a minor matter and more serious matters or 'appeals' are dealt with by a council of chiefs (ibid.: 99).

> *that both systems, protocols, procedures, are observed in the whole process.* Yesterday, we believe that we observed the two procedures for the two systems and we feel that we are quite satisfied with what we've done yesterday [my emphasis]. (Pacific Beat 2006)

An underlying principle of the *kastom* system as enunciated by the chiefs and as practiced in the vast majority of cases, is that it is restorative. This means that dispute resolution is focused on restoring those relationships that have been broken by the disputes. Two of the main aims of any *kastom* meeting are: *blong mekem [tufala pati] shake han mo kam gudfala fren bakegen* (to make the two parties shake hands and become good friends again), and to allow the defendant to *mekem gud fes* (literally 'clean (the person's) face' so as to regain respect in the community). The purpose of this second aim is to allow the defendant to once again become a functioning member of the community.

However, at times the restorative principles are not followed and the *kastom* system is used as a means of punitive control. An example of this is given by a youth in Port Vila in 2007 who stated:

> I will tell you about a case of a relative of mine. She had "flatem" [had sexual intercourse with] all the men around her and made lots of women very angry with her. The chiefs tried everything they could to stop her – they cut off her hair, and they all whipped her. Then finally they sent her back to the island. She stayed there for ten years and she saw how hard life was there, not like getting paid money for sex, and now she has come back to Vila ten years later a changed woman. Now she stands next to the chiefs to assault the women who have children with no fathers! (Forsyth 2009: 108)

Another central principle of the *kastom* system is that of restoring peace and harmony to the community. At times this principle conflicts with the restorative notions of the *kastom* system; for example victims who may not really be happy with the decision are forced to accept it and "shake hands" for the good of the community. This principle may also conflict with notions of individual rights, as prioritized by the state justice system, because the peace of the community is prioritised over individual justice.

While the *kastom* system resolves the majority of disputes, it also faces significant challenges, largely as a result of Vanuatu's development as a nation state from what was a stateless society, and the pressures of rapid social change over the past decade as a result of globalisation. For example, there has been a shift from a *kastom* based traditional economy, over which chiefs had a great deal of control, to a cash economy; and the population is increasingly mobile, which takes people out of the sphere of influence of their chief. Chiefs regularly complain that people refuse to listen to their orders, to come to meetings or pay the fines levied upon them. In addition, community members challenge the chiefs on the basis that they have no authority under the Constitution; the police prevent chiefs from using force to enforce their orders; and people take disputes to the state system if they are not satisfied with the chiefs' decision, thus undermining their authority. Another difficulty associated with the *kastom* system today is that in many places it discriminates against women and youth, both procedurally by denying them a voice and also substantively, for example by fining a woman more than a man in a case of adultery. There is also a widespread perception that some chiefs are biased, and even more problematically, there is no real way of dealing with biased, unfair, lazy or incompetent chiefs. As a result, many ni-Vanuatu face the dilemma of believing in the *kastom* system and its advantages, but not being able to benefit from it because of the character of their particular chief.

Despite these challenges, the *kastom* system is generally well-supported by the population today, including by women and youth. People appreciate its many benefits, including its essentially restorative nature, its geographic and financial accessibility; its familiarity; its ability to bring about peace and the fact that it is 'their' system.

The relationship between kastom *and the state system*

Since colonisation, ni-Vanuatu have thus been faced with at least two systems of conflict management that they can draw upon, depending upon particular circumstances (such as the accessibility and strength of both in a particular location) as well as personal preferences (such as support for or mistrust in *kastom* chiefs, the state, or the colonial powers, and beliefs about which system will lead to a more advantageous outcome). The legitimate scope of the two systems has never been formalised, instead the unofficial division of jurisdiction has been left to individual institutions and administrators to negotiate. The results of this process have and do vary considerably over time and place (Forsyth 2009: 139-174). Until very recently (as discussed below) there was little active dialogue between the two systems, or interchange of different legal views. This was due in part to the lack of centralisation of the *kastom* system, endemic political instability and the difficulties of communication in Vanuatu generally, and also to the lack of institutional spaces for such dialogue to occur. During the colonial period, District Agents and Assessors were formally charged with liaising between the two systems, and found themselves confronted with particular situations requiring them to reconcile procedural and substantive differences between the two systems (Rodman 1977: 525-537). With independence, such roles disappeared, and with them the opportunity for conflicts between the systems to arise and be articulated on the level of legal principle.

The current linkages between the systems are thus largely informal, dynamic and subject to continuous negotiation. Although this means that the relationship can easily adapt in response to the needs of each particular system and to define its own norms and procedural framework, it leads to unrestricted "forum shopping" (where parties seek to bring their dispute in the forum they believe will give them the most advantageous outcome) and is problematic in many other respects. For example, many complainants who bring their dispute in one system feel (for reasons founded or unfounded) that they could have got a better outcome with the 'other' system, which undermines reconciliation processes and finality of disputes. Also confusion about which disputes should be dealt with by which system means that actors in both systems often try to avoid responsibility for difficult cases, such as those involving domestic violence, by claiming the other system is responsible. Finally, the informal linkages mean that where people refuse to obey chiefly orders by claiming that they will 'appeal' to the state, the chief has no real way to enforce his decision (see Forsyth 2009: 175-197, 254).

An increasing cause of tension is the state's heavy reliance upon the *kastom* system, especially in rural areas, coupled with its reluctance to contribute any resources or recognition in return. The chiefs are becoming tired of being treated as the unpaid and unacknowledged assistants of the state system, and are increasingly vocalising demands for legislative recognition of chiefly powers. In the past, the state system has been able to brush off such demands by trotting out platitudes about the authority and power of the chiefs resting in community respect. However, it is unlikely that this response will be tenable for much longer, especially given the evidence that community respect is partially unravelling for the chiefs.

Thus we can see that both the state justice system and the *kastom* system are vital for ensuring conflicts are managed in an effective and legitimate way in Vanuatu. However, each system is currently facing significant challenges, its operation undermines the other in many respects, and they are largely missing out on the opportunity to be enriched by, and learn from, each other.[4] Recognition of this means that any justice reform initiative should consider building the capacity and legitimacy of state and non-state systems, as supporting one to the exclusion of the other is unlikely to be effective (OECD 2007: 18). One way to do this is to develop linkages between all relevant systems, for the reasons outlined in the introduction to this article. Baker also argues that this:

> offers the opportunity of state oversight according to defined standards and within an affordable national budget, whilst at the same time linking state systems to non-state providers who may well enjoy local ownership, sustainability and effective procedures (Baker 2010: 609).

Investigating how such linkages might be created is the subject of the next section.

Initiatives Linking State and *Kastom* in Vanuatu

In the past five years there have been a number of initiatives that have forged, or attempted to forge, closer links between the state and *kastom* systems, although this has not necessarily been the primary or even articulated goal of the initiative. In the following section I demonstrate the interest in such links by actors in both state and *kastom* systems, and the important role that can be played by donors and academic institutions in facilitating the building of such links. I will also highlight some of the challenges involved in the creation of such links.

[4] For a detailed analysis of the way in which each is undermining the other see Forsyth (2009: 182-196).

Kastom-*generated links*

(a) National legislation

The NCC has become increasingly proactive in the past eight years in seeking to organise the different levels of chiefly councils and to get the state to assist chiefs with enforcing their authority, such as making people pay *kastom* fines. To this end, a *National Council of Chiefs Bill* was drafted, largely by the NCC but with assistance from a law professor, to set out the roles and powers of chiefs. When the Bill reached parliament in 2006 it was debated for two days, and was amended to such an extent that it did not result in any real increased recognition of chiefly powers by the state. The only significant change was to give the NCC the authority to reshape existing island and urban councils of chiefs. To date its efforts to do this have met with mixed success.[5] The Secretary of the NCC commented that the Act as finally enacted by parliament was like a dog that had had all its teeth removed and yet was still expected to go and hunt pigs (Forsyth 2006).

This exercise demonstrates the extremely contentious and politicised nature of discussions over chiefly powers in Vanuatu. It also shows that although state leaders may make general statements about the importance of traditional leaders and *kastom*, when it comes to engaging in any real power sharing then they are reluctant to give any responsibility away, and so this is a process that involves much time and dialogue. Although the highly contested nature of these issues does make it difficult for donors to become engaged, there is a potentially very useful role for them in funding research and workshops to assist in making sure the debates are as informed as possible. It is likely that much more could have been achieved with the Bill if there had been more support for the NCC in preparing and workshopping the legislation with those involved in the state justice system (police, prison officers, prosecutors, judges, Ministry of the Justice officials etc), as well as with interest groups, such as those representing women and youth, before presenting it to parliament.

[5] For example, the Port Vila council of chiefs was dissolved in 2007 amid significant disagreement.

(b) Kastom *Governance Partnership Project.*

The *Kastom* Governance Project was initiated following an informal meeting between the Secretary of the NCC and a member of Australian Centre for Peace and Conflict Studies (ACPACS), and then Australian Development Agency (AusAID) was brought in as a donor in 2005 (ODE 2010: 13). The overall aim of the project is to support *kastom* so as to "support the way of life of Ni-Vanuatu: environmental sustainability, economic prosperity, peace, justice, equity" (ODE 2010: 28). The central activities of the project are research on aspects of the *kastom* governance system by ACPACS and *storians* (workshops) which facilitate dialogue on *kastom* leadership, change, development and conflict resolution between chiefs, community leaders, women and youth representatives, provincial government officials and police. The *storians* also involve creating action plans to put into practice some of the ideas generated at the workshop. A project leader describes these *storians* as being:

> structured contexts for facilitated conversations around questions that community leaders regularly face but rarely have an opportunity to work through together in a reflective context. That is, they are understood as 'difficult conversations' that could lead to innovative action." (Westoby 2010: 15)

Although hampered by delays caused by a variety of internal process problems, the *kastom* governance project offers a number of positive lessons in how external agencies such as a university can assist a non-state system to contribute to conflict management. One positive feature of the initiative is the amount of agency that was given to the chiefs in the design and operation of the project. The project design was based upon "a year of conversation" (Westoby and Brown, 2007: 77-78) during which time, trust and mutual respect was established between ACPACS and the NCC. Since then, the NCC has played an important role in the design of the project. A project developer observed that the project consciously tried to avoid a common mistake in approach to development in the Pacific Islands which involves "teach[ing] them how to 'do' our institutions better" and instead to recognise "communities and customary leaders' efforts to be self-determining - creating spaces that enable people to negotiate ways through the currents of rapid change that enable them to hold what they value" (Westoby 2010: 15, 18). The participatory nature of the project was also enhanced through the training of local facilitators who were gradually given greater and greater responsibility for the implementation of the workshops. The strong sense of ownership of the activities by the NCC, and the facilitator-only role that ACPACS assumed, also mitigated much of the risk of AusAID (and the Australian government) being perceived as interfering in such a highly charged political issue (ODE 2010: 34).

The project also illustrates a number of difficulties in working with a non-state system. First, is the difficulty of determining whom to engage with, a particularly difficult question in a decentralised system. The project dealt with this by working through the NCC. However, this was not entirely satisfactory as it privileged those chiefs who are associated with the national system. It also meant that some important community leaders were not involved, and this led to difficulties in the implementation of the action plans (ODE 2010: 22).[6] Second, it demonstrates that a truly participatory design process requires time to establish trust, to build relationships and to discuss how things will be. Third, the implementation of the action plans was found to be "patchy" (ibid.). This illustrates the difficulty of implementing the many good ideas that occur in the relaxed space of a workshop when there is a return to 'real life' and, perhaps, an encounter with a competing political agenda. In order for this to be successful, there needs to be continual support and follow up, as is apparently planned for the next phase (ibid.: 23).

The final challenge is how to support the human rights of marginalised groups such as women and children, whilst at the same time permitting the participants to determine the direction that the workshops and the action plans take. There is a potential for the project to "strengthen a chiefly system that includes practices detrimental to women" (ibid.). This issue will inevitably arise in every discussion about reforming the *kastom* system because of a widespread belief that traditionally the *kastom* system was strongly patriarchal and authoritarian. It is therefore common for many chiefs today to blame their lack of authority on the greater rights allowed to women and youth, and to try to shore up their authority by increasing controls over them. Although the anthropological record does not support this belief (Tor and Toka 2004), these views are firmly entrenched and have led to considerable friction when NGOs have come into communities with a rights-oriented training and development agenda. Indeed, a workshop organiser observed that: "chiefs often stated in *storians* that many of these 'development' agents were contributing to, and partly causing, conflict within communities" (Westoby 2008: 50). It is therefore clear that adopting a rigid rights based

[6] The ODE (Office of Development effectiveness of AusAID) report does not specify who these community leaders are.

approach will risk alienating participants and undermining any project. This observation is supported by Merry's study of *bulubulu* (traditional forgiveness) in Fiji where she found that a rights discourse backfired in a project intending to stop people using *bulubulu* to avoid prosecution for rape, and led to an increase in *bulubulu* rape cases and the discrediting of human rights and feminist discourses (Merry 2006: 122).

A better approach is to establish a foundation of trust between participants and facilitators to initiate conversations about gender and youth, giving space for all participants to reflect on the issues raised. Braithwaite (2010) similarly talks about the need to "vernacularise" restorative justice discourse into the language of local traditions in a way that shows respect to those traditions. This will at the very least lead to a more nuanced understanding of the issues involved, and the conflicts can be approached "conversationally rather than coercively." For example, at one workshop I attended the chiefs complained that the youth were causing problems in the community. The youth leader responded by saying that they were frustrated that they had no opportunity to play sport, in particular football, because of lack of space due to land disputes. This discussion presented the chiefs with the solution of resolving the land dispute and making a football field. Thus, involving as many female and youth community leaders as possible in the design and implementation of projects, as well as encouraging them to attend as participants, helps to ensure different viewpoints are articulated and creative conversations can be had. The use of local facilitators is also an important way to mediate conflicts in a culturally sensitive manner. This follows Braithwaite's suggestion to train local trainers to have a 'double consciousness' of indigenous ways of thinking about justice and of the global movement for restorative justice (Braithwaite 2010: 2012).

(c) Local level initiatives by chiefs

A number of individual chiefs as well as chiefly councils have made moves to amend their local *kastom* system by incorporating certain features of the state system. The most widespread example of this is the writing down of their *kastom* laws as so-called 'by-laws' (White and Lindstrom 1994: 229). Such by-laws typically set out the various offences that contravene *kastom* laws and provide a penalty in terms of livestock or foodstuffs or woven mats. These by-laws are recorded for a variety of reasons, including that if the laws are written down the people cannot question the chiefs' authority – i.e. it is written "in black and white" - and that if a chief goes to court then he has to be able to justify his decision

(Forsyth 2009: 106). There are many other examples of deliberate borrowing from the state system, including: the keeping of minutes of *kastom* meetings; the creation of village police; and the introduction of the concept of payment of fees to get chiefs to hear cases. In at least one village there are village police who wear a special uniform and work on behalf of the chief to provide security and to take statements from people making complaints. They say they wear the uniform in order to "*mekem spirit blong wok blong mifala strong, igat pawa*" (make our work spirit strong and give power). These borrowings are symptomatic of the widespread open-mindedness and willingness to embrace new ideas that exists among chiefs. This attitude is illustrated by one of the by-laws from a ward council in Penama Province which, roughly translated, states:

> The Council does not agree that women should wear shorts but we understand that they have the right to so she can wear shorts so long as they come down to her knees and she does not wear them in front of her brother or some other relatives or else she will be fined.

These borrowings are also likely to be in response to a desire to co-opt state power and to enforce chiefly authority. Chiefs often state that they want training and assistance to enable them to *leftemap* (lift-up) their system. This positive attitude towards change could be capitalised on by international donors in developing a project that seeks to support chiefs in learning about, and adapting and adopting beneficial features of the state justice system in order to enhance the quality of *kastom* conflict management. As I have argued elsewhere (Forsyth 2009: 225) such adaptations, which will ideally be mutual, will enhance the ability of different actors and institutions to gradually start to all steer conflict management reform in the same direction.

State-Generated Links

An important issue in terms of the legitimacy of the state courts is the extent to which *kastom* payments are taken into account in sentencing for criminal offences. If the courts do not take the *kastom* penalty into account, the defendants are left with a sense of grievance at having been subjected to two punishments, and the chiefs feel that their work has been overlooked or, worse, undermined. On the other hand, there can be concerns that people merely make *kastom* payments as a way of 'buying their way out of trouble.'

In 2006 the Penal Code (Amendment) Act was passed. It requires that state courts *must* take into account any compensation made or due by the offender under *kastom* as a mitigating factor in sentencing. This changed the previous position, which allowed courts to take *kastom* into account but did not require them to do so. There are, however, still problems with the way courts take *kastom* payments into account.[7] First, the court is not permitted to halt or terminate the proceedings because the *kastom* system has already dealt with the matter. Second, there is very little inquiry into whether the parties are satisfied with the settlement, or whether or not the payment was appropriate according to the *kastom* of the relevant area. Further, the courts have hitherto been inconsistent in their approach to determining the extent to which a customary payment can mitigate a criminal sentence. In discussing these inadequacies and highlighting others, Paterson and Jowitt make the following suggestions for reforming the way courts take *kastom* into account in sentencing:

> First, the judges could, at their annual conference, discuss these issues and resolve that judicial practice will change. Alternatively, a conference or workshop could be convened to discuss these issues and pass resolutions which could be regarded by the courts as expressions of community attitudes. Third, legislation could be enacted to provide guidance for the courts. (Paterson and Jowitt 2008: 47)

This initiative demonstrates that when making linkages between the two systems it can be insufficient to simply outline broad principles and leave it to the stakeholders, who in this case were the judges and lawyers, to implement them on a case-by-case basis. This may lead to disparity and unfairness. Instead what is required is an opportunity for all who will be involved in implementing the new or reformed link to participate in developing a uniform policy, identifying in as detailed a way as possible how it should work. In addition, there must be a built-in evaluation process to follow up on the results of the reform after a certain number of years have passed, so as to determine if it has helped or hindered the particular objective(s) of the initiative.

[7] For an interesting discussion of how other courts in the region have dealt with the issue of taking into account customary remedies see New Zealand Law Commission (2006: 180-184).

Donor and Other Outsider-Generated Links

(a) Community Justice Supervisors

In 2005 the New Zealand Aid Program (NZAID) began a major Correctional Services Project in Vanuatu. The Project devised a number of reform proposals that "create opportunities for linkages between *Kastomary* processes and the Courts" (NZ AID 2005: 34). It established a taskforce of senior ni-Vanuatu employed in the state justice system and the Malvatumauri and held "extensive consultations . . . with a number of stakeholders and interest groups in five or the six provinces" (ibid.). A central proposal was the establishment of a Community Probation Service, which would adopt a "Community Justice Process". This process is said to build on and strengthen the Vanuatu tradition of community participation in the justice process and to preserve and enhance the existing practice of chiefs resolving disputes in what the Project refers to as a traditional context. The process is based on the idea that at a number of points there are opportunities for matters to be referred back to community leaders, principally chiefs and pastors, for resolution and reconciliation. The most visible aspect of this to date is the establishment of the position of Community Justice Supervisors (CJS) in the Correctional Services Act of 2006. The supervisors are generally chiefs or pastors and they voluntarily supervise community work sentences handed down by the Court. They are also often involved in the 'pastoral' care of offenders and checking that their relations with the community are harmonious. In many cases they have already been involved with the offender in a *kastom* process. According to an overseas advisor to the project, a recent workshop demonstrated that there is "obviously strong support for the model" and his perception was that chiefs feel there is a good fit between the two models (of state justice and *kastom* conflict management).[8]

This project is an important one given the limited detention facilities in Vanuatu, that are currently overcrowded and have been criticised for human rights abuses (Forsyth 2009: 157-159). In 2010 there were 125 detainees and 260 offenders were being managed in the community by 60 CJSs (Whibley-Smith 2010). Involving the chiefs in probation thus: frees up valuable prison space; reflects the importance of *kastom* practices in Vanuatu; acknowledges the value, status and

[8] Email correspondence with key informant, overseas advisor, 16 June 2010.

knowledge of respected community members; makes the offender accountable to their own community and; contributes to the rehabilitation and reintegration of offenders. CJSs are also functioning as important linkage points between the community and the state justice system (Whibley-Smith 2010). Although there has not to date been detailed research into the efficacy of the program, preliminary research indicates some problems over boundary issues, including past issues impacting on the CJS/Offender relationship and the other responsibilities of CJSs impeding their work (Whibley-Smith 2010). Unfortunately there is no detailed information available on these issues.

(b) Vanuatu Judiciary Conference

At my suggestion, and facilitated by funding from NZAID, in 2006 the Vanuatu Judiciary held their annual conference on the topic of the relationship between the state justice system and the *kastom* system at the University of the South Pacific. This was the first time that the judiciary, chiefs, police lawyers and academics had come together to discuss the issues relating to the existence of the two systems of dispute resolution in Vanuatu. As such, it was very much an exploration of the issues involved, a discussion of the possible tensions, and a sharing of ideas about future directions that could be explored. The first part involved a description of the current relationship between the two systems, and was facilitated by a series of papers presented by members of the judiciary, police and the chiefs as well as through group discussion. The point that was emphasized by the Secretary of the NCC and other speakers was that the resources spent on the provision of justice all go to the formal system and none to the *kastom* system, and yet the majority of the population have their disputes resolved by the latter. The second part was devoted to a discussion of the current problems with the relationship, which was managed through a series of papers and then by group discussion in small groups. There was a great deal of agreement amongst the participants in relation to what the problems are, some of the most significant being: lack of communication between the two systems; lack of clear pathways between the two systems; lack of clear guidelines about which system should deal with which cases; the fact that the two systems undermine each other in a variety of ways; and also the problem of people being punished twice for the same offence, once by the state system and once by the *kastom* system (see Forsyth 2006).

The final part of the conference was concerned with a consideration of what steps could be taken to improve the relationship between the two systems and involved small groups considering a series of questions designed to provoke and focus discussion, as well as plenary discussion of the findings of each group. Perhaps unsurprisingly, the participants were far more divided in their views about the possible solutions (Forsyth 2006). For example, when considering the question of sharing of jurisdiction, some groups proposed that the decision of which system should deal with a particular case should rest with the chief. Another group suggested that in urban areas, state law should apply whereas in rural areas, *kastom* law should apply unless there is no *kastom* law that covers the situation. Other groups proposed that chiefs should deal with minor matters and the state with serious matters. Some groups felt that *kastom* should always be used to deal with matters relating to natural resources, even in urban areas. There was also disagreement about whether individuals should have the right to opt-out of being dealt with by the *kastom* system, with some feeling there should be no opt-out as this undermines the chiefs' authority, while others stated that there should be freedom of choice. Others said that a person should always be able to go to the state system afterwards. Although undertakings were made by chiefs, the police and the judiciary about moving forward with issues identified during the conference (see Forsyth 2006), little headway has in fact been made. Like the action plans in the *Kastom* Governance project, this demonstrates the important role academics can play in facilitating discussions between different actors involved in conflict management, by creating the space and the conditions for such dialogue to occur. However, it also shows the necessity to have follow-up support to assist participants in actioning undertakings made.

The next section proposes a theoretical framework that centres on the creation of linkages in reform and development programming.

A Conflict Management Web Framework

As stated in the introduction, the reality of legal pluralism in the field of conflict management in countries such as Vanuatu necessitates donors working with both state and non-state systems. There are three possible approaches to doing this: subordinating the non-state system into the state system, creating a new, third system based on the incorporation of elements of the state and non-state system (a hybrid approach) and the creation of a conflict management web as proposed here. The advantages of this approach over the other two are set out at the end of this section.

The conflict management web framework proposed here responds to observations such as Baker's that worldwide there has been "scant understanding of links [between state and non-state systems] by the development community and in particular by those engaged in police and justice reform programmes" (Baker 2010: 601) The new conceptual framework proposed here is thus intended to assist international donors and others to understand and develop appropriate linkages between state and non-state systems in this field. The framework is based upon a number of key insights from network theory (Wellman 1983), nodal governance (Shearing and Wood 2003) and regulatory space metaphors (Scott 2001). It recognises that there are multiple state, non-state as well as hybrid actors (meaning neither fully state, nor non-state) and institutions, which possess a range of relevant resources that are currently acting in the conflict management arena, and that there are formal (mandated by state law) and informal relationships or ties between them. It also recognises that these relationships are "complex, dynamic and horizontal" (Scott 2001: 330), and cause the various actors and institutions involved to undergo "processes of assimilation, transformation and adoption" (Baker 2010: 613). Moreover, the relational ties within a network are crucial to determining the "strength, cohesion, collaborative intensity and sustainability" (Baker 2010: 600) of the network as a whole.

However, the web approach presented here also differs in some respect from these theories. It has an explicitly normative as well as an empirical focus (see Wellman 1983: 162), as it is geared towards achieving cohesion of the overall structure, not merely to understand the various linkages that exist. Also, unlike classic social network theory, it does not view the attributes of individuals as being less important than their relationships and ties with other actors within the network. Indeed, evidence from fieldwork in Vanuatu suggests that personal characteristics of key individuals are often essential in any development initiative, and are often inextricably linked with their ability to create and maintain relational ties.

The key features of the conflict management web framework are as follows. First, it focuses on identifying, strengthening and, where necessary, building, mutually supporting linkages between different actors and institutions actively involved in conflict management (or indeed any other field). This avoids the adoption of a hierarchical, state-centralist approach to reform and frees up reform initiatives to consider how, for example, state institutions can be positively influenced by and kept in check by non-state actors and institutions (see Scott 2001: 337). It also helps to ensure that agents of reform (be they state governments or international donors) are not duplicating the efforts (or worse, inadvertently undermining the efforts) of another reform project. Second, this framework emphasises the sharing of information about what reform initiatives work and why between various state and non-state actors in the field and also donors, NGOs and academics. This will foster home grown adaptation and innovation to replace the current tendency to look immediately outside for ideas and models. In turn, this is likely to increase the legitimacy of conflict management institutions and actors, which has been identified as an important issue in state-building and reducing conflict and violence (World Bank 2011: 84). Action learning and reflection are thus central to the framework, meaning that those involved in reform should regularly assess the benefits of their projects to inform themselves, and others in the web, about how to better implement reforms.[9]

Third, this framework promotes multiple, small-scale, locally based reform projects, thus taking the focus away from centralised institution-building projects. Ideally, such projects can be on a longer time-scale than would be possible if national coverage were attempted as there will not be as much pressure for short term results as less will be riding on the outcome. Small-scale projects can also be intensely local and collaborative and give as much agency as possible to the participants involved to determine the types of reforms to discuss and to implement. An approach that favours multiple projects recognises that many reform initiatives will fail, and also promotes creative (risky) reform initiatives by not having all of the reforming agency's eggs in the one basket. The World Development Report similarly suggests: "pilot many different types of approaches to see which work best; accept a higher failure rate; evaluate rigorously and adapt quickly; and scale up approaches that are working" (World Bank 2011: 32). If many different approaches are tried, the failures of some will be counter-balanced by the successes of others.

Finally, the conflict management web framework promotes a decentralised approach to conflict management, which can be of great use where, as in Vanuatu as discussed above, the state alone does not have the ability (or the will) to meet the conflict management needs of citizens. This works in four ways: it provides alternative paths to conflict management where state courts are over-burdened or non-functional; competition provides incentives to state justice institutions to improve their performance; it can help to avoid the problem of "capture" of

[9] A collaboration-strengthening pyramid such as suggested by Braithwaite (2002: 115 - 127) may also assist in this evaluation and strengthening process.

donor-funded judicial reform efforts by elites (White 2009); and it can act as a check on power in the hands of a single justice institution where that institution is abusing its power (Braithwaite 1997).

So, what are the actual implications of this for states, international donors and others wishing to undertake justice reform projects? First, it means approaching conflict management reform in a holistic way, taking account of *all* the actors and institutions involved in the field in a given jurisdiction, including international donors, academics and NGOs. This is an explicit recognition of the political nature of, and role played by, donors in a locally dynamic system. Developing links may be difficult where there are competing agendas at play, or competition for scarce resources (financial or social capital for example), but developing even weak links between competing actors and institutions may foster dialogue that will in the long term produce a more positive relationship between them. Granovetter (2005: 34) argues that greater density of links between nodes: "makes ideas about proper behaviour more likely to encountered repeatedly, discussed and fixed." It may also be difficult in countries where customary or religious systems have broken down or are discredited, although there may be other new grass-roots initiatives that have sprung up to replace them. Of course, in situations where there are no viable non-state actors or institutions to work with, the conflict management web framework may not work and it may be necessary to consider a different framework, such as creating a hybrid structure based on newly created institutions, such as the PNG village courts (see Evans et al. 2011).

Second, it means that all projects will need to start with a network analysis of the different institutions and actors involved in conflict management and the links between them. This is more than a standard stocktake of visible actors and formal counterparts, and will inevitably require in-country fieldwork rather than a desk based literature review. As demonstrated above, much of what actually happens in practice in conflict management in developing countries cannot be understood from the literature alone. Relying solely on written materials will prioritise state agencies and may result in overlooking important grass-roots initiatives that could be built upon. This analysis will involve investigating whether any existing institutions or actors have agendas that the particular reform project can strategically align with, before starting to create a new reform project from scratch. It will also mean creating opportunities for dialogues to occur between donors, academics and those involved in conflict management about what initiatives are currently underway and need support, such as the conversation that started the *Kastom* Governance project. It is also a project that requires an anthropologically informed approach, i.e. an understanding of the local political economy and how things actually work in practice in-country, rather than just technical legal skills.

Of course this is likely to be an expensive and time-consuming process and does not easily fit into the current incentive structure for donors (Gibson et al. 2005; World Bank 2011: 26). However, a potential aid may be the tools developed in an IT context to deal with decentralised sources of information, such as a wiki, an interactive website that facilitates the sharing of information by many people. If each country developed a conflict management web wiki that could be used to share information about what projects were happening and reviews of them and associated resources, this would go a long way to reinforcing many existing links between actors and institutions involved in conflict management. It may be that a state government could seek donor funding for establishing and maintaining the wiki, and require everyone involved in the justice sector to keep the site updated as a condition of project approval. Although many rural communities do not have access to the Internet, this is changing fast with the huge global expansion of mobile and broadband networks. In Vanuatu, community leaders in even remote areas often have links with people who do have access, and so reliance on a web-based tool will not necessarily exclude more remote actors from the conversation.

One of the major challenges that the conflict management web framework raises is determining what degree of co-ordination and strategic alignment is desirable and practically attainable. The provision of conflict management services often involves local and national political issues, competing agendas, and as demonstrated in section one, different views of what the aims of conflict management should be. Further, having different justice providers can lead to problems associated with forum shopping as discussed above. The question of the governance of networks is a large one and beyond the scope of this article. It seems highly unlikely that any organisation or institution would be willing or able to take on such a role, especially in countries where the state is weak. A single source of oversight may also cut across many of the benefits of the decentralised approach. A better solution in the comparatively simple context of a single nation state is to adopt a self-steering approach (Schout and Jordan 2005) that focuses on developing and strengthening the links between the different actors and institutions involved, both in terms of substantive issues of conflict management and reform project co-ordination. Dialogue about potentially competing reform agendas will promote an articulation of the different agendas at stake, which in turn may assist in finding some middle ground, when all sides see what resources can be fruitfully shared (for example the *Kastom* Governance project includes gender as an issue that is discussed in the workshops), although this may need time (for example the relative failure of the *Chiefs Bill*). The more networking and communication that occurs between the actors that engage in spinning different strands of the justice web, the greater is the chance that the web as a whole will have coherence. Braithwaite and Drahos argue that webs of dialogue are effective for both weak and strong actors and can result in defining a problem, agreeing on principles and rules to solve it, and enforcing those rules "with impressive results" (Braithwaite and Drahos 2000: 32).

The creation of linkages to form a dense web has a number of advantages over both subordination and hybridization, the two other approaches to legal pluralism often used in developing countries. Most of these advantages stem from the fact that the web approach treats non-state institutions as autonomous or semi-autonomous, thus freeing the state from the need to regulate or administrate them, and leaving much greater scope for their autochthonous development. This is fundamentally different to a hybridized system, such as the PNG village courts, which involve the creation of what are essentially state institutions, although they incorporate elements of customary institutions.

There are six other advantages of the conflict management web approach to the other two approaches. First, the web approach responds to the idea of harnessing voluntary and legitimate social ordering, and only resorting to state sanctions when this fails (Braithwaite 2002: 29). Second, it recognises that state forms of ordering themselves need to be subjected to oversight by other social institutions, and thus in a healthy regulatory system, mutual monitoring is both necessary and legitimate. Third, linkages can facilitate a more efficient sharing of resources between institutions and actors, whilst leaving space for each to perform the role that it does best. Fourth, linkages can promote dialogue about existing or potential conflicts of agenda in a non-hierarchical manner, leaving more room for creative compromises than if a top-down approach is adopted. Fifth, linkages can facilitate different orders learning from the other, which can raise standards and legitimacy on both sides (Baker 2010: 609; Forsyth 2009: 225-238). While the end result of reform based on a web approach may well be similar to a hybridized system, it will have been achieved in an organic manner, driven by the needs and experiences of the actors involved, rather than having had its form pre-determined (and state-directed) from the start. It is thus likely to have far more legitimacy and ability to rely on local forms of ordering than a state-created hybrid system. Moreover, the web approach has the advantage that any new system that may be developed will emerge in an organic manner, lowering the potential for problems (for example, inter-operability and competition) from the creation of a third system, as may occur where a new hybrid system is introduced.

Conclusion

This article has argued that two different types of linkages need to be made to improve the quality of conflict management in a country such as Vanuatu, where crucial resources (financial, human, organisational etc.) and legitimacy are dispersed between state and non-state institutions. The first type is between those involved in conflict management at both state and non-state levels. Such linkages will facilitate a more effective sharing of resources, as trust and understanding builds between the key actors involved in the administration of each system (Granovetter 2005: 34). The aim is to develop what Santos calls *interlegality* (Santos 1987: 298), where there is: "continuous interaction in the main between different legal perceptions, thereby influencing and shaping new normative orders adapted to considering cultural diversity" (Svesson 2005: 51-52). International donors have an important role to play in facilitating these linkages by creating opportunities for dialogue to promote knowledge exchange between key actors, such as the *Kastom* Governance project and the Judiciary conference.

The second type of linkage that needs to be improved is that between donors, NGOs, state governments and non-state actors and institutions about the different justice reform initiatives that are taking place in a country. This could foster a greater harmonisation of agendas, lessen the risk of one initiative undermining another, allow resources to be used more efficiently, promote discussion about different visions for reform, and help to identify existing initiatives by non-state actors that would benefit from better resourcing.

This article proposes that a conflict management web framework may be adopted as a conceptual and practical tool to assist in developing both types of linkages. This approach is based on analysing the nature and extent of the ties currently linking all actors and institutions involved in conflict management in a particular country, including those who provide material and organisational resources, such as international donors. The understandings gained from such an analysis can then be used to program reform initiatives that can be strategically aligned with autochthonous initiatives currently underway, or which create new linkages that promote a more efficient sharing of the existing resources and social capital. This will increase the chances of any reform fully capitalising on existing resources, being legitimate and sustainable, and being owned and driven by local actors and institutions.

References

BAKER, Bruce

2010 'Linking state and non-state security and justice.' *Development Policy Review* 28: 597-616.

BOEGE, Volker, Anne BROWN, Kevin CLEMENTS, Anna NOLAN

2008 'On Hybrid Political orders and Emerging States: State Formation in the Context of 'Fragility.' Accessed at http://www.berghof-handbook.net/documents/publications/boege_etal_handbook.pdf

BRAITHWAITE, John

1997 'On speaking softly and carrying big sticks: neglected dimensions of a republication separation of powers.' *University of Toronto Law Journal* 47: 305-361.

2002 *Restorative Justice and Responsive Regulation*. UK: Oxford University Press.

2008 *Regulatory Capitalism: How it Works, Ideas for Making it Work Better*. UK: Edward Elgar.

2010 'Traditional Justice.' Unpublished Paper presented at the Project on Restorative Justice, Reconciliation and Peacebuilding at the University of Notre Dame, September 2010.

BRAITHWAITE, John and DRAHOS, Peter

2000 *Global Business Regulation*. UK: Cambridge University Press

CHANOCK, Martin

2000 'Introduction.' Pp. 1-31 in Sally Moore, *Law as Process: An Anthropological Approach (1978)*. Classics in African Anthropology. Hamburg, Germany: Lit Verlag.

EVANS, Daniel, Michael GODDARD and Don PATERSON

2011 'The Hybrid Courts of Melanesia: A Comparative Analysis of Village Courts of Papua New Guinea, Island Courts of Vanuatu and Local Courts of Solomon Islands.' Justice and Development Working Paper Series, Vol. 13, 2011. Accessed at http://siteresources.worldbank.org/INTJUSFORPOOR/Resources/HybridCourts.pdf

FORSYTH, Miranda
2006 *Report on the Vanuatu Judiciary Conference 2006: The Relationship Between the Kastom and State Justice Systems*. Accessed at http://www.paclii.org/vu/2006_jud_conf_report.html
2009 A *Bird that Flies with Two Wings: Kastom and State Justice Systems in Vanuatu*. Canberra: ANU ePress. Available at http://epress.anu.edu.au/wp-content/uploads/2011/05/whole_book1.pdf
GIBSON, Clark, Krister ANDERSSON, Elinor OSTROM and Sujai SHIVAKUMAR
2005 *The Samaritan's Dilemma: The Political Economy of Development Aid*. USA: Oxford University Press.
GRANOVETTER, Mark
1973 'The strength of weak ties.' *American Journal of Sociology* 78: 1360-1380.
1983 'The strength of weak ties: a network theory revisited.' *Sociological Theory* 1: 201-223.
2005 'The impact of social structure on economic outcomes.' *Journal of Economic Perspectives* 19: 33-50.
GUPTA, Joyeeta
2002 'Global sustainable development governance: Institutional challenges from a theoretical perspective.' *International Environmental Agreements: Politics, Law and Economics* 2: 361-388.
HUYSE, Luc and Mark SALTER (eds.)
2008 *Traditional Justice and Reconciliation after Violent Conflict*. International Institute for Democracy and Electoral Assistance.
MARANGO, Thompson
2011 'Minimal Budget Hinder Police Operation.' *Vanuatu Daily Post*, Wednesday 9 February 2011, 3.
MERRY, Sally Engle
2006 *Human Rights and Gender Violence: Translating International Law into Local Justice*. Chicago: University of Chicago Press.
NZ AID (NEW ZEALAND AID PROGRAM)
2005 *Proposed Vanuatu Community Probation Service: Summary Report*.
NEW ZEALAND LAW COMMISSION
2006 *Converging Currents: Custom and Human Rights in the Pacific*. Study Paper 17.
ODE (OFFICE OF DEVELOPMENT EFFECTIVENESS)
2010 *Vanuatu Kastom Governance Program*, Draft Report. AusAID.

OECD (ORGANISATION FOR ECONOMIC CO-OPERATION AND DEVELOPMENT)
2007 'Enhancing the Delivery of Justice and Security: Governance, peace and Security.' Accessed at *www.**oecd**.org/data**oecd**/27/13/38434642.pdf.*
PATERSON, Don and Anita JOWITT
2008 'More on customary reconciliation ceremonies in sentencing for criminal offenders.' *Journal of South Pacific Law* 12/2: 39-47.
PACIFIC BEAT
2006 'Vanuatu: Chiefs Step in to End Jail-break Impasse.' 10 May 2006. Accessed at http://abc.gov.au/ra/pacbeat/stories/s1635039.htm
RODMAN, William L.
1977 'Big Men and Middlemen: the politics of law in Longana.' *American Ethnologist* 4(3): 525-537.
SANTOS, Boaventura de Sousa
1987 'Law: A map of misreading; toward a postmodern conception of law.' *Journal of Law and Society* 14: 279-302.
SCOTT, Colin
2001 'Analysing regulatory space: fragmented resources and institutional design.' *Public Law*, Sum: 329-353.
SCHOUT, Adriaan and Andrew JORDAN
2005 'Co-ordinated European Governance: Self-Organizing or Centrally Steered?'*Public Administration* 83: 201-220.
SHEARING, Clifford and Jennifer WOOD
2003 'Nodal governance, democracy and the new 'denizens.' *Journal of Law and Society* 30/3: 400-419.
SVENSSON, Tom
2005 'Interlegality, a process for strengthening indigenous peoples' autonomy: the case of the Sami in Norway.' *Journal of Legal Pluralism* 51: 51-78.
TOR, Roselyn and Anthea TOKA
2004 *Gender, Kastom and Domestic Violence: A Research on the Historical Trend, Extent and Impact of Domestic Violence in Vanuatu.* Vanuatu: Department of Women's Affairs. Accessed at http://www.vanuatuculture.org/documents/Gender&Kastom.pdf
WALKER, Polly and Selwyn GARU
2009 'A few more arrows': Strengthening mediative capacity in Vanuatu.' Pp. 94-110 in Dale Bagshaw and Elisabeth Porter (eds.), *Mediation in the Asia-Pacific region: Transforming conflicts and building peace*. London, U.K.; New York, U.S.A.: Routledge.

WELLMAN, Barry

1983 'Network Analysis: Some Basic Principles.' *Sociological Theory* 1: 155-200.

WESTOBY, Peter

2008 'Dialogue and disentanglement: navigating the territory of diverse discourses of community development within Vanuatu.' *New Community Quarterly* 6: 81-92.

2010 'Community-based training for conflict prevention in Vanuatu: reflections of a practitioner-researcher.' *Social Alternatives* 29: 15 - 18.

WESTOBY, Peter and Anne BROWN

2007 'Peaceful community development in Vanuatu: a reflection on the Vanuatu Kastom Governance Partnership.' *Journal of Peacebuilding & Development* 3/3: 77-81.

WHIBLEY-SMITH, Angela

2010 'Community Justice Supervisors: Incorporating *Kastom* into Vanuatu Probation.' Powerpoint presentation on file with author.

WHITE, Brent

2009 'Rotten to the core: project capture and the failure of judicial reform in Mongolia.' *Arizona Legal Studies Discussion Paper* No. 09/24.

WHITE, Geoffrey and Lamont LINDSTROM (eds.)

1994 *Culture, Kastom, Tradition: Developing Cultural Policy in Melanesia*. Hawaii: The East-West Centre.

WORLD BANK

2011 *World Development Report: Conflict Security and Development*. Accessed at http://wdr2011.worldbank.org/sites/default/files/pdfs/WDR2011_Full_Text.pdf

DECENTRALISED POWER AND TRADITIONAL AUTHORITIES: HOW POWER DETERMINES ACCESS TO JUSTICE IN SIERRA LEONE

Paul Jackson

Introduction

This article addresses the influence of international intervention on access to justice in rural Sierra Leone and links it to the decentralisation of power. Decentralisation was implemented in 2004 across Sierra Leone and resulted in a strong debate about the nature of political power at the local level (Fanthorpe 2006; Richards 2005; Jackson 2006). This was partly the result of the previous governance structure of Sierra Leone and in particular a colonial bifurcation that placed Paramount Chiefs in political power outside the Western Area of Freetown (Jackson 2005; Sawyer 2004.[1] At the same time, Sierra Leone was a post-conflict state having emerged from a very damaging and brutal civil war with significant external donor support. As such, Sierra Leone has enjoyed a certain status as a success story, of a state

[1] Paramount Chieftaincy was established in 1938 by the Native Administration Act. Chiefdoms delivered services including education, agriculture and justice. Chiefdom Councils were established in 1964 under the Tribal Authorities Act, re-established in 2003 and then became subject to a 2009 Chiefdom Act. They consist of a Paramount Chief, Section and Town Chiefs, an electoral college of councillors, and an administrative staff including court functionaries and chiefdom police. A distinction should be made between the lower ranking chiefs and paramount chiefs who are state agents and exercise executive, administrative and judicial powers. For a comprehensive discussion see Fanthorpe (2006); Fanthorpe et al. (2011); and Jackson (2006).

that has been resurrected and reconstructed by the international community (Evans et al. 2002; Fitzgerald, 2004; Ginifer and Kaye 2004; Poate et al. 2008). The international community therefore had an interest in making the state work and as a result international intervention has largely governed much of the macro-reconstruction efforts of the state, particularly in governance, justice and security (Jackson and Albrecht 2011).

Central to this article is a focus on the political dynamics of legal pluralism, specifically the interaction between 'formal' and 'informal' justice, and the significance of power relations at the local level following decentralisation.[2] The relationship between local power, decentralised authority and justice at the local level is not frequently articulated, particularly in the context of donor supported post-conflict reforms and what impact these have on justice processes at the local level. Reforms in the area of decentralisation, and justice/security sector reform, are often not seen as having a close link, probably because justice/security is seen as separate from political power issues, i.e. the former interventions tend to have a more 'technical' focus.[3] It is the contention of this article that justice interventions alter power structures and it is the politics arising from these structures that play an important - if not *the* important - role in the outcomes of such reforms. The coexistence of formal and informal systems at a local level reinforces the power structures that support an elite in the countryside and prevent access to justice for those who are excluded from that elite. Legal pluralism may be seen as a problem (elites manipulating the system) or as a potential solution (providing a choice between remedies) for those seeking justice.

If access to justice is so influenced by power arrangements, donor programmes in support of justice must become better at understanding and working with local politics, including abandoning dichotomies that are of little use in understanding reality (formal/informal, modern/traditional). Whereas many post-colonial African

---

[2] This paper is based on fieldwork carried out in Sierra Leone between 2002 and 2007 for DFID and the World Bank, where the author was an adviser to the Government of Sierra Leone, and more recent research on local government in post-conflict environments for the UNDP. There are several definitions of 'formal' and 'informal', but this paper follows Manning (2009) in taking formal as having a formal legal mandate.

[3] See, for example the OECD/DAC (2005) Guidelines on Security Sector Reform, which are deliberately technical in approach and form the current 'orthodoxy' on security and justice interventions.

Governments had seen the chiefs as something of an impediment to modernising strategies, many chiefs have also enhanced their role particularly since the 1990s and have formalised their governance role. However, on the ground the picture is frequently far more complex than a simple dualistic approach to traditional authority being either formal or informal and it is the negotiation of those relationships and links that remains important. As a result successful programmes need to empower the marginalised within local power structures. Dismantling or reducing the power of the chiefs is impractical in the short term and so programmes need to work with them. What they should not do, however, is to enhance their power at the expense of access to justice for the marginalised.

This article argues that local power arrangements are important in determining people's access to justice in Sierra Leone and they also have a strong impact on the outcome of justice processes. Furthermore, these links are usually overlooked within internationally supported local government and justice reforms, where traditional authorities like Paramount Chiefs are able to negotiate local political institutions to maintain biases against lineages and social categories, particularly youth and gender. Many international donor programmes emphasise the development of formal justice systems, but traditional or customary law still provides the majority of justice decisions for the population, particularly in the districts (Jackson 2006; Baker 2008; Manning 2009). As Baker and Scheye (2007) observe, there are a number of core assumptions underlying current international approaches to justice sector reform, including: first, that a lack of a formal justice system is tantamount to a lack of justice *per se*; second, that the formal state justice system is what people want; and, third, that a formal state system of justice is sustainable. To these three, in the case of Sierra Leone, I would add that there is also an assumption that the traditional and formal systems are somehow unaffected by local power structures. In reality, I argue, traditional authorities are important to justice outcomes, because of: the nature of traditional authority; their relationship with decentralised power structures; power over those holding decentralised roles; and, traditional roles over land.

This article begins by briefly outlining the context of international intervention and the approaches that were taken in both decentralisation and also in security and justice following the end of the war in 2002, and primarily for DFID. It then moves on to map the justice actors at district level and how they interact. In particular it shows how justice institutions are linked into local power structures and how these structures can be influenced by local power brokers, particularly political elites. The article then goes on to map power and rivalries within and between political elites at the local level and how people may be able to negotiate these networks. However, the analysis concludes that those with resources are better able to negotiate these networks than those with few resources. International interventions around decentralisation and justice and security sector reform have either made little difference or reinforced local elite power. The implication for intervention is that strategies for the provision of support need to develop mechanisms to enhance the ability of local people to negotiate the power and justice structures at a local level.

The Context of Intervention

Since independence from Britain in 1961 the main feature of Sierra Leone's political system was an increasing centralisation of power and resources in Freetown coupled with a dualism between Freetown and the rest of the country. This dualism has been reinforced by a continuation of the colonial bifurcation of western legal systems in Freetown and of a form of indirect rule in the countryside based on a system of District Officers and Chiefs. Following the end of the Margai era in 1968, the then mayor of Freetown, Siaka Stevens, became Prime Minister and following a period of military interventions, he assumed full Presidential powers in 1972, a position he held until his nominated successor, Major General Joseph Momoh took up power in 1985. Throughout this period Sierra Leone drifted towards dictatorship, concentrating resources in Freetown resulting in the widespread alienation of many parts of the population (Richards 1996; Jackson and Albrecht 2010, 2011).

Eventually, political pressure on Momoh forced a constitutional review in 1991. That same year the Revolutionary United Front (RUF) was formed by Foday Sankoh, and began a campaign of violence along the Liberian border. The stated aim of the RUF at this time was to end corruption, but in reality on the ground this was quickly supplanted by a logic encompassing control over resources and, effectively, a revolt against centralized social and political control, particularly of the countryside (Richards 2005; Fanthorpe 2006; Jackson 2006). As the RUF revolt took hold, Momoh's Government was replaced in a coup by the National Provisional Ruling Council (NPRC) led by Valentine Strasser, which became increasingly ineffective in the face of the RUF, leading to the employment of a South African mercenary firm Executive Outcomes in 1995. Militarily this was successful, but the NPRC were less so and were eventually forced to hand over power in an election held in 1996 when Ahmad Tejan Kabbah of the Sierra Leonean People's Party (SLPP) was elected President.

Two months later discussions between the SLPP and the RUF led to the Abidjan Peace Accords of 1996, but the unwillingness of either party to agree on disarmament or to international monitoring arrangements led to a breakdown in the peace by early 1997. Another coup in Freetown led by the Armed Forces Revolutionary Council (AFRC) meant that President Kabbah was forced into exile in Guinea. This in turn led to the next cycle of violence that incorporated ECOMOG, a Nigerian-led regional peacekeeping force combating the AFRC, the involvement of a British firm, Sandline, in illegal arms dealing with the SLPP and the eventual return and reinstatement of President Kabbah backed by a significant UN military presence in 1998.

UN intervention was plagued by a number of issues immediately after deployment, leading to a hostage crisis in April 2000 where several UN units were surrounded by a reanimated RUF. The eventual intervention of UK forces in May 2000 and the reorganisation of the UN military presence within UNAMSIL II, led to the UK-led *Operation Palliser,* which started as a non-combatant evacuation operation, then transformed into a military campaign until January 2002, despite direct orders to the contrary (Albrecht and Jackson 2009; Jackson and Albrecht 2011).

The context of the intervention then was challenging. Out of a total population of around 6 million, some 50,000 people were estimated to have been killed, around 500,000 had become refugees and around 500,000 were classified as Internally Displaced Peoples (IDPs) (Horn, et al. 2006). At the same time, the governance infrastructure of state institutions symbolising the power structures that RUF fought against, had been entirely destroyed. In the countryside there were no government records or buildings and the chiefs had largely fled or been killed. In sum, the situation was one of rather literal state building. There was no existing state left at almost any level (Jackson 2006). The state, in fact, had been key to the conflict in the first place. As the Truth and Reconciliation Commission stated:

> While there were many factors, both internal and external, that explain the cause of the civil war, the Commission came to the conclusion that it was years of bad governance, endemic corruption and the denial of basic human rights that created the deplorable conditions that made the conflict inevitable. Successive regimes became increasingly impervious to the wishes and needs of the majority. Instead of implementing positive and progressive policies, each regime perpetuated the ills and self-serving machinations left behind by its predecessor. By the start

> of the conflict the nation had been stripped of its dignity. Institutional collapse reduced the vast majority of people into a state of deprivation. Government accountability was non-existent. Political expression and dissent had been crushed. Democracy and the rule of law were dead. By 1991, Sierra Leone was a deeply divided society and full of the potential for violence. It required only the slightest spark for this violence to be ignited. The Commission traced the roots of these lapses through the post-independence period and into the colonial period.
>
> This context provided ripe breeding grounds for opportunists who unleashed a wave of violence and mayhem that was to sweep through the country. Many Sierra Leoneans, particularly the youth, lost all sense of hope in the future. Youths became easy prey for unscrupulous forces who exploited their disenchantment to wreak vengeance against the ruling elite. The Commission holds the political elite of successive regimes in the post-independence period responsible for creating the conditions for conflict (TRC 2004: 1).

The post-colonial Sierra Leonean state had been in a state of decay for some years before the outbreak of hostilities in March 1991. War, neglect, patronage, and the increasing use of violence by the state meant that by the late 1990s the provision of security had become splintered into numerous factions, community by community across the country. It is commonly accepted that the failure of the state to honour its patrimonial promises and the failure of institutions to provide justice in the countryside significantly contributed to brutal and seemingly inexplicable violence as well as two military coups (Keen 2005; Peters 2006: 7; Richards 1996). At the same time, the colonial bifurcation of the state had led to an enriched core around Freetown and an impoverished periphery in the countryside where the development of an alienated youth created the conditions for the conflict (Richards 1996; Jackson 2005, 2007). The restoration of a functioning state that could control a monopoly of violence was therefore perceived by international donors as an imperative in the early stages of intervention and the military nature of the initial intervention coloured the way in which those external actors, particularly the UK, structured that intervention (Jackson and Albrecht 2010).

The context of complete state collapse led to an initial priority of state re-establishment, security provision and the construction of basic justice systems that could manage conflict locally. The 'Chiefdom Restoration Project', which was primarily driven by security needs and was controversial amongst international governance advisers within Sierra Leone, was identified as being important as part of the restoration of governance in the countryside, but more particularly as part of the security agenda in recreating the responsibility of the chiefs to 'report strangers' (Jackson and Albrecht 2011 Denney 2011).[4] That support should be directed towards an identifiable central authority was never questioned in the case of Sierra Leone, not even as that authority's ability to enforce a degree of security across its territory had weakened to the point of non-existence. The key driver of intervention was therefore reconstructing a state that was perceived to have fallen into decay over a period of some thirty years, around twenty of them being characterised by violence. Even so, it was perceived that doing so would be possible within a relatively short programme horizon.[5]

Post-War Justice Sector Reform

Initial interventions both before and immediately after the war within Sierra Leone were heavily dominated by re-establishing security through the disbandment of the RUF and the formation of a new military, and the reconstruction of the SLP (Jackson and Albrecht 2011 Denney 2011). One of the unintended consequences of a focus on policing was that reforms of other institutions forming part of the justice sector moved forward more slowly. This lag in the development of justice alongside security has been a characteristic of the reform process right from local courts, formal legal systems, and prisons to Ministerial development. Even by 2008 the police themselves were regularly commenting that weaker capacity across justice institutions was undermining effectiveness through an inability to process cases (Howlett-Bolton 2008).

Support to the justice sector can basically be divided into two periods, before and after 2005. After 2005, the development of the Justice Sector Development Programme (JSDP) brought together the SLP, the judiciary, the prison service and the Ministry of Internal Affairs in a comprehensive programme across the sector.

---

[4] The author was part of these discussions. In fact the programme came to an unfortunate end by the time of the Local Government Act in 2003.

[5] This idea has continued throughout the planning horizons used by DFID within planning and evaluation in Sierra Leone and is reflected in many of the internal planning documents.

Before 2005, the main involvement of external donors in the justice sector was the Law Development Project. Started in January 2001 this concentrated on reconstructing infrastructure and developing logistics including refurbishment of the main court in Freetown and magistrate courts in Bo and Kenema.

However, the capacity to use these courts had not necessarily been developed and it was relatively late that training of twenty registrars, administrators, under-sheriffs and bailiffs began. The legacy of a failing justice system that had built up over several years was still being felt in Sierra Leone as late as 2008. In particular, there was a huge backlog of cases, including those awaiting trial, imprisonment or enforcement decisions, poor record keeping, and insufficient space in prisons.

In common with many countries, there have also been issues in incorporating traditional systems within the justice system as a whole. It is clear that the traditional system, operated by Paramount and Section Chiefs, offers access to many more people than the formal state system. The traditional system has been seen as part of the justice sector reform supported by donors at least partly because the formal system does not reach into the countryside.[6] Local citizens have made limited use of traditional systems in Sierra Leone to effect reconciliation and peacebuilding within local communities, although the extent of this remains under-researched (Baker 2006).

It is easy with hindsight to criticise the lack of progress in justice reform. However, it should be recognised that the justice sector had been subject to a very long decline. Reconstructing a legal system takes time and investment. By 2008 there were approximately 200 members of the Sierra Leone Bar Association and virtually all of them resided in Freetown. This leaves access to justice extremely difficult for those who live in the countryside. Given the fact that the RUF may be seen as a rural-based organisation, the lack of justice in the countryside must be seen as extremely risky in a fragile country (Jackson 2006).

By 2004, it had become obvious that whilst the Law Development Programme (LDP) had provided infrastructural improvement and training for the judiciary, huge capacity problems remained and the justice sector as a whole remained the poor relation of other security programmes (Jackson and Albrecht 2011). Despite the fact that discussions regarding the integration of the justice and security

[6] The commonly cited figure – but very difficult to verify – is that around 80% of people access justice through traditional mechanisms.

systems had taken place as early as 2002, other elements of the justice sector, namely prisons, probation, legal reform, non-state justice and legal advice, had not benefited from any external support or development assistance.

Also, prior to the JSDP, which started in 2005, no assistance had been given to the Ministry of Internal Affairs, which governed the justice sector. This has had implications in terms of a lack of representation for the police and justice sector at Ministerial level, and access to Government resources for justice in general. In conjunction with the decentralisation process this has produced a situation where there is considerable variation in interpretation of customary law at the local level, with lack of coherent and effective central oversight. A broad and detailed consultation at village level carried out by DFID concluded that there was a general desire among the populace for better governance rather than the abolition of the chiefdom system (Fanthorpe et al. 2011). This provided a direction for all subsequent governance activities in local administration, including the re-establishment of local government in 2004. However, the same section of the report goes on to outline the key dilemma in relying on the chiefdom system to deliver justice. It states that: "[...] the fact that chiefdom administration was in deep crisis is clear for all to see in the reports on the pilot consultations. Due process in chiefdom administration had virtually disappeared due to the combined effects of war, resource starvation, and opportunism" (Fanthorpe et al. 2011: 56). The report goes further to state that "Chiefdom administration is not working" (ibid.: 5).

Given these comments, it is perhaps surprising that the chiefdoms have been identified as a key element in driving the population into conflict by enhancing their economic, social and political alienation (Jackson 2005). The rule of a male gerontocracy in the countryside complete with degraded and corrupt links to elements of the state and particularly to the diamond trade in diamond-bearing areas meant that the chiefdom system had been in decline for a long time before the war eventually destroyed large parts of it. It was not an accident that the first targets sought out by RUF fighters during the war in almost every case, was the chief, closely followed by the District Officer.

Mapping Justice and Power Structures at District Level

While there has been an emphasis on the chiefs, it is important to recognise that the reality of local justice for most people in Sierra Leone is not a bifurcated system with two mutually exclusive and antagonistic systems (formal versus informal), but a hybrid consisting of a number of differing choices with a wide variety of differing possible outcomes. This is not only reinforced by the apparent contradiction of having a 'modern' government system coexisting with a 'traditional' one, but also by the willingness of local people both to exercise a preference for the lowest possible level of justice (i.e. the most local to them) and also to 'shop around' for the desired forum for any given situation (Kelsall 2006).

A detailed survey of local institutions and their complex relationships is beyond the scope of this paper[7]. However, it should be acknowledged that this consists in reality of variations of shades of grey rather than a sharp division between 'formal' or 'informal', with the District Magistrates' Court at the formal, state, end of a spectrum and the informal family elements at the other end. The Government of Sierra Leone (GOSL) itself estimates that around 70 per cent of people in the country cannot access the formal state system and rely on the customary system through the local courts or informal mechanisms at local level (such as talking to the chief) that remain undocumented.

Magistrate's Courts

The judiciary itself consists of a High Court and district level Magistrates' courts. The High Court is based in Freetown but visits the three Provincial Capitals of Makeni, Kenema and Bo. There is a 'Law Officers Department', which serves as an office for public prosecutions and is responsible for all prosecutions within the formal system. However, there are just ten prosecutors in the whole country, with seven based in Freetown and one each in Bo, Kenema and Makeni, so in practice prosecutions within Magistrates' courts are handled by police prosecutors (Castillejo 2009).

Typically located in district capitals, these courts are presided over by a mixture of magistrates, court clerks and Justices of the Peace (JPs) who usually receive training in largely uncodified common law. Magistrates' courts typically hear serious cases involving larceny, assault, sexual assault, fraud, and arson. The Ministry of Justice estimates that around 70% relate to land disputes (Castillejo 2009).[8]

---

[7] See Manning 2009 for a detailed survey.

[8] A study by Kelsall (2006) showed that larceny consisted of 36%, with assault and sexual assault comprising another 27%.

There are significant problems with the magistrate court system, including completion times and adjournments. These are frequently caused by a failure of those involved to come to the court, mainly because many people put their own family business above attendance at court but also because many witnesses do not have the means to come to court, or have the fee (Kelsall 2006; Casillejo 2009). There is also a chronic shortage of magistrates and lawyers within the system. Magistrates are not only underpaid but are also frequently *un*paid as salaries are often delayed (Castillejo 2009). This presents a risk to the whole legal structure through bribery, allowing those with money immunity from prosecution. There have also been several instances where either Chiefs or other powerful individuals have exercised significant influence over sentences or had cases thrown out of court (Kelsall 2006; Jackson 2006; Castillejo 2009).

The financial imbalance in access to justice is exacerbated by a system that does not provide legal representation for parties. There is only a public defender in capital cases that get to the High Court. At the same time the Sierra Leone Bar Association states that there are one hundred lawyers in private practice in Sierra Leone, but only seven are outside Freetown (Castillejo 2009). If a case gets to the High Court without a defence lawyer any defendant is likely to spend considerable amounts of time in prison on remand[9]. The considerable costs of going to court are also exacerbated by paying for travel to a district court or medical examinations and reports.

One response to this is to use the formal system as a means of leveraging settlement in the local court or with informal authorities. Known in Sierra Leone as 'subterranean movements', this seeking of alternative remedies to those imposed by a court is reportedly common (Kelsall 2006; Fanthorpe 2006; Jackson 2006).

Local Courts

Customary courts are known as 'local courts' in Sierra Leone and are regulated by the Local Courts Act. These courts administer customary law which varies across chiefdoms, which have the power to establish customary bye-laws. Typical cases heard in the local courts include conflict resolution, family matters, conflicts over money, loans or small frauds, and land issues. But such courts should not deal

[9] The current JSDP within Sierra Leone, a DFID funded justice support programme, has identified this (interview with current JSDP manager, 2011).

with larger crimes or major theft (Kelsall 2006). Local courts are also investigative, i.e. whereas a magistrate's court hears pre-prepared cases presented by lawyers or police, a local court may hear 'truth-telling' by those involved, who are forced to swear on a variety of objects, including the Bible or the Koran.

Sentencing is open to negotiation through bargaining and the sentence is essentially a process of negotiation between the court, the accused and the plaintiff with the aim of ensuring that fines are fair and can be paid (Fanthorpe 2006; Kelsall 2006). This is not always benign and may establish bye-laws that may contradict human rights or constitutional law, or impose unusual punishments or excessive fines. As Castillejo (2009) reports, the level of fines may be more representative of the financial needs of the chiefdom than the actual offence since court fines are a key source of chiefdom income.

In practice chiefs wield a lot of power over local political and justice processes (Fanthorpe 2006; Richards 2005). They are the hub of local elites; control land through exercising trusteeship; dispense local justice; and have access to resources through tax collection and granting of land rights (Jackson 2005). They also appoint the Court Chairmen and the four other court members, so the court itself is an instrument of the Chief (Castillejo 2009).

While the jurisdiction of local courts is mandated by the state, in practice they hear many cases that they should not and they are known to levy fines in excess of the maximum allowed by law (Castillejo 2009). Oversight of these courts is minimal and there are also variations between different localities. Appeal is rare since this would make the case a formal case being put to a magistrate's court at district level. In addition, local courts are frequently closely tied to chiefs through kin or social networks, allowing an element of elite capture of the local legal system (Jackson 2005; Kelsall 2006; Manning 2009).

The customary system is said to have a number of advantages, including cost, accessibility, understanding and relative speed in dispensing justice that is usually based on mediation (Jackson 2006; Castillejo 2009). However, there are a number of issues that raise concerns. Whilst the costs of bribery are frequently cited as being an issue in the Magistrates' courts as well as the Local courts, the Local courts frequently levy a fee for a hearing and also impose disproportionately high fines that are well beyond their legal mandate and represent the financial needs of the chiefdom (Castillejo 2009). Those who are unable to pay are then forced to leave the chiefdom or go to prison, so the costs of failure in a court can be very high. Local courts, then, contrary to common perception, are both expensive and high risk, particularly for particular groups who are traditionally excluded, like women and children (Richards 2003; Jackson 2006; Castillejo 2009).

Local Government Reform: Rivalries between Decentralised and Traditional Power

A key policy decision of the post-war Government was to decentralize power from Freetown to a rejuvenated local government structure. This process led to the Local Government Act and local government elections held in May 2004. Most analysts agreed that the centralized system of government was a major contributing factor to the war during the 1990s and the World Bank, UNDP and DFID in particular, placed a strong emphasis on decentralization and reconstruction of the shattered local state as part of their post-war reconstruction efforts (Jackson 2005, 2007; Fanthorpe 2006).

Following the war, in 2003, the Ministry of Local Government and Community Development (MLGCD) canvassed public opinion on local government.[10]The consultation included debates about the limitation of chiefdom power, representation of excluded groups and non-party elections. However, the consultation process itself did not produce uniform agreement on all of these issues and the only significant addition was the creation of a new district council in the Western Area. In addition, a proviso was included, giving strong supervisory powers over local government to the three Resident Ministers who head the Provincial Administration.[11] The centre thus retained significant control over the new councils.

The position of the Local Council Chief Administrator (LCCA) is critical. This position effectively controls the entire bureaucracy of the council and also acts as secretary and main contact for the councillors. The appointment of competent individuals has therefore been extremely important in the early stages of decentralization. Certainly the competence of staff more generally, particularly in some of the more remote districts, has been problematic due to the difficulties in recruiting good staff outside Freetown.

---

[10] See Jackson (2006) for a more detailed discussion of the process and context.

[11] These have headquarters in Bo, Makeni and Kenema respectively

The change of roles within the chiefdoms, instigated by the Local Government Act, has caused significant friction with the new local councils. The Government is keen that chiefs and councils work closely together and the provision in the Act by which councils set tax rates and chiefs collect and share revenue is designed to encourage this. The problem, however, is really that the Act is not clear about the relationship between chiefs and councils in a number of key areas, including development funding, Ward Committees and Chiefdom Committees, local taxes, and the nature of responsibility with regard to land and natural resources. Whilst local development activity is the responsibility of the Council, access to human and physical resources, particularly land, remain the preserve of the chief. Councils and Chiefs have to work together, but there are no guidelines as to how this should happen.

The biggest conflict remains financial. The Act transfers several sources of revenue from the chief, to the local council, including some local taxes, fees and licenses[12]. Local councils have the authority to determine the rate of local tax and the level of precepts. All revenues have to be paid into local authority accounts and will be subject to audit. At the same time, the collection of the tax remains in the hands of the chiefdoms, which have to declare the amount of tax collected. Local councils can also disburse monies directly to chiefdoms for development purposes. In several local councils there have been reports of local councillors collecting their own taxes, while in at least one council, the council sacked the Chief Administrator and divided up the tax receipts amongst themselves (Jackson 2006). This remains a core issue and a recent report on the effectiveness of decentralisation concludes that the main constraint remains central government's insistence on maintaining the powers of the chiefs since without effective tax authority local councils are unable to construct a social contract with the population (Fanthorpe et al. 2011). This is exacerbated by lack of willingness of central government to decentralise functions, a reliance on patronage for appointment and the political parties' policy of using local government as a means of developing political support (Fanthorpe et al. 2011).

Confusion and rivalry over power was not helped by poor implementation of the Act itself or measures such as fiscal decentralisation. As a result there is a local rivalry between the administrative staff posted by the central government, the chiefs and the local councillors (Jackson 2007). This has been further exacerbated by the involvement of local MPs as they try to gain local political traction

[12] The main tax is the 'head tax', a form of poll tax.

(Fanthorpe et al. 2011). The escalation of political conflict in the countryside is a symptom of the lack of an effective oversight mechanism. Notionally, the Ministry of Local Government oversaw disputes relating to chiefdom, crime, gambling, bye-laws and land. With the abolition of District Offices, this workload has increased exponentially and the Ministry was unprepared. There is little record keeping, few staff and no clear procedures. In effect there is little or no oversight from the centre (Cutting 2004).

In terms of justice provision, this leaves the citizen with a nominally wide choice, but that apparent choice is actually limited by the close linkages between those who may be dispensing justice. It is also telling that during the consultations on the draft Local Courts Act in 2006, one Paramount Chief directly equated justice with power by stating that "[...] if you take the authority of the local courts away from the Paramount Chiefs, they won't have any power" (Manning 2009). In some chiefdoms there is a close alliance between the LCCA, the chief and senior councillors, meaning that the magistrates' and local courts can be placed under significant pressure to bring about particular outcomes, usually in favour of the family or interests of the local political elite (Castillejo 2009). Kelsall (2006) also reports a case of a man's daughter being beaten by another child where hospital fees are paid, but the man also seeks compensation for the beating. The Treasury Clerk is a friend of the offender's mother and intervenes, promising to settle the case privately. The case is not settled, however, and the man either has to go to the District appeal court or the magistrates' court, where he will have considerable costs for fees, a letter and for an arrest. He could, of course, go to the Treasury Clerk's boss, the Local Court Supervisor, but he is a relative of the Treasury Clerk (Kelsall 2006).

Powerlessness and Access to Justice

The previous section outlined the nature of political power and pointed to the close link between local political power and justice. This becomes clear when we examine the lack of access to justice of specific groups within society. In urban areas, there may be an option of a formal justice mechanism, usually a Magistrates' court or an appeal court, but in rural areas the majority of the population rely on access to local courts, presided over by a board appointed by the Paramount Chief. This leaves the Chiefdom as the only real actor 'beyond the tarmac road' (Baker 2008). The local courts mainly investigate and make judgements based on customary law, and chiefs also have the power to set bye-laws in conjunction with predominantly male elders. This means that citizens do not necessarily know the bye-laws that apply to them or that they may contravene human rights (Castillejo 2009). At the same time, there appears to be little chance that a poor person could bring a successful case against a chief or a member of a chief's family.

One additional factor is the continuing importance of kin groupings to rural society. Chiefs are themselves constrained by ruling family and kin linkages as well as traditions within the rural hierarchy.[13] Family history is frequently taken into account in selecting people for formal positions so descendants of chiefs are more likely to gain positions of influence than are relative newcomers. Kinship also has the effect of restricting power to a particular ethnic group - the *indigenes* - or the original founders. Because chiefdom and kinship is so tied to the land, legitimacy is usually tied to the length of time that a particular family has occupied a piece of land.

This places certain groups of people in an increasingly powerless position. *Non-indigene* (stranger) women and youth are in particularly vulnerable positions with almost no representation and no power to influence decisions in local courts. Paramount Chiefs are frequently cited as hearing cases when they have no mandate to do this, and individuals who oppose the chief are likely to be ostracised from the community (Richards et al. 2004; Fanthorpe 2006; Richards 2005; Castillejo 2009). Young men are expected to obey their elders whilst (male) elders wield power in families, social groupings, and justice forums like the courts. 'Youth' in Sierra Leone, as elsewhere, is a social category, having more to do with social status, belonging and kinship relations than with age (Fanthorpe 2001; Richards et al. 2004; Richards 2005). 'Youth' in Sierra Leone means 'anyone younger than the elders' and is linked to land control, wealth and marriage; those who lack those things remain classed as 'youth'. Even the legal definition of youth relates to those under 35. The social exclusion of these 'youths' was identified as a key driver of the conflict (Richards 1996; Fanthorpe 2001, Richards 2005).

Women have also been marginalised by the customary system of justice, although this varies between the north and south of the country (Castillejo 2009). The customary system tends to govern domestic issues that concern many women while women also face higher barriers to entry to the formal sector in terms of financial and social issues. The management of domestic affairs, dominated by men, is

[13] This is partly where the secret societies come in since they perform a regulatory function in society, including influencing the Chief.

institutionally biased against women and frequently violates women's constitutional and human rights. Many of practices continue within the customary system despite the introduction of human rights legislation, including women having the status of 'minors' in many local courts (Castillejo 2009). During research within the Chiefdoms in 2002, there were comments from women that expressed pleasure at being asked their opinion because they "[...] are not considered worthy of taking any challenging responsibility other than cooking and nursing children." (Fanthorpe et al. 2002: 31). The same report goes on to report that polygyny (one man with several conjugal relationships), leviratic marriage (inheriting a brother's wife), collecting 'marriage tax' whilst girls were still at school, hearing serious rape cases in local courts rather than district courts (and therefore treating it as a minor case) and patrilineal inheritance were all rigorously supported by local courts (Fanthorpe et al. 2002).

Impact of External Donor Intervention and Power

The majority of international donor support has been concentrated on strategic developments within Freetown and the development of the Ministries. With the exception of the Moyamba pilot district the UK's Justice and Security Development Programme has had very little impact beyond Freetown, but a new version of this programme seeks to expand more generally on the relationship between state and non-state, the Chiefs and the role of civil society in terms of mediation and justice (Albrecht 2010). At the same time, there has been a development of several legal NGOs designed to improve access to justice within the existing mechanisms at the local level. These include Timap for Justice and the National Forum for Human Rights. Many NGO programmes consist of a barrister and several paralegals, who offer advice, mediation and case work. In some cases, NGOs will also represent people up to the national court level. As such, paralegals operate as a vital information source for people whose preference is for the lowest settlement level but who also may not understand all of their options.

The development of NGOs and civil society organisations (CSOs) has been a deliberate attempt to construct a series of oversight mechanisms within civil society, partly to compensate for the extremely weak justice oversight mechanisms at state level (Castillejo 2009). The JSDP developed a 'demand-side strategy' to develop the capacity of civil society to provide oversight at local level but also to develop projects that are likely to attract donor funding (DFID 2010). However, there are questions about the capability of civil society to do this, their access and also their independence from those local institutions they are supposed to be investigating (DFID 2010; Castillejo 2009).

Civil society may provide leverage to those seeking redress or compensation without going to court. Representation to a paralegal costs nothing, but shows intent and therefore may make a settlement out of court more likely. Kelsall (2006) documents a case in which a ten year old daughter of a local dignitary had been raped by a middle aged man. Timap had taken the case to the police and the family of the girl then tried to drop the case because the perpetrator had paid customary compensation. As Kelsall (2006) further points out, a cynical reading of this is that the family took the case to Timap as a form of leverage, knowing that the customary court would increase the offer of compensation to prevent a formal court case. This is useful leverage for the plaintiff (although the girl's thoughts are not documented) but it sits uncomfortably with the idea of punishing human rights violations.

Secondly, NGOs and this form of demand-led legal support and oversight represent a threat to the power of the chiefs (Richards 2003; Jay and Koroma 2004). In this way, civil society can form a local opposition to the chiefs and therefore a threat. However, there are real questions about *who* actually constitutes civil society. There is certainly a legitimate concern that many civil society groups are not representative, may be chasing donor funding rather than developing independent strategies and may also be comprised of different versions of the same local elites who have had access to education (Castillejo 2009).

However, it is clear that organisations like Timap do empower local people. The state law lacks hegemony in Sierra Leone as it is geographically limited to urban areas, is socially limited (by secret societies) and is also institutionally compromised (glacial speed, financially limited, lacking capacity). As such, any external intervention is likely to be similarly limited. However, where Timap and others have been successful has been in helping individuals to act within the framework of state law through providing access to knowledge, legal advice, advocacy and mediation (Kelsall 2006). Certainly where the state law is applied in Sierra Leone, this type of NGO intervention has improved access to justice (DFID 2010 Castillejo 2009).

This leaves the international community with a series of choices about how to move forward. Given the lack of hegemony of the state law across Sierra Leone, the donor community is in a good position to broaden the existing mandate of the state law through geographical expansion coupled with support to overcome the institutional flaws of lack of capacity and resources. At the same time, there clearly has to be recognition of the strength of local institutions, including secret societies and customary law in those areas currently outside the remit of the state law as codified. In part this is already being recognised with DFID producing an Improved Access to Security and Justice Programme in Sierra Leone that explicitly recognises the importance of the customary system as well as formal legal institutions (Albrecht 2010).

Conclusions

This article has explored the relationship between justice provision and local government in post-conflict Sierra Leone. It shows how national reforms and international interventions in the justice/security sector associated with decentralization have altered power structures and that these altered power structures have subsequently come to play a significant role in determining the outcomes of these reforms and interventions. Local political power structures remain dominated by paramount Chiefs and traditional elites and continue to exclude significant groups from justice and power. Chiefs, as agents of the state, can count on the support of central government agencies in their insistence that they retain considerable power over local institutions and, in this, they represent a desire of centralised political power to exert authority at a local level (Fanthorpe et al. 2011). These local power dynamics have a strong bearing on the extent to which rural citizens can gain access to justice despite efforts to decentralise power and legally empower marginalised groups. Reform efforts have overlooked the inherent political dimensions of justice provision, which in rural Sierra Leone are deeply embedded in informal social structures, including kinship relations and secret societies, but which have also been influenced by more recent local government reforms and the continuing influence of the chiefs.

For most people, justice is not dispensed from formal, modern systems but from a dense network of institutions at the local level, which may or may not be codified or even visible. These institutions constantly change and are subject to a variety of controlling bodies, which regulate the meaning and enforcement of common law. Indeed, even the formal institutions of local and magistrate courts draw on common law rather than state law in many of their cases, and this is open to interpretation and influence according to changing local customs. Different social structures exercise influence over justice processes and outcomes. These biases exist despite the public, national agreements, for example to enforce human rights legislation. Local power is at least partly exercised through the appointment to courts and through the role of elders within villages, many of which are relatively old and also male. As documented, this leads to institutional bias within the customary system, particularly against women and those classified as youth.

Overall, these political dynamics leads to a dilemma for international support in the justice sector. Whilst some argue that international support should forget formal, western justice and support the local systems (Baker 2008), it is clear that there are considerable issues with this style of justice and abuse of the traditional system may have significantly contributed to the war in the first place (Richards et al. 2004; Jay and Koroma 2004; Jackson 2005). For the powerless, this means that they have no effective access to justice.

The core issue, then, must be to encourage external support that empowers people to access justice within the legal frameworks within which they operate. In other words, there has to be an acknowledgement that a formal legal framework lacks hegemony and is unlikely to be available to every community within Sierra Leone. At the same time, this does not mean that people within those communities should be just subject to the whims of local political elites or the biases of the chiefs. This implies a huge improvement in capacity and reach of the formal, state legal system and in the ability of those involved to be able to access support, knowledge and advice to enable them to use it.

The political reality of the local situation in Sierra Leone is that both the chiefs and central government civil servants are attempting to access what David Booth (2010) refers to as 'strangulation by politics', whereby there is a campaign for the reinstatement of colonial era institutions characterised by a central state exercising power through 'indirect rule' and thereby retaining control over the local districts (Fanthorpe et al. 2011). This stands in contrast to the decentralised vision of local political power making local decisions, but it does go some way to explain the persistence of dependency politics at local level and the almost complete dependency on the chief for access to land, services and justice.

This does, however, have its limits, and it is clear that human rights, development and good government have all become part of the day-to-day lexicon of the government. The current government's agenda, for example, refers to the idea of a social contract between a government that delivers services and a population that pays taxes. This means a return to the chiefdom system of the pre-war period is unlikely. Its implication, given the persistence of chiefs, is that both the formal and informal systems are going to coexist for some time.

This does not mean that external intervention should merely acknowledge that local situations are complex, but that there needs to be a subtle shift in the way in which support for those excluded from the contemporary system is designed. Specifically, the lack of legal and political hegemony of the state means that any formal system will be not only difficult to access, but is also likely to vary in quality across the country. This is likely to be exacerbated by availability of staff and how embedded local staff are within local communities controlled by chiefs and will also vary geographically. Whilst it is commonplace to discuss chiefs as if they were a homogenous national group, this is not true and there are considerable variations in different regions and districts (Fanthorpe et al. 2011).

The experience for individuals within districts is likely to be unpredictable and uneven as well as varying in quality and outcome. It is very difficult to predict what may be the best course for a particular individual to pursue both within either formal or informal system, or indeed in those districts where research has shown that jurisdiction between formal and customary courts is also variable.

Given this, the analysis of the local system within Sierra Leone suggests a strong refocusing away from just concentrating on support for the courts and towards supporting individuals within the system in finding the best way to negotiate the reality of local justice systems. This may encompass 'justice shopping', whereby support could be given in order to maximise the outcome for individuals regardless of which system is being used, or improving education, support and financial resources to enable better 'justice navigation' by individuals. This would provide a practicable solution in the medium term as the formal legal system, along with conventions such as human rights, develops more fully. It provides a means whereby individuals may be empowered within real systems as those systems evolve, rather than either leaving them to the mercy of a formal system that is the preserve of the few, or a customary law system dominated by local elites.

References

ALBRECHT, Peter
2010 *Betwixt and between – chiefs and reform of Sierra Leone's justice sector.* DIIS Working Paper 2010:33.
ALBRECHT, Peter and Paul JACKSON
2009 *Security System? Transformation in Sierra Leone 1997-2007*, Global Facilitation Network for Security Sector Reform and DFID.

BAKER, Bruce
2006 'The African post-conflict policing agenda in Sierra Leone.' *Conflict, Security & Development* 6 (1): 25-50.2008 'Beyond the Tarmac Road: Local Forms of Policing in Sierra Leone and Rwanda.' *Review of African Political Economy* 35: (118), 555-570.
BAKER, Bruce and Eric SCHEYE
2007 'Multi-Layered Justice and Security Delivery in Post-Conflict and Fragile States.' *Conflict, Security and Development* 7 (4) 503-528.
BOOTH, David
2010 *Towards a Theory of local governance and public goods' provision in sub-Saharan Africa*. Africa Power and Politics Working Paper no. 13.
CASTILLEJO, Clare
2009 *Building Accountable Justice in Sierra Leone*. FRIDE Working Paper 76, Madrid: FRIDE.
CUTTING, Joel
2004 *Overview of the Ministry of Local Government and Community Development Capacity Needs in Relation to the Decentralisation and Local Government Reform Programme (Government of Sierra Leone)*. DFID, Sierra Leone.
DENNEY, Lisa2011 'Reducing poverty with teargas and batons: The security-development nexus in Sierra Leone.' *African Affairs* 110 (439): 275-294.
DFID (DEPARTMENT FOR INTERNATIONAL DEVELOPMENT)
2010 *Building the State and Securing the Peace*. DFID Policy and Practice Paper, London. (unpublished draft).
EVANS, Roderick, David JONES and Graham THOMPSON
2002 *Sierra Leone Security Sector Reform Project II: Output to Purpose Review*. Defence Advisory Team Output to Purpose Review, 25 June–5 July. DFID.
FANTHORPE, Richard
2001 'Neither Citizen nor Subject? "Lumpen" agency and the legacy of native administration in Sierra Leone.' *African Affairs* 100: 363-386.
2006 On the Limits of Liberal Peace: Chiefs and Democratic Decentralization in Post-War Sierra Leone. *African Affairs* 105: 27-49.
FANTHORPE, Richard, Alice JAY and Victor Kalie KAMARA
2002 *A Review of the Chiefdom Governance Reform Programme, Incorporating an Analysis of Chiefdom Administration in Sierra Leone*. Unpublished DFID report, Freetown.
FANTHORPE, Richard, Andrew LAVALI and Mohamed Gibril SESAY
2011 *Decentralization in Sierra Leone: Impact, constraints and prospects*.

Unpublished DFID Sierra Leone Report.
FITZGERALD, Ann M.
2004 *Security Sector Reform in Sierra Leone*. Shrivenham: Global Facilitation Network for Security Sector Reform.
GINIFER, Jeremy and Kaye OLIVER
2004 *Evaluation of the Conflict Prevention Pools: Sierra Leone*. Evaluation Report EV647. London: DFID,
HORN, ADRIAN, Funmi OLONISAKIN,and Gordon PEAKE
2006 'United Kingdom-led Security Sector Reform in Sierra Leone.' *Civil Wars* 8(2) 109-123.
HOWLETT-BOLTON, Anthony C.
2008 *Aiming for Holistic Approaches to Justice Sector Development*. Security System Transformation in Sierra Leone, 1997-2007. Working Paper Series Paper No. 7, Global Facilitation Network for Security Sector Reform and International Alert. Birmingham: University of Birmingham.
JACKSON, Paul
2005 'Chiefs, Money and Politicians: Rebuilding Local Government in Post-War Sierra Leone.' *Public Administration and Development* 25: 49-58.
2006 Reshuffling an old Deck of Cards? The Politics of Local Government Reform in Sierra Leone. *African Affairs* : (106) 95-111.
JACKSON, Paul and Peter ALBRECHT
2011 *Reconstructing Security after Conflict: Security Sector Reform in Sierra Leone*. Basingstoke: Palgrave Macmillan.
JACKSON, Paul and Peter ALBRECHT (eds.)
2010b *Security Sector Reform in Sierra Leone 1997 - 2007: Views from the Front Line*. Geneva Centre for the Democratic Control of Armed Forces. Berlin: LIT Verlag.
JAY, Alice and Momoh Taziff KOROMA
2004 *From 'crying' and clientalism to rights and responsibilities*. Study for the Government of Sierra Leone and European Commission on Accountability in Sierra Leone. Freetown.
KEEN, David
2005 *Conflict and Collusion in Sierra Leone*. Oxford: James Currey.
KELSALL, Tim
2006 *Law and Legal Institutions in an Upcountry Sierra Leonean Town*. Unpublished report prepared for Timap for Justice and the National Forum for Human Rights, Sierra Leone.
MANNING, Ryann E.
2009 'The landscape of Local Authority in Sierra Leone: How 'traditional' and 'modern' justice systems interact'. Pp. 110-137 in Yongmei Zhou (ed.),

Decentralization, Democracy and Development: Recent Experience from Sierra Leone. World Bank Country Study. Washington: World Bank.

OECD/DAC (ORGANISATION FOR ECONOMIC COOPERATION AND DEVELOPMENT/ DEVELOPMENT COOPERATION DIRECTORATE)

2005 *Security System Reform and Governance*. DAC Guidelines and Reference Series. Paris: OECD.

PETERS, Krijn

2006 *Footpaths to Reintegration. Armed Conflict, Youth and the Rural Crisis in Sierra Leone*. PhD Thesis. Wageningen University, the Netherlands.

POATE, Derek, Paul BALOGUN, Ines ROTHMANN, Mark KNIGHT and Fatmata SESAY

2008 *Country Programme Evaluation: Sierra Leone*. Evaluation Report EV690. DFID.

RICHARDS, Paul

1996 *Fighting for the Rain Forest: War, Youth, & Resources in Sierra Leone*. Oxford: James Currey.

2006 'To Fight or to Farm? Agrarian Dimensions of the Mano River Conflicts (Liberia and Sierra Leone).' *African Affairs* 104: 571-590.

RICHARDS, Paul, Khadija BAH and James VINCENT

2004 *The Social Assessment Study: Community-driven Development and Social Capital in Post-War Sierra Leone*. Unpublished paper commissioned by the Community Driven Development Group of the World Bank for the National Commission for Social Action of the Government of Sierra Leone.

SAWYER, Amos

2004 'Violent conflicts and governance challenges in West Africa: the case of the Mano River Basin area.' *Journal of Modern African Studies* 42 (3): 437-463.

TRC (TRUTH AND RECONCILIATION COMMISSION)

2004 *Final Report of the Truth and Reconciliation Commission of Sierra Leone*. Freetown.

DELIVERING JUSTICE: THE CHANGING GENDERED DYNAMICS OF LAND TENURE IN BOTSWANA

Anne Griffiths

Introduction

Poverty reduction has been at the heart of global initiatives promoted by International and transnational organizations, such as the United Nations (UN), the World Bank and the UK's Department for International Development (DFID) (UNDP 2008; World Bank 2006; UNDP 2005; DFID 2004, 2008; SIDA 2002). In recognising that women and children feature disproportionately among the poor worldwide (Ruzvidzo and Tiagha, 2005), these agencies have expanded the concept of poverty to include not only material deprivation but also powerlessness that stems from a lack of access to justice. In addressing the latter in its 2008 report, the Commission for the Empowerment of the Poor (2008) identified land as one of the four pillars of legal empowerment.

This article explores women's access to land in Botswana and the changes that have ensued over time derived from institutional, legal and social transformations, brought about in part by the role played by NGO's. Based on field research carried out in the 1980s (See Griffiths 1997) and in 2009-2010 under a grant from the Leverhulme Trust it examines the factors that have led to a situation where women are now clearly represented in land transactions[1]. These include enhanced

[1] I am indebted to the Leverhulme Trust and to the government of Botswana and all those who participated in the research, especially my research assistants, Phidelia Dintwe, Phenhyo Churchill Thebe, Kawina Power and Boinelo Baakile.

education as well as informal and formal sector employment that have enabled some women to be more proactive, along with a shift in social attitudes towards women's role in society that is harder to define but stands in marked contrast to views expressed by interviewees in my earlier research. Understanding the social dimensions of change and their effects is important, but is something that is often overlooked by international donors who have a tendency to focus on reforming laws and institutions without having a clear grasp of how these interact with the social dynamics of their environment.[2] Yet such knowledge is crucial if rhetoric is to be distinguished from reality and ideological assertions are to be tested against empirical facts. For without this understanding policies may give rise to unexpected outcomes and detrimental effects that run contrary to the intentions of donor programmes and policies (Weilenmann 2009).

Within Africa, rights to land have always been the subject of contestation, fuelled by changes in demography, the mobility and density of populations and economic development. A key resource for family and household livelihood, land has been the subject of ongoing debate especially in the broader context of nation building and development. Earlier debates were polarised about the extent to which customary land tenure represented an obstacle to national progress that was associated with the kind of agricultural investment in and productive use of land that in turn is associated with clearly defined and enforceable property rights. These rights were promoted through individual, registered title that is derived from Western style law.[3] Over time the neo-liberal economic agenda, that underpinned the move towards registrations of title, became broadened to adopt a more holistic approach to development and poverty, including attention to human rights, good governance, accountability and informal justice.[4] Nonetheless, problems still arise

[2] See Manji (2010) on the difficulties of drafting legislation to protect women's access to land in the face of opposition from commercial lenders and the problems of reconciling financial inclusion with the aim of international development to end poverty.

[3] For discussion of these debates see Griffiths (2007).

[4] An example is provided by a Report on "Non State Systems of Justice" issued by the UK Department of International Development (DFID 2004) that, among other factors, recognizes the need to address historical context, the role of the non-state legal order, human rights compliance, and myths held about non-state legal orders.

as to how these concepts are to be defined and assessed with regard to implementation. For example, one project call issued by the UN in 2008 for a study of informal justice world wide, constantly associated 'informal justice' (including customary law) with what it referred to as 'deficits' in the democratic process. This is done without every clearly identifying what is meant by 'justice', or the characteristics that are associated with its 'formal' and 'informal' character. The call also failed to address how a 'democratic process' was to be identified. This lack of clarity stems from a conflation of ideological or normative assertions that are taken to be commensurate with reality on the ground. This 'reality' however cannot be taken for granted but must be constructed through empirical observations that investigate how questions of land, poverty and access to justice are handled in specific contexts. My research is an attempt to bridge that gap. A variety of methods were employed in the data collection, including archival research, examination of court and land board records, participant observation of disputes, interviews with government personnel, members of NGO's and local people as well as extended oral life histories of families from Molepolole village, updating earlier research. In 2009 a new dimension was added, namely a study of the Kweneng Land Board and of the Land Tribunal that deals with appeals from Land Boards.

The Botswana government acknowledges that: "studies worldwide have shown that the impact of population growth on poverty is strongest at the micro-level, that is, at the level of households and communities", recognising that "poverty remains one of the major development challenges for Botswana" (Botswana Government 2003a: 24). The government also accepts that women bear the brunt of poverty, especially given female-headed households that are prevalent in the country (Botswana Government 1981a: 21; UNICEF 1993). In 2002-3, 30% of the population lived below the national poverty line. Among this group nearly two out of three were rural and most of them were women, with female-headed households proving to be the most vulnerable in both rural and urban areas (van Klaveren et al. 2009: 31-32). Under these conditions the question of women's access to land is highly pertinent given that land is not only central to the state's strategies for development but also crucial for the livelihoods and well-being of individuals, households and families.

Legal and Historical Background to Land in Botswana

Two years after acquiring Independence Botswana passed the Tribal Land Act of

1968 (Cap. 32:02, Laws of Botswana). It was the first piece of legislation to propose substantial changes to the dominant Tswana tribal systems of land tenure, which had been left intact after the proclamation of the tribal reserves during the colonial era (Ng'ong'ola 1997: 14). This was necessary in order to more readily accommodate "more modern practices of land use, such as more exclusive allocation and utilisation of tribal grazing ranges" (Morolong and Ng'ong'ola 2007: 146). These developments were perceived as enabling a young country to provide for a land administration system that was just and that could assure all Batswana of access to land by being more accountable to elected politicians that were newly in place. This was to be done by dislodging the authority of chiefs by vesting ownership of tribal land in land boards specifically established in each tribal area to whom authority was delegated for dealing with land rights, including judicial powers over land disputes previously vested in chiefs. With an eye to progress the rules regulating land covered a complex mix of statutory and customary provisions that vary according to how land is classified under one of three categories, as tribal, freehold or state land under statutes such as the Tribal Land Act (TLA), the State Land Act (Cap. 32:01) and the Town and Country Planning Act (Cap. 32:09). As Tribal Land accounts for 70% of land in Botswana it is on this sector that my study is focused. Some of the provisions in relation to the TLA reflect a continuity with the past, leading Morolong and Ng'ong'ola (2007: 143) to observe that when it comes to Botswana "the unique features of contemporary tribal or customary land tenure in Botswana can be retraced to the manner in which the country's plural land tenure system was constructed during the first few decades of colonial rule". Under the TLA, Land Boards were established for specified 'tribal areas' that corresponded with the nine native reserves proclaimed during the colonial era. However, under section 13, the Act handed over powers to Land Boards in relation to allocation, use and cancellation of land rights that had been previously vested in chiefs under customary law. Thus Land Boards replaced Chief and tribal authority control over the allocation and distribution of land.[5]

Institutional Features: Kweneng Land Board and its Powers

Kweneng is one of twelve Land Boards in Botswana that under the Tribal Land

[5] Informally, chiefs and headmen continue to have some influence, especially in handling family agreements on inheritance that deal with land transfers.

Act administers customary grants of land and common law leases. Tribal land is now held by the land board or by individuals either as a customary grant or a lease. Neither of these types of tenure confer "ownership" on the recipients as this vests in the Land Boards who hold it "[...] in trust for the benefit and advantage of citizens of Botswana" under section 10(1) of the Act. This wording reflects the 1993 amendment to the Act opening up jurisdiction for Land Boards to all citizens regardless of their 'tribal' affiliation. While the Act does not define customary rights, these are commonly assumed to cover residence *(motse),* arable agriculture *(tshimo)* and grazing *(moraka)*. In dealing with tribal land, Land Boards could issue customary land certificates for residence, arable agriculture and grazing but not for hunting. These certificates, however, could not be given for non-customary uses such as trading, manufacturing, business or commerce. To deal with these activities, Land Boards were given powers to allocate common-law rights under leases. The introduction of common law leases on tribal land was designed to commercialise land rights in rural areas. One of the most important reasons for pursuing common-law title and leases is that they can be used as a security for development loans. Ordinary customary grants cannot because they are not regarded as marketable securities by formal lending institutions because the land has not been adequately surveyed to meet these institutional requirements.

Kweneng Land Board (KLB) is based in the village of Molepolole, which lies at the centre of the Bakwena polity or 'tribe'. It was established before colonial overrule by Sechele I (c.1833-1892) who consolidated a disunited Bakwena around a large central settlement with outlying domains evident in Molepolole today. Always large, it has grown from a settlement of around 30,000 in the 1980s to over 50,000 in 2008, making it the largest village in Botswana today. It is both the capital and regional centre of Kweneng district where I carried out fieldwork between 1982 and 1989.

My study in 2009-2010 focused on this Land Board because in its 5,000 km^2 jurisdiction it administers the entire spectrum of land allocation in Botswana from rural cattle posts to peri-urban and urban residential and industrial areas. Situated close to the capital city, Gaborone, it is located in an area where nearly one third of Botswana's 1.9 million people live. In this area, land use and tenure is a pressing issue given the growth in population (Botswana Government 2003a: 18) and the expansion of urban centres like Gaborone. This gives rise to competition for the acquisition of plots of land, not just for domestic or agricultural use, but also for commercial purposes (Kalabamu and Morolong 2004).

When Land Boards were established in 1968 the objective was to balance a number of interests reflecting tribal authority and governmental political control that would democratise land institutions. To achieve this membership of these boards derived from a number of sources including local elections within the jurisdiction of the Land Board as well as appointees from the Ministry of Lands and Housing and the Ministries of Agriculture and of Commerce and Industry. When I carried out my research in 2009-2010 there were nine working members of KLB, four of whom were women.

Access to Land: Social Dynamics of Gendered Family Networks

My earlier research from 1981 to 1989 pointed to the need to move beyond abstract assertions about land tenure in law, to acquire a detailed understanding of the concrete ways in which individuals and families acquire access to and control over land in all its forms in practice (see Griffiths 1997). In an African context it is clear that "people's ability to exercise claims to land remains closely linked to membership in social networks and participation in both formal and informal political processes" (Berry 1993: 104). My life histories from the 1980s highlighted the difficulties women face in gaining access to or control over property, including land, under customary law. This is due to the gendered position women occupy in kinship networks and the economic, political, ideological and social domains that shape the world in which they live. The research also underscored the need to recognize the social context of law as well as the degree to which customary and Western-style law are mutually constitutive and underpinned by the gendered norms and values that operate in daily life. This is something that is often overlooked by policy makers, as is especially evident in law reform and in the current focus on informal, traditional or customary law and its perceived failure by donors to meet human rights standards.

My earlier research on life histories also highlighted the circumstances under which some women were successfully able to claim resources, including land, while others faced constraints that disempowered them. These life histories, collected in 1984, 1989 and 2009-2010, through oral testimonies and data from field notes provided by anthropologist Isaac Schapera, cover five generations of the founding families of Mosotho *kgotla*[6] in Molepolole village. In 2009-2010 I

[6] A *kgotla* is the assembly centre (both the physical location and the body of members) of a group of households presided over by a male headman or ward

focused on updating the genealogies of two particular family groups, the Makokwe family group and the Radipati family group, who are both descended from a common male ancestor, Koosimile, because these groups, although related, demonstrate very different life trajectories. Makokwe who was born in the first house, had access to a resource base that revolved round subsistence agriculture, raising livestock and migrant labour of an unskilled nature on an intermittent or contract basis. These characteristics, shared by many other families in Botswana, associated them with what Parson (1981) termed 'the peasantariat'. The members of this kin group were increasingly distanced from the elite cattle owners and higher income wage earners (Botswana Government 1981a: 8). In contrast to his brother, Radipati, who was born into the third house, was an educated man. His descendants, unlike other families in Mosotho *kgotla*, have focused on attaining education and the acquisition of skilled and secure employment, which among the younger generation is predominantly government based. This has set them apart from other families, and through the position of the younger generation who represent a growing elite in Botswana, places them among those whom Cooper (1982) has referred to as 'the salariat'. For family members the networks of which they formed part had an impact upon their access to and control over resources. For women among the Makokwe family, the gendered division of labour within the household placed them in a weaker position than that of their male counterparts. For while their labour was an essential part of the family enterprise, it was generally of a domestic and agricultural nature that was not valued on a par with that of men who provided essential cash remittances for households or who maintained control over cattle at the cattle post. In contrast, among the Radipati family, women's access to education and stable formal employment has given them a greater range of resources, including land, as well as giving them a greater degree of independence from reliance on male networks of support. However, in the 1980s when I began my research they represented a minority of women within their generational cohort.

---

head; in the past, but no longer, all household heads were related through the male line. It forms part of the organization of Tswana society that revolves around the construction of a *morafe* or polity. *Kgotlas* are structured through a tightly organized hierarchy of progressively more inclusive administrative groupings, beginning with households that make up a *kgotla* and extending through wards, which are the major units of political and legal organization of the *morafe* as a whole. At the centre is *Kogsing*, the Chief's ward where the Chief's *kgotla* is situated.

Bearing this in mind, I expected to find a dearth of women when it came to land transactions when I began my research in 2009-2010. In order to obtain a broader picture, beyond qualitative life history data, my research incorporated a study of land certificates and leases from Kweneng Land Board. I was extremely priviliged to be granted access to these records, which have proven hard to locate over the years but which provide important information about who is acquiring land certificates and the extent to which women are featuring in these transactions. As far as I am aware this is the first study of its kind to investigate land certificates and leases and it fills an empirical gap in knowledge about dealings in land. For as Ng'ong'ola, Professor of law at Botswana University, observed to me in 2004:

> Land Boards claim to follow a gender neutral policy on allocations. But it would be interesting to apply your type of [data] analysis to the actual situation on the ground. There is not much information on how women have been fairing in their dealings with Land Boards.

My study examined 4041 certificates and 1200 leases over a ten-year period from 1999 to 2009, which was combined with the observation of women appearing as claimants and appellants before Kweneng Land Board for all types of land use.[7] Contrary to my expectations, women were in fact featuring in the processes of acquiring certificates and leases.[8] Overall, over half of the land certificates were registered in women's names (2,063 out of 4,041), including certificates over residential plot allocations, transfers and extensions, as well as field allocations/registrations, transfers and extensions. There were only thirty-seven cases where the sex of the certificate holder was unclear. A smaller number of women feature when it comes to fields. Out of a total of 1,611 certificates, women accounted for 44%, that is, 716 certificates. This is interesting because in my

[7] Given the state of the records it was not possible to sample a set number from each year or to conduct a random sample from the records. Thus it was not possible, for example, to access 2,000 records with regard to fields with 200 records from each year over a ten-year period. Instead, we had to work with what was available. For further details see Griffiths (n.d.a).

[8] While information was incomplete in a number of cases, especially for the years 1999 to 2005, it was possible to identify the sex of the certificate or leaseholder from their Omang or identity card, where the fifth number signifies a man if it is 1 and a woman if it is 2.

earlier research I found that where women did access land it was through inheriting fields from their mothers or grandmothers. Kalabamu and Morolong (2004) state that women in 2004 were more likely to get fields as men were more interested in other types of property like cattle and cattle posts. In discussions with government personnel, NGO's and local people in 2010 there was a view that women may be handing over their fields to men because they lack the resources to work them and/or because of fears about personal safety in isolated areas where women may feel vulnerable. As the Deputy Director of Social Services explained in an interview:

> Women are not really into farming because fields today are so far from the village that when they go there they have to live alone. There have been a number of cases reported of older women being raped at the farm lands and women are scared. In the past old people were used to farming but for a poor single mother who will be alone at the lands it will not be safe for her.

Women also feature in leases. Out of 600 residential leases there were 292 women and 305 men with only 3 applicants whose sex was unclear or who represented an 'other' category such as a company. Women did not feature as prominently in the 600 commercial leases with 347 men to 196 women, but they were still present (with only 57 in the 'other' category). Not only are women in possession of certificates and leases, but they also feature on the waiting list for land in Kweneng district. On one list, for Gamodubu and the surrounding area that is close to Molepolole, there were 10,856 names up to May 2010, consisting of 5,944 women and 4,901men (with 11 where the sex was unclear). Overall, my most recent research demonstrates that women (from 21 to 84 years of age) are clearly acquiring land through the acquisition of customary certificates and leases to a much larger extent than has generally been recognised, although what little empirical research exists currently in Botswana points towards this conclusion (Kalabamu 2006 and 2009). The factors motivating women to obtain land and underlying their success in acquiring certificates are discussed below.

Factors Mobilising Women's Acquisition of Land

Local people, land board and government personnel, and staff from NGOs view women's current acquisition of land as being attributable to a range of factors. These include changes in the law that involve repealing legislation, such as the

Abolition of Marital Power Act, number 34 of 2004, providing that women married under community of property laws are no longer subject to their husband's exercise of marital power over matrimonial property. This means that married women can now acquire land certificates in their own right. Or it may involve amendments to existing legislation, such as the insertion of section 18 into the Deeds Registry Act (Cap. 33:02) to bring it into line with the provisions of the foregoing Act. These changes also involve the government's acknowledgement of the need to pursue gender equality, fostered by international human rights legislation and judicial decisions forcing the government to deal with gender discrimination. For example, *The Attorney General v. Unity Dow,*[9] (dealing with discrimination against married women and the citizenship of their children) and the *Student Representative Council of Molepolole College of Education v Attorney General*[10] (where a policy excluding pregnant female students from College for a year was held to be discriminatory). However, while the Botswana government has finally ratified the Convention on All Forms of Discrimination Against Women and its Optional Protocol, it has so far failed to ratify – or even sign - the Protocol to the African Charter on Human and People's Rights on the Rights of Women in Africa. The development of women's awareness of their rights through enhanced education and increased participation in both formal and informal sector employment is also deemed to have played a very important role. In this regard, and more generally, the work done over the last twenty-five years by NGOs such as Emang Basadi (Stand Up Women) and Ditshwanelo (Centre for Human Rights) was also cited as having had a significant impact.

Both the men and women whom I interviewed express the view that there has been a shift in attitude towards women. A male Land Board member commented:

> I tend to think as the country develops more women have access to resources. Our mentality was initially that a woman belongs in the kitchen. That view has now changed. We recognize that women have contributed to the economy, not just as child minders, and that women are getting access to jobs that were predominantly male in the past.

The Acting Deputy Land Board Secretary, a woman, also observed that: "today

---

[9] Court of Appeal, Civil Appeal No. 4/91 or 1992 LRC (Const) 574.

[10] Civil Appeal No 13 of 1994 [1995] (3) LRC 447.

there is recognition that women have a role to play in the socio-economic development of the country". However these perspectives are resisted in some quarters with the NGP Emang Basadi's office bearers noting that while "things have changed men resist this". They observe that men are frustrated because "their voices are now faint" and that this gives rise to gender-based violence. In part they attribute this to the fact that as women become more proactive "men may feel displaced from their roles and responsibilities" including their role as breadwinner. Men view this role as under threat "because women never used to work formally".

The Deputy Permanent Secretary at the Ministry of Labour and Home Affairs acknowledges: "the lifestyle has changed in Botswana". He attributes this to the number of programmes[11] that provide assistance so that "when you look at women and economic empowerment there are so many packages [available] that you see many women coming up". The senior adjudication officer of Kweneng Land Board, a woman, explained that: "married women used not to own properties, the husband owned them but this is no longer the case". She also observed that more women today are educated and "have the ability to hold their own money". She attributes women's advancement to their access to education and their ability to "stand on their own". In the past women had to get permission from the husband to apply for a plot. The requirement has been removed "because of human rights". She also observes that in the past "men had the money power".

Legal changes have contributed to this development. The legal advisor to the Ministry of Lands and Housing explained that: "women are no longer in a position where they cannot get land". According to him, in the past before the Tribal Land Act: "women could not get land in their own right when chiefs were allocating land." After this Act was passed: "there were still some problems for women who were married in community of property because they could not get land in their own right"[12]. This was because "men could use marital power against their wives and so stop them from acquiring land independently. They used it to deny women

[11] These include programmes for education and training in a number of sectors including agriculture and business as well as grants fostering self-employment, some of which are financed by government and some of which are jointly financed by government and international donors.

[12] This is under Roman Dutch law, which gave the husband marital power over a married couple's estate so that the wife could not hold or administer property in her own right until the Abolition of Marital Power Act was passed in 2004.

access to land. When this was abolished [in 2004] women could no longer be denied land on this basis." Taken together with the 1993 amendment to the Tribal Land Act, that provided that land boards were no longer restricted to allocating land to "tribesmen" of a particular polity but were charged with allocating land to "citizens" of Botswana, he is of the opinion that "today the system is working well for women". He sees the 1993 amendment as "placing everyone on an equal footing".

NGOs, such as Emang Basadi and Ditshwanelo, have made a major contribution in raising public awareness about gender issues and human rights. This is acknowledged by the Acting Deputy Land Board Secretary who observes that they "have promoted women's empowerment and the government seems to be supporting them". A female land board member stated in her interview that Ditshwanelo has made a contribution to women featuring in land certificates and leases because:

> [...] they run workshops. One of their recommendations was that having a spouse should not be a hindrance for women to acquire land. The Land Board adopted that recommendation. At the time I joined the Land Board women had to acquire their husbands' consent to apply for land. This was also the case for transfers. Now there is no problem related to women acquiring land [in their own right].

Women, however do not represent a homogenous whole and my preliminary analysis suggests that there are certain characteristics that enhance women's potential to acquire land. For presentational purposes I will split them into three categories although the characteristics they embody may well overlap and be interdependent. First, there are the unmarried, proactive female household heads with children, who are employed and/or run small businesses; I shall refer to these as the 'Can Do Women'.[13] Second, there are the family carers and investors who within their family group are unmarried and whose siblings agree to them inheriting the family yard because of their caring responsibilities and/or lack of resources or because of the foregoing and their economic investment in the home. This category will be referred to as the 'Family Investors'. Third, there are those

[13] This term is derived from the way one of my interviewees described his female relatives.

women whose married male friends financially assist them to acquire land because they want to set them up in "small houses". I refer to this category as the 'Small House Women'. What these characteristics and categories entail is discussed in greater detail below.

(a) The 'Can Do Women'

There are more women demographically in Botswana than men, which has been the case for a number of years (Botswana Government 1995, 2004:8). Similarly, in Kweneng district, women are 52% of the population (Botswana Government 2009b: 7). Women in the district generally outlive men (Botswana Government 2009b: 11). Many of these women remain unmarried but have children. This is not a new phenomenon. Schapera (1947: 175) noted that with the advent of migrant labour during the colonial era marriage became postponed until a later stage in an individual's life cycle; that taken together with a decline in polygyny (Schapera 1950: 45; Schapera and Roberts 1975: 266; Kuper 1970: 473; Comaroff and Roberts 1977) lead to increased numbers of adults remaining attached to their natal household, especially unmarried women with children (Kocken and Uhlenbeck 1980: 53; Molenaar 1980; Griffiths 1988; 1997: 22-28; Molokomme 1991). More recently, the 2006 Demographic Survey records that 64.6% of the population has never married and that women head 46.6% of the households in the country (Botswana Government 2006: 26). The public are well aware of this, as one female sub-Land board member observed: "most women are not married so they go ahead in applying for land [because they have no husband to depend on]". She also commented that: "Batswana women have children before marriage. Then they think of having their own place. They don't want to stay in the family home [because this may cause quarrels]". Indeed, the Acting Deputy Land Board Secretary notes that: "even if women are married, we recognize that divorce rates are high and that a woman might [apply for land because] she might be chased away and obliged to return to her family home".

While many of these female-headed households feature among the poorest in the country, there are those that have been able to escape the net of poverty to maintain themselves and their families. There are a number of factors that have contributed to this. The first factor is enhanced formal education (Botswana Government 2009a) that not only applies to women but to the country as a whole, where three quarters of the population have attained education to a primary, if not to a secondary school level (van Klaveren et al 2009: 44). The second concerns changes in women's formal employment patterns that indicate that more women are becoming represented in this sector (Botswana Government 2006). This has been accompanied by an increase in women's informal sector employment much of which is conducted from women's homes or along the roads (Botswana Government 2007). While NGOs like Emang Basadi have lobbied for greater women's access to employment, there are others, like the Women's Finance House that assist low income women in acquiring skills and the start up capital to finance small business ventures, such as trade kiosks, hair salons and selling airtime. For greater detail on these developments see Griffiths (n.d.a).

Finally, self-help and the proactive engagement of unmarried women have helped them to access land. The Director of Housing notes that: "there has been a move to women being more proactive and taking advantage of situations that exist because women have to fend for their families". The Deputy Director of Social Services attributes the fact "that more and more women are applying for land now" to "women becoming more independent", adding that: "In the past women held marriage as an ideal but now over time women have seen other single women who have made it in life without a man. They can see that they can make it without a man". She also observes that: "there are many independent women who are now doing well on their own, even those with low literacy levels. Perhaps they are doing well with small businesses and their success can motivate other women". This is a perspective that is held by one of the female Land Board members who attributes the number of women featuring in land certificates to the fact that "many women are unmarried".

In a collective interview with sub-Land Board members there was an acknowledgment that most of the younger generation who are unmarried tend to apply for land on their own behalf. In this context one of them stated: "my own observation is that women tend to apply for land at an early age, unlike their male counterparts". He expanded on this theme to say: "a man may only get started at thirty-eight, maybe after getting married. Men tend to wait a lot of the time until, at a late stage, they realize now I'm a man I want to go out on my own [i.e. away from my parent's yard]."

To place these general observations in context from the life history data, Radipati's daughters, Goitsemang and Olebogeng, provide an example of proactive, unmarried women acquiring land. They are residents of Mosotho kgotla in Molepolole and form part of Radipati's family whose life histories I pursued in 1984, 1989 and 2010. Unlike other women of their generation, Goitsemang aged

73 and Olebogeng aged 66 (in 2010) received an education beyond that of most of their contemporaries. According to Goitsemang when her father died in the 1950s her mother Mhudi managed to find the money to continue her education beyond Standard 4 Primary School. This was unusual because: "parents did not regard education as important. They are only realizing now that education means a lot. They considered cattle more important".[14] As a result she was able to train as a nurse and work in South Africa until she returned home to help nurse her sick sister Salalenna. She then found employment in Gaborone with a construction company during the construction boom that was taking place in a post-independent Botswana. She worked her way up the company starting as a store worker and was promoted to a wages clerk and then to a personnel officer, a position that she held until she left in 1984 in order to return to Molepolole to look after her mother full time.

By this time she had acquired two plots of land in Gaborone. According to her nephew Bongi (Olebogeng's son)[15] these plots were acquired through the government self help housing association scheme (SHAA).[16] Such assets put her in a privileged position compared to many women of her generation. Through education she was able to obtain employment that not only enabled her to acquire resources for herself but also assisted her youngest sister, Olebogeng, who had also completed primary school, to find employment with the same company. She was able to nominate Olebogeng to replace her when she was transferred to Morupule Colliery where the company was putting up houses for Anglo-American in 1972. As a result Olebogeng was employed with the company up until 1989 when it was taken over. Like Goitsemang, she too has acquired land in Gaborone under the SHAA scheme, and this land is located next to her sister's plot.[17] Olebogeng currently lives in the natal household in Mosotho kgotla. Goitsemang also lives there but she regularly goes to stay with her unmarried daughter Patricia at the other end of the village where most of the younger generation have developed plots of land that they have acquired from the Land Board.

---

14 Quote from interview in 1989.

15 From an interview in 2010.

16 This programme applies to both tribal and state land.

17 While there is no comprehensive disaggregation of sexes with regard to statistics, the Director of Housing noted that in her experience most of those applying for SHAA and for the poverty alleviation and housing schemes are women.

Like many women in Botswana they have never married but have had children. These children have gone on to stable and secure employment. Goitsemang's nephew, Bongi, for example trained as a lawyer (like his uncle David) and in 2010 was acting as a legal advisor to the Office of the President. He acknowledges that his mother Olebogeng's life has been hard because she and her siblings inherited very little from their father Radipati, but that she, like his grandmother Mhudi (who died in 1988), is a 'can do' kind of person. He pays tribute to his grandmother saying that although "her children did not have a high level of education", from his perspective, "she made sure that all the grandchildren stayed with her and she instilled education in us like crazy". He observes that no other family from Mosotho kgotla is as well educated as his and in his view "education has taken us from the fringes of poverty". Goitsemang and Olebogeng find themselves in a different position from other women who may have found it more of an uphill struggle to acquire land, or more importantly to develop it, due to limited resources within their social networks.

(b) The Family Investors

A second group of women who acquire land are those whose siblings agree to them inheriting the family yard because of their lack of resources and/or their role as caregivers for family members, or because of their economic investment in the premises. Under customary law certain norms apply to the distribution of an estate. It is generally accepted that daughters inherit fields and that the family yard goes to the youngest son. At the five *kgotla* meetings held in Molepolole in 2010 there were some discrepancies as to the treatment of these assets, with some maintaining that the family yard went to the youngest child regardless of sex (Mokgopeetsane and Ntloolengwae wards) while others were firmly of the view that it went to the youngest son (Dikoloing, Lekgwapheng and Mokgalo wards). In the case of fields, some said it went to the eldest rather than the youngest daughter (Dikoloing and Ntloolengwae wards), but all agreed that she had to be unmarried. Where there was an additional field belonging to the father, there was consensus that this went to a son, although once again there was some disagreement as to whether this was the eldest or youngest son. What these discussion reveal are the ways in which people respond to living conditions on the ground that reveal the malleable, flexible nature of customary law.

From my earlier research it is clear that transmission of property among families is focused on maintaining the future generation with an emphasis on preserving assets where available for children. Given the patrilineal nature of Tswana society where descent is traced through the male line - through the man's father where the parents are married, and through the woman's father where they are not – it is not surprising that male offspring are privileged over female offspring when it comes to inheritance under customary law, with the eldest son receiving the greatest share of all the property in recognition of the responsibilities that he adopts as head of the family. For this reason, as head of the household, he not only had the role of custodian with regard to his children, but also had responsibilities for representing and maintaining extended kin (beyond his immediate nuclear family) where he was the senior male among the social network of family members.

Under this system, among children, daughters inherited less than their brothers because it was envisaged that they would marry, and go to live among their husbands' relatives where their husbands would establish their own *malwapa* (residential yards; sing. *lolwapa*). Through marriage, these women's children would be affiliated with their husband's family group, tracing descent through the male line where property devolves from father to son. What daughters tended to inherit was their mothers' personal property such as clothes and domestic utensils. They might also inherit fields that had been worked by their mothers. In contrast, brothers inherited the plough, cattle, any guns that their father may have had and other family property, including land. Among siblings property was not shared equally but depended on their birth order within the family.

However, these formulations of customary law derived from archival and oral sources were never rigidly adhered to as my 1980s research demonstrated (Griffths 1997: 46). This continues to be the case, as in 2010 it transpired that among Makowe's descendants a married daughter, Kgomotso, was allocated a family ploughing field but she requested that it go to her older, married brother Ranko, since she had acquired another field to plough from a *rakgadiagwe* (patrilineal aunt). What emerges from these histories is that in some cases families follow established norms, as in the case of Rammutla, who is the youngest son of Nkgadikang, who was Makokwe's second son. He inherited his parent's residential yard when his father died and had the certificate transferred into his name although his mother is still alive and living with him and his wife in the yard. On the other hand other arrangements may be made. It is interesting to note that the two children from Nkadikang's first marriage, a boy and a girl, took over their mother's property when she died and sold the developments on it, splitting the proceeds between them.

Thus there is a flexible approach to inheritance that incorporates adherence to traditional norms as well as allowing for other approaches to the distribution of property. Distributing property according to consensus reached among family members has always been a feature of customary law, but what is clear is that the basis upon which such agreements are made is open to a broader range of factors driving the process of negotiation than in the past. This flexibility is apparent from the land certificates that demonstrate that women are inheriting land although they are neither the eldest nor the youngest child and do not conform to earlier depictions of customary law norms. What appears to be at work here is an example of Erhlich's (1936) 'living law'. For what is happening is that siblings are agreeing to a different form of distribution through the signing of affidavits that are submitted as part of the transfer process. These affidavits signed by chiefs or headmen testify to the fact that the deceased's family have agreed to the land being transferred to the transferee. This must be done before the Land Board can certify a change in title to the land certificate, issuing a new certificate in the transferee's name. In discussing inheritance, headmen and land overseers acknowledge that families may reach their own arrangements with regard to the allocation of the family yard and fields. When asked if they find many of these agreements being made, the members of Dikoloing ward comment that: "due to modernisation it happens a lot". A young woman from Lekgwapheng ward gave an example drawn from her aunt's experience. She told us that the certificate was written in her aunt's name because the family agreed that it should be done that way and wrote letters agreeing to this to the Land Board. The headman of Mokgopeetsane Ward, Kgosi Benjamin, noted that where an inheritance is concerned the family: "come to me bringing all their names and I must write a letter to the Land Board".

In Ntlooengwae ward the headmen explained that the reason why women are appearing on certificates today is because "sometimes when one of the siblings looks after the other siblings or parents the plot will be transferred to the person who was looking after other family members" and women often take on this caretaking role. Or, he explained: "maybe the yard was developed by that particular person and having invested a lot in that plot the certificate will be transferred to the person who developed the plot". This was the case with Radipati's daughter, Goitsemang in the 1980s. Although no formal land certificate was involved, Mosotho *kgotla* members supported Goitsemang against her brother David's attempts to take control of the yard because of the financial investment she had made in it.

These practices may be attributed in part to changes in labour patterns within familial and household networks. In the 1930s for example, the Makokwe family were linked into co-operative networks that extended across several households and had contributed to the livelihoods of individuals and family members through the pooling of resources among and between generations. This involved staggering contracts at the South African mines to acquire money to invest in livestock and seeds for subsistence agriculture. It also involved sharing plough oxen and pooling labour as well as herding cattle at the cattlepost.

In recent years other options for maintaining livelihoods, outlined earlier in the paper, have loosened these co-operative ties and dependencies. The widow of Ntologelang, one of Makokwe's sons, observes that her grandchildren "are not keen to work jointly like their parents used to do" and that "they are only interested in taking care of their immediate families" although they do come together for "weddings and funerals". The advent of the plough and of government programmes providing free seed and ploughing services for up to five hectares of land mean that households are no longer so dependent on the extended networks for support that they used to be. Another widow of one of Makokwe's sons, Nkadikgang, commented that: "since we resorted to using tractors the spirit of brotherhood that hovered upon us died a natural death as we stopped helping each other". Other potential sources for securing livelihoods, such as access to other forms of employment, for example in the construction or service industries, and the development of informal sector businesses have created other opportunities. This has created a situation where the youngest living son of Makokwe, Ramokaki, bitterly reflects that he is facing challenges as a subsistence farmer, not only because he is old and sick[18] but because "only two of my grandchildren are keen to help me take care of my livestock".

What appears to be emerging are smaller, more nucleated family units where support is concentrated among fewer members. This is especially the case where resources are scarce.[19] Women have always taken on the role of caregivers within the family but the older generation appear to accord this role more recognition than they have in the past. This forms part of a more general move towards a

18 He never quite recovered his health after working at the South African mines from 1957 to 1970.

19 Motzafi-Haller (1986) notes the way in which in extreme cases poverty over time impacts on families and households by creating a truncated set of relationships brought about by the downsizing of family membership through abandonment.

reassessment of and recognition of changing gender roles within the society (Kalabamu 2003), and a more egalitarian approach to inheritance rights (Kalabamu 2009). In *kgotla* discussions and interviews in 2010 they observed that daughters could be depended upon to a greater extent not only to provide care-giving services but even economic support because sons were expending their resources elsewhere, often on women and children outside their immediate family group.

When it comes to inheritance, Ntlooengwae ward members note that: "siblings meet and agree as to whom the land should be transferred". In reaching these decisions the wealth and status of the siblings plays an important role with the result that "the poorest sibling who may be unemployed will be given the yard because the other siblings are in work and have already acquired other plots". Where family members have adequate access to resources and feel secure, they can afford to redistribute property according to need. Such an approach is not uncommon. There are examples of this kind of distribution taking place among Makokwe's descendants. His only daughter, Olebeng, the youngest child in the family, was given control over the natal household in Mosotho *kgotla* in the 1980s because her older brothers had all married and established their own households. She lived there for many years until she married in 2001 (in late middle age) and went to stay at her husband's homestead. It is not only women who benefit from these redistributions. Note the case of Ranko referred to earlier who benefited from his sister, Kgomotso, transferring her inherited field to him because he had no access to a field and she had acquired another elsewhere.

A member of the Molepolole sub-Land Board provided an illustration of the kind of factors that are taken into account in dealing with inheritance. He is the eldest child in a family with eight children, including six girls and two boys. He explains that in his family he and his siblings "have given our mother's house in Tshosa ward to our younger sister. This is because she is still young and doesn't have a lot of money. Most of us are old enough to look after ourselves". It turns out that this sister is not the youngest in the family. Of the four sisters who come after him, one is a nurse, one is an engineer who studied in the UK, one is a civil engineer in Gaborone in the Roads Department and the fourth sister is working for the Land Board. They are all married. Then comes the sister who is not married and who is working in Jwaneng "in a very simple job in one of the shops". His brother has graduated from University and is now working for the Citizen Empowerment Development Agency. The youngest child, "a sister, is studying information technology at the University of Botswana and will be graduating this year (2010)". He explains that they did not give the plot to their youngest sister "because she will be able to pursue a good living". In the family's view "my youngest sister will be able to look after herself [while] my [other] poor sister is not married and not getting a lot of money."

Such considerations are not confined to practices in Molepolole and Kweneng District. The senior adjudication officer for Kweneng Land Board, who is not from the district, is one of eight children in a family of six girls and two boys. She and her siblings have done well in life. In her own case, she and her deceased husband who was a senior police officer managed to acquire residential, commercial and agricultural land throughout the country in the course of employment transfers. She has no worries about there being sufficient property for her children to inherit. However, there is one sibling, a sister who did not progress beyond Form 3 at school and who has not managed to get a job. This sister now takes care of their elderly parents. All the siblings support her care-giving by contributing 200 Pula (about £20) a month for her upkeep. It is expected that when the parents die she will inherit the family yard because of her straightened circumstances.

(c) The Small House Women

Given the sensitive nature of the subject matter, it is hard to get information on the third category of unmarried women who receive financial assistance to acquire and develop land from married men. It was drawn to my attention by one of the male main Land Board members who observed that while not wishing to take anything away from women's achievements because "women are working and sweating for themselves", he does "know of a few women who are involved with married men. [These men] get fed up of going to motels and lodges and encourage the women to get a plot and develop it so they can visit them there." He noted: "there are a few like that. If you were to check you would find that they don't have the means themselves to develop the plot but there are developments going on [paid for by the men]". These relationships may represent a longstanding tradition in Botswana where women enter into relationships that are accorded some recognition but do not count as marriages (Schapera 1947: 173). In these cases the woman is referred to as a '*nyatsi*' (often glossed as 'concubine'). In these circumstances there is no legal obligation, as there would be in a marriage, for the man to support the woman as a wife. However, he may voluntarily provide financial assistance during the relationship by building her a house or developing land she has acquired as a form of security for her and any children they may have in the event of the relationship coming to an end. The subject of small houses features regularly in the

Botswana press and highlights family conflicts that arise in relation to the distribution of resources among family members. While the women associated with these houses are often taken to task for exacerbating family breakdown, almost nothing is said about the men who engage in these relationships. Discussion surrounding this category of women raises questions about the extent to which women featuring on certificates or leases actually have control over the land in question or are dependent on others for managing and developing it. In other words, what status does a person acquire by being named on a certificate, or rather what does this 'title' convey in relation to land?

Actual Control of Land and Informal Transactions

My recent research, outlined above, supports the thesis that there have been marked changes over time that have contributed to a greater number of women acquiring certificates and leases in relation to land in contemporary Botswana. Similar findings are emerging in relation to women and land in South Africa (Budlender et al. 2011). However, the question arises as to what extent being named on a certificate translates into actual control of land by those categories of women, mainly unmarried, who now tend to acquire land.

With regard to tribal land, certificates and leases do not represent ownership of the asset, as that remains vested in the Land Board for the benefit of Botswana citizens. What they represent is a right to use and develop the land. For this reason, land itself cannot be sold, but transfers for money can and do take place where the 'title' holder may sell developments on the land to another person. It is well known in Botswana that all kinds of informal transactions take place in relation to land that are not apparent from the existing formal documents. Kalabamu and Morolong (2004: 161), for example, noted that in a district of Gaborone there is a gender bias that leads unemployed women to apply and get plots that are later registered in their partners' names on the assumption that women do not have adequate financial resources to develop the land. Such practices may give rise to an activity referred to as "fronting".[20] This is a situation

[20] For bringing this to my attention, I am indebted to Professor Kalabamu from the Department of Architecture and Town Planning and Mr Dumba, who worked for over 20 years at the Ministry of Lands and Housing and currently in Home Economics, Faculty of Education, at the University of Botswana.

where people who do not qualify for the land in question find someone to front for them. This may come about because, for example, with the SHAA programme their income exceeds the threshold for the grant. This strategy enables them to acquire land and develop it. They then get the 'title' holder, who is acting as a proxy, to transfer it to them in due course. This is not a new phenomenon. When commercial ranches were put out to tender in the 1970s, a Commission of Inquiry held in 1980 discovered that many of those who were successful in their tenders were in fact acting as proxies for certain Chiefs who already had substantial interests in cattle and land. This enabled the Chiefs in question to consolidate their interests and expand them without having to adhere to the restrictions placed on the tendering system. The problem of fronting and speculative dealings in land is one that has long been acknowledged by the government (Botswana Government 2003b: 11).

As noted earlier, title to customary land through certificates and leases does not confer ownership. This means that land certificates relating to the family yard and inheritance are not regarded as conferring absolute rights on the titleholder. When explaining that the youngest son in the family inherits the family yard under customary law, the members of Mokgalo ward explained: "this does not mean that he gets complete control of it. If his sister marries and gets divorced she can come back to stay in the yard, or even a man who gets divorced. The last born can't chase them away because they also have the right to stay in that yard". The members of Dikoloing ward also noted that: "the property is for all family members regardless of certificate being in one person's name". These views on the status of land certificates were endorsed by senior members of Bakwena Tribal Administration, including the Senior Chief's Representative, the Chief's Representative and Senior Headman, Patricia Sechele.[21] This attitude was also reflected in interviews with family members. When I asked Bongi Radipati, for example, what he envisaged would happen to the family compound in Mosotho *kgotla*, he responded that it would:

> [...] fall into the children's hands because my family have steadfastly refused to change this [that is put it in the name of one

[21] In 2010 there were 52 headmen in Molepolole. Out of these three were women of whom Patricia Sechele is the most senior. She is the daughter of the late Mac Sechele a member of the Kwena royal family and former Chief Regent. When I began my research in the 1980s there were no headmen who were women.

> person]. So all six children have an equal and undivided share and it will remain like that. We all gather here at Christmas and at the other long holidays and we call it our home. It will never pass into private hands.

Nonetheless, having your name on a certificate or lease does given an individual a degree of authority and power when it comes to dealing with the Land Board, especially in the case of transfers where the Board has to approve the sale of developments on the land to transferees.[22]

Diverging Family Profiles: Effects of Social Stratification on Resources

It is clear that social networks continue to play an important role in facilitating access to and control over land. In this process it appears that gender is less of a consideration than it once was compared with the social stratification of families and households that emerged out of their encounter with colonialism and that continues to operate today.[23] For as the histories of members of the Makokwe and Radipati family demonstrate, access to resources varies according to affiliation within networks that are configured out of different domains embracing both the peasantariat and the salariat. This gives rise to dimensions of "class" created out of a constellation of factors that contribute to the accumulation of human/social as well as economic capital. These factors include education, employment (formal and informal), and the capacity to enhance self-development and proactively pursue opportunities. While social mobility, as Radipati's family illustrate is attainable, what makes this possible are the advances made over generations that derive from families' genealogical histories. For what is key is the resource base upon which individuals and their families can draw. Where there is a degree of affluence and sufficient resources are available for family members there is more room for negotiation and consensual decision-making. This is illustrated by the earlier discussions on inheritance.

---

[22] Many disputes involve allegations of a titleholder wrongfully transferring land without the consent of the family where this land forms part of a family's inheritance.

[23] For a detailed discussion of the historical, political and economic dimensions giving rise to this see Griffiths (1997: 17-27 and 62-105).

Where, however, resources are not so accessible and under pressure conflicts are more likely to arise. Given that the first allocation of residential land is free, a number of unmarried, unemployed young women at Lekgwapheng Ward explained that they had been motivated to apply to the Land Board for land due to "overcrowding" at home. They observed: "when people are living in an extended family there are disputes and as a result chiefs will work overtime to deal with these disputes in extended families". They accounted for this on the basis that "many of the young women who are unmarried have children. When they go out and work and leave their children with a younger family member, these family members sometimes do not treat the children equally and this causes quarrels in the yard". For this reason, these young women express the view that "we have to have our own yards, especially when we have children". Overcrowding is a common problem in Molepolole. It also occurs in Mokgpeetsane ward where one unmarried man (20 years old) explained that he has applied for land because it has become "very crowded" in the family yard where he lives. He is one of eight children living there together with his unmarried sisters and their children. Although unemployed, he is hoping that if he gets a plot his employed, older brothers will help him to develop it. In such situations tensions may arise leading to those with "title" seeking to chase away other siblings. These tensions not only promote disputes among siblings but also arise between widows and their mothers-in-law and/or sisters-in-law. Quarrels may also arise between a cohabitant of a deceased male partner who seeks to retain the residential yard and the deceased's family who seek to remove her from the premises[24]. In the past an unmarried woman had almost no chance of claiming the yard but in recent years there is an indication that this is no longer an unsurmountable barrier[25].

Apart from the difficulties applicants face in being allocated land, due to long waiting lists, there is also the problem of having sufficient resources to develop it

[24] It is beyond the scope of this article to deal with disputes but it is important to note that they may take any number of paths that see them criss-crossing between the local kgotla, the Chief's *kgotla*, the Customary Court of Appeal, the Land Tribunal, the Magistrate's and High Court, even going as far as the Court of Appeal.

[25] See Banynabotlhe Gaebotlhe (female cohabitant of deceased) vs Kemolaole Modise (mother of the deceased male cohabitant), Customary Court of Appeal MO 211/2009, heard at Chief's kgotla on 23rd February, 2010 where the cohabitant was awarded the deceased's yard.

when their applications are successful. Many of the young women from Lekgwapheng Ward who were awaiting allocation did poorly at secondary school and when they left they did not find any kind of employment (formal or informal). Nor have they had any support from the fathers of their children who are also unemployed. So, even if they do acquire land, in their present circumstances they lack the resources to develop it. Given the current pressure on land, repossession of undeveloped land is on the agenda. Kweneng Land Board had a policy of repossessions that was not actively pursued. However, the Board Secretary observed in May 2010 that they are now trying to "intensify this" as a result of the annual Performance Agreement signed between Kweneng Land Board and the Ministry. Many land boards now promote a policy of repossession on the basis of failure to develop residential land within five years of allocation, impacting on those who, for whatever reason, lack the capacity to develop land that they have acquired.

Concluding Observations: Implications for Justice Delivery

At the beginning of this article I stressed the need for policy-making in development circles to take account of empirical data in framing proposals for intervention. For without this data there is a danger that ideological assertions are treated as matters of fact, that if acted upon can give rise to unexpected outcomes that undermine the intentions and expectations of donor programmes. As a result of an empirically based study, my recent research on women's access to and control over land demonstrates that women in Botswana today are in a much stronger position regarding acquisition of resources, including land, than they were twenty-five years ago. This study, that has a longitudinal perspective derived from ongoing fieldwork over years, has enabled me to trace continuities and changes in governance structures at all levels that shape and are shaped by women's engagement with them. Such a perspective provides an understanding of the context in which changes in women's relationship to land have come about through enhanced education and informal and formal sector employment that coupled with legal reforms has enabled them to become more proactive in their pursuit of land. An historical dimension reveals how these processes of transformation have, in part, involved the changing social dynamics of families and households that mark a shift in attitudes towards inheritance. This allows, for example, women as carers or investors in the family natal compound to inherit it on their parents' death. Such arrangements can be viewed in a number of ways, as an example of consensual agreements that have always been a feature of customary law, or as reflecting a change in customary norms under the current conditions of family life in Botswana that are in tune with Ehrlich's (1936) living law. This is evident not only in the case of unmarried women but also with regard to married women and widows. For, in applying customary law, headmen in Molepolole today accept that "when the husband dies everything is transferred to the wife including the brand of cattle". Of course this observation does not prevent the *de facto* seizing of assets, regardless of who is legitimately recognised as having control over them. What is interesting is that this view expressed by headmen about widows' rights demonstrates a change in attitude from my earlier research where it was the deceased person's brothers and uncles who were said to oversee the estate and determine the transfer to beneficiaries, and who were often accused of property grabbing. This alteration in approach is corroborated by findings in the Chief's *kgotla* for 2009 that demonstrate that women, particularly widows, followed by daughters, are being appointed to administer the estates of deceased persons (Griffiths n.d.b). Under the Succession (rights of the Surviving Spouse and Inheritance Provisions) (Cap. 31:03) statutory law has recognised women's rights to inheritance as a surviving spouse for some time. Its provisions, however, do not apply to estates that are dealt with under customary law.[26] Nonetheless, norms of succession are being incorporated more generally into the operation of daily life. This is not surprising as my earlier research demonstrated the mutually constitutive nature of law that extends beyond the boundaries of an institutional setting.

These changes in justice provision for women feature not only in terms of public institutional delivery, but also in terms of more private family arrangements. Such developments owe much to the work of NGOs. These organizations, of which there are many in Botswana,[27] have campaigned tirelessly on a number of fronts for general social change as well as for changes specifically geared towards women. They have extensively lobbied government, provided skills training and seed capital to promote business development at a number of levels, as well as running workshops in local areas nationwide to promote a better awareness of social issues such as property ownership for women, maintenance for children, and gender-based violence. Unfortunately, the continued operation of these services

[26] See s. 3 of the Act.

[27] Others in addition to those previously cited include Reteng (with a focus on indigenous minority groups), Skills Share Botswana (promoting indigenous women's projects), Gender Links (focusing on gender and the media) and Bonela (dealing with HIV, Ethics and Law).

was under threat in 2010 for a number of organisations due to insecure funding. New contracts needed to be negotiated with donor agencies and the likelihood of their renewal was open to question given Botswana's elevation to a middle ranking country from an international aid perspective and the effect of the recent global recession on donors' finances. As the government of Botswana is unlikely to have the resources to take these services over, either in terms of manpower or finances, or in terms of motivation, withdrawal of support from these NGOs will seriously impair service delivery on the ground. This will have implications for future development in the country.

In acknowledging the transformations that have taken place my research has also highlighted the continued importance of family networks in promoting access to resources needed to acquire control over land. These networks represent diverging constituents that reflect the impact of social stratification derived from family genealogical histories. This has implications for identifying social inequality and targeting programmes to deal with it that must be based on an understanding of the factors that give rise to it. The research reveals that in the process of acquisition, development and control over land, social networks continue to play a key role. For women's access to land and control over it is affected by whether or not the family networks of which they form part have sufficient resources to assist them, both in developing land allocated to them by the Land Board, or in transferring land to them as inheritance. As noted earlier, where there are sufficient resources available to family members there is more room for negotiations and consensual decision-making, whereas where this is not the case, disputes and conflicts are more likely to arise with a danger of repossession by the Land Board. Understanding the factors that shape these networks and that contribute to individuals' upward or downward mobility is crucial if governments, international agencies, and NGOs are to create effective programmes for dealing with poverty reduction and access to justice.

A step towards achieving this goal in development is for donor agencies to rigorously address the following questions when proposing the formulation of policy considerations and/or interventions. Firstly, what are the underlying assumptions on which such policies or interventions are based? Secondly, for what ends are these policies or interventions being pursued, including assumptions about outcomes? Thirdly, what are the sources of data that are being drawn on to inform the analysis and how and why have they been selected? Finally, what are the constraints and limitations or biases of the proposed approaches to policy and interventions (and conversely their strengths)? A careful consideration of these dimensions should help provide a more grounded approach to development, one that is based on an understanding of fact and not fiction.

References

BERRY, Sara S.
1993 *No Condition is Permanent: The Social Dynamics of Agrarian Change in sub-Saharan Africa.* Madison: University of Wisconsin Press.

BOTSWANA, GOVERNMENT OF
1981a *National Development Plan (NDP 6) 1981-1991*: 21. Gaborone: Ministry of Finance and Development Planning.
1981b *Report of the Commission of Inquiry into Ngwaketse Development Area Ranches and Government' Decision on the Recommendations of the Commission* 1981. Gaborone.
1995 *Household Income and Expenditure Survey 1993/94,* Main Report, Volume 1.
2003a *National Development Plan (NDP9) 2003/04-2008/09*: 18. Gaborone: Ministry of Finance and Development Planning.
2003b *Ministry of Lands and Housing,* Mathuba, B. M. Botswana Land Policy. Unpublished Paper presented at an International Workshop on Land Policies in Southern Africa, Berlin Germany, May 26th - 27th May 2003.
2004 *Household Income and Expenditure Survey 2002/03,* Main Report, Volume 1. Central Statistics Office: Gaborone.
2006 *Botswana Demographic Survey 2006*, Central Statistics Office: Gaborone.
2007 *Informal Sector Survey Report (ISS)*, Central Statistics Office: Gaborone.
2009a *Education Statistics 2000, Stats Brief,* Central Statistics Office: Gaborone.
2009b *Kweneng District Development Plan* (KDDP6) 2003-2009, Kweneng District Council, Kweneng District Development Committee. Ministry of Local Government.

BUDLENDER, Debbie, Sibongile MGWEBA, Ketleetso MOTSEPE and Leilanie WILLIAMS
2011 *Women, Land and Customary Law.* Community Agency for Social Enquiry, South Africa.

COMAROFF, John L. and Simon A. ROBERTS
1977 'Marriage and Extra-marital Sexuality: The Dialectics of Legal Change among the Kgatla'. *Journal of African Law* 21: 97-123.

COMMISSION FOR THE LEGAL EMPOWERMENT OF THE POOR

2008 *Making the Law Work for Everyone - Volume 1,* New York, United Nations Development Programme. Accessed at http://www.undp.org/legalempowerment/report/index.html

COOPER, David

1982 *An Overview of the Botswana Class Structure and Its Articulation with the Rural Mode of Production: Insights from Selebi-Phikwe* (Dated 1980). Cape Town: Centre for African Studies, University of Cape Town.

DFID (Department for International Development)

2004 *Non-State Justice and Security Systems*. Policy Division.

2008 *Guidance Note, Justice and Accountability*. A DFID Practice Paper.

EHRLICH, Eugen

1936 *Fundamental Principles of the Sociology of Law.* Translated by W. L. Moll. Harvard Studies in Jurisprudence, no. 5. Cambridge, Mass: Harvard University Press. (Originally published 1913).

GRIFFITHS, Anne

1988 'Support among the Bakwena'. Pp. 289-316 in Franz von Benda-Beckmann, Keebet von Benda-Beckmann, Eric S. Casino, Frank Hirtz, Gordon R. Woodman and Hans F. Zacher (eds.), *Between Kinship and the State: Social Security and Law in Developing Countries.* Dordrecht: Foris Publications.

1997 *In the Shadow of Marriage: Gender and Justice in an African Community.* Chicago and London: University of Chicago Press.

2007 'Making Gender Visible in law: Kwena women's access to power and resources'. Pp 139-163 in Anne Hellum, Julie Stewart, Shaheen Ali, Amy Tsanga (eds.), *Human rights, plural legalities and gendered realities: Paths are made by walking*. Harare, Zimbabwe: Weaver Press.

n.d.a. 'Families, Networks and Lifecycles: Legal Pluralism and Women's Access to Land in Botswana.' *Acta Juridica* forthcoming.

n.d.b 'Managing Expectations: Negotiating Succession under Plural Legal Orders in Botswana'. In John Eekelaar and Mavis Maclean (eds.), *Families: Deviance, Diversity and the Law,* forthcoming.

KALABAMU, Faustin Tirwirukwa

2003 *Changing Gender and Institutional Roles in Self-Help Housing in Botswana: The Case of Lobatse.* The Institute of Southern African Studies. Lesotho.

2006 'Patriarchy and women's land rights in Botswana'. *Land Use Policy* 23/3: 237-246.

2009 'Towards egalitarian inheritance rights in Botswana: the case of

Tlokweng'. *Development Southern Africa* 26/2: 209-223.

KALABAMU, Faustin Tirwirukwa and Siamisong MOROLONG

2004 *Informal Land Delivery Processes and Access to Land for the Poor in Greater Gaborone, Botswana*. DFID Contract No SSR Project R8076.

KOCKEN, E.M. and G.C. UHLENBECK.

1980 *Tlokweng: A Village Near Town*. ICA Publication no. 39. Leiden: Leiden University, Institute of Cultural and Social Studies.

KUPER, Adam

1970 'The Kgalagari and the Jural Consequences of Marriage'. *Man* 5: 466-482.

MANJI, Ambreena

2010 'Eliminating Poverty? "Financial Inclusion", Access to Land, and Gender Equality in International Development'. *Modern Law Review* 73(6): 985-1025.

MOTZAFI-HALLER, Penina

1986 'Whither the "True Bushman": The Dynamics of Perpetual Marginality'. Pp. 259-328 in F. Rotland R. Vossen (eds.), *Proceedings of the International Symposium on African Hunters and Gatherers*. Sprache and Geschichte in Afrika, vol 7, no. 1. Sankt Augustin: Monastery of Sankt Augstin.

MOLENAAR, Marja

1980 *Social Change within a Traditional Pattern: A Case Study of a Tswana Ward*. M.A. thesis, University of Leiden.

MOLOKOMME, Athaliah

1991 *"Children of the Fence": The Maintenance of Extra-marital Children under Law and Practice in Botswana*. Research report no. 46. Leiden: African Studies Centre.

MOROLONG Siamisung Thoki and Clement NG'ONG'OLA

2007 'Revisiting the Notion of Tribal Land'. Pp. 142-175 in Charles M. Fombad (ed.), *Essays on the Law of Botswana*. South Africa: Juta Law.

NG'ONG'OLA, Clement

1997 'Land Rights for Marginalized Ethnic Groups in Botswana, with special reference to the Basarwa'. *Journal of African Law* 41: 1-26.

PARSON, Jack

1981 'Cattle, Class, and State in Rural Botswana'. *Journal of Southern African Studies* 7: 236-255.

RUZVIDZO, T. and H. N TIAGHA

2005 'The African Gender Development Index'. Pp. 22-47 in Christi van der Westhuizen (ed.), *Gender Instruments in Africa*. Pretoria, South Africa:

Institute for Global Dialogue.

SCHAPERA, Isaac

1947 *Migrant Labour and Tribal Life: A Study of the Conditions of the Bechuanaland Protectorate*. London: Oxford University Press.

1950 'Kinship and Marriage among the Tswana'. Pp. 140-165 in Alfred R. Radcliffe-Brown and Cyril Daryll Forde (eds.), *African Systems of Kinship and Marriage*. London: Oxford University Press for the International African Institute.

SCHAPERA, Isaac and Simon ROBERTS.

1975 'Rampedi Revisited: Another Look at a Kgatla Ward'. *Africa* 45(1): 258-279.

SIDA (SWEDISH DEVELOPMENT COOPERATION AGENCY)

2002 *Swedish Development Cooperation in the Legal Sector*.

UNDP (United Nations Development Programme)

2005 *Programming for Justice: Access for All. A Practitioner's Guide to a Human Rights-Based Approach to Access to Justice*. Bangkok: UNDP.

2008 *Strengthening the Rule of Law in Conflict/Post Conflict Situations. A Global UNDP Programme for Justice and Security 2008-2011*. UNDP.

UNICEF (UNITED NATIONS CHILDREN'S FUND)

1993 *Children, Women and Development in Botswana: A Situational Analysis*. Report prepared by Mandeleo (Botswana) for the Government of Botswana and UNICEF.

VAN KLAVEREN, Maarten, Kea TIJDENS, Melanie HUGHIE-WILLIAMS and Nuria R. MARTIN

2009 *An Overview of women's work and employment in Botswana*. Working Paper 09-81, Amsterdam Institute for Advanced Labour Studies, University of Amsterdam.

WEILENMANN, Markus

2009 'Project Law - A Legal intermediary between local and global communities: A Case Study from Senegal'. *Anthropologica* 51: 39-51.

WOLRD BANK

2006 *Equity and Development*. World Bank Development Report.

STATUTUORY PROVISIONS BOTSWANA

Abolition of Marital Power Act
State Land Act (Cap. 32:01)
Town and Country Planning Act (Cap. 32:09)
Tribal Land Act (Cap. 32:02)

THE JOURNAL OF LEGAL PLURALISM
and Unofficial Law
Gordon R. Woodman (Editor in Chief)
HUMAN RIGHTS AND
LEGAL PLURALISM
YÜKSEL SEZGIN (Guest Editor)
The Journal of Legal Pluralism and Unofficial Law Nr. 60
LIT